New Yiddish Library

*The New Yiddish Library is a joint project of the
Fund for the Translation of Jewish Literature and
the National Yiddish Book Center*

*Additional support comes from the Kaplen
Foundation and the Felix Posen Fund for the
Translation of Modern Yiddish Literature*

SERIES EDITOR: DAVID G. ROSKIES

The World According to Itzik: Selected Poetry and Prose

ITZIK MANGER

TRANSLATED AND EDITED

BY LEONARD WOLF

WITH AN INTRODUCTION

BY DAVID G. ROSKIES AND

LEONARD WOLF

YALE UNIVERSITY PRESS

NEW HAVEN & LONDON

"The Ballad and the White Glow," "The Crucified and the Verminous Man," "For Years I Wallowed," "Hagar Leaves Abraham's House," "In the Train," "Jacob Teaches the Story of Joseph to His Sons," "November," "The Patriarch Jacob Meets Rachel," all by Itzik Manger, translated by Leonard Wolf, from *The Penguin Book of Modern Yiddish Verse*, by Irving Howe, Ruth R. Wisse, and Khone Shmeruk, copyright © 1987 by Irving Howe, Ruth Wisse, and Chone Shmeruk. Used by permission of Viking Penguin, a division of Penguin Putnam, Inc. Excerpts from "My Last Day in Eden," "My Friend Pisherl," "In King David's Estates," "A Terrible Tale of the Messiah-Ox," "The Turmoil over the Flight of the Messiah-Ox," "Our Mission," and "Anyella" from *The Book of Paradise* by Itzik Manger, translated by Leonard Wolf. Translation copyright © 1965 by Leonard Wolf. Reprinted by permission of Hill and Wang, a division of Farrar, Straus and Giroux, LLC.

Printed in the United States of America.

Library of Congress Cataloging-in-Publication Data

Manger, Itzik, 1909–1969.
[Selections. English. 2002]
The world according to Itzik: selected poetry and prose / Itzik Manger ;
translated and edited by Leonard Wolf ; introduction by
David G. Roskies and Leonard Wolf.
p. cm. — (New Yiddish library)
Includes bibliographical references.
ISBN 0-300-09248-2 (cloth : alk. paper)
1. Manger, Itzik, 1901–1969—Translations into English. 2. Bible.
O.T.—History of Biblical events—Poetry. I. Wolf, Leonard.
II. Title. III. Series.
PJ5129.M26 A27 2002
839'.18409—dc21

2001007306

A catalogue record for this book is available from the British Library.

The paper in this book meets the guidelines for permanence and durability of the Committee on Production Guidelines for Book Longevity of the Council on Library Resources.

10 9 8 7 6 5 4 3 2 1

This book is dedicated to the memory of Uriel Weinreich, scholar, Yiddishist, and friend, who introduced me to the work of Itzik Manger

—L. W.

◆ ◆ ◆ *Contents*

PROSE

LET US SING SIMPLY

Let us sing simply, directly, and plain
Of all that's familiar and dear.
Of agéd beggars who curse at the frost
And of mothers blessing the fire.

Of indigent brides with their candles who stand
At sightless mirrors, forlorn,
Each of them seeking the intimate face
They loved and that laughed them to scorn.

Of those who cast lots and who steal the last coin
Of their victims with speech that's obscure;
And of wives who, deserted, curse at the world,
Slinking away through back doors.

Of housemaids whose fingers are worked to the bone
And who hide from their mistress's sight
The morsels they save for the soldiers who come
On their visits to them every night.

Let us sing simply, directly, and plain
Of all that's familiar and dear.
Of indigent mothers who curse at the frost
And of beggars blessing the fire.

Of young women in summer forced to abandon
Their bastards on doorsteps, and quail
At the sight of a man in a uniform
Who is able to send them to jail.

Of hurdy-gurdies that grind and grind
In poor courtyards on Fridays all day,
And of thieves surprised at their work who must
Flee over the rooftops away.

Of ragpickers picking their way through debris,
Who dream of the treasure they'll find,
Of poets who foolishly trusted the stars
Then promptly went out of their minds.

Let us sing simply, directly, and plain
Of all that's familiar and dear.
Of agéd folk who curse at the frost
And of children blessing the fire.

◆◆◆ *Introduction*

DAVID G. ROSKIES AND LEONARD WOLF

In modern Yiddish literature, what often seems naive proves to be extremely sophisticated. Poets of folklike verse are revealed to be consummate craftsmen and the comic writers are invariably the most deadly serious. Proofs of this paradox are the fables-in-verse of Eliezer Steinbarg (1880–1932) and the whole comic oeuvre of Sholem Aleichem (1859–1916). Among a somewhat younger generation of writers, however, only one created a corpus of ballads and Bible poems so seamless that they might have been written by the anonymous "folk"; a body of autobiographical fiction so innocent and playful as to make the Jewish child into a harbinger of hope; and satires that carried such a punch, they could stave off the fear of destruction. His name was Itzik Manger (né Isidore Helfer). The present selection of poetry, prose, and literary essays is the first attempt in English to give Manger his due as a modernist folk bard, divinely inspired prankster, and consummate poet of exile and homecoming.

Czernowitz, the multiethnic city of his birth in 1901, was also the birthplace of Paul Celan, Dan Pagis, and Aharon Appelfeld. Like other aspiring young Jews of his time, Manger looked to German literature as the pinnacle of European civilization. At the Kaiser-Königlicher Dritter Staats-Gymnasium, Manger's fellow pupils crowned him "Poet" for having given Goethe's ballad "The Loyal Eckardt" a theatrical form.

Then Manger was expelled for bad behavior.[1] Other pranks soon followed, one of his favorites being the invention of a mock biography. Here is what, decades later, he submitted to the noted lexicographer Zalmen Reisen, who dutifully published it in the augmented edition of his *Lexicon of Yiddish Literature, Press, and Philology* (1927).

MANGER, ITZIK (1900–) Born in Berlin as the son of a tailor, an immigrant from Romania. Came to Jassy at age fourteen where he learned Yiddish and until very recently, worked at his [tailor's] trade.

The son of a German-speaking tailor in Berlin via Romania? Who else could boast of such a mixed-up pedigree? And to have mastered Yiddish in so short a time! Manger even made himself a year older so as to usher in the twentieth century. In a more lyrical moment, at the age of twenty-eight, Manger described himself to an interviewer as "born in a train between two stations. It may be that's how I acquired the wander-demon in me. When I was myself a child, my youngest little brother died in my arms. My first encounter with the mystery of death. That was the first time that I looked directly into the dark, dead eyes of the ballad. A year later that moment was transformed into my ballads."[2] That would have made Manger a child-balladeer, unless we accept the commonly held notion that he never really grew up. To add the finishing touch, soon after granting this interview, he changed his name from the formal-sounding Yitskhok (Isaac) to the folksy, child-like Itzik.

Still later, Manger described himself as salt of the Yiddish earth, the earth that lay at the foothills of the Carpathian Mountains, where the saintly Baal Shem Tov, founder of Hasidism, was reputed to have roamed. There every horse-and-buggy ride with one's grandfather carried mythic overtones. Every vivacious aunt doubled as a surrogate mother. At home, "the master, the master's wife, the journeyman tailors, and one or two apprentices were as one family." The workplace, he would recall, "was filled with song and laughter. Everyone sang." The best of the singers was a journeyman named Leybele Becker, who taught young Itsikl to recite Friedrich von Schiller's "Die Glocke," Goethe's "Erlkönig," and Heinrich Heine's "Zwei Grenadieren," and would lend out his secular books. The tailors sang haunting Yiddish love songs to still their grieving hearts. And on the festival of Purim, the chief rhymester and improviser was the master tailor, Hillel Manger, himself ("Childhood Years in Kolomey"). Is it any wonder that his eldest child would grow up to become the last Yiddish troubadour? That Itzik would one day take Warsaw by storm, becoming the boy wonder of the Yiddish Writer's Club?

This much seems to be true. A love of literature permeated the Manger home. His younger brother, Notte (1903–1942), was also a tailor, but one of those rare people who, though self-taught, had a sophisticated understanding of classical and contemporary European as well as Yiddish poetry. Notte's influence on Manger's life and writing cannot be overestimated. Manger admired his brother's knowledge and taste in literature and made a persona of him in a series of lyric poems, "The Journeyman Notte Manger Sings." In *The Book of Paradise,* Manger's fictional autobiography, the artist Mendl Reyf captured the likenesses of "the two infatuated angels" Siomke and Berl, who worked for the patch-tailor Shlomo-Zalman. They are the spitting image of the two earthly brothers Itzik and Notte Manger. Manger's mother, the daughter of a mattress maker, was a pious woman who imbued him with a love of the folksongs she sang. And Manger's father, whose "bohemianism" and bouts of depression kept the family on the move, coined the Yiddish expression *literatoyre,* a felicitous and extremely naughty pairing of "literature" and "Torah."[3] In this home, apparently, religion and art, piety and profanity were easily reconciled. No Kulturkampf, no adolescent rebellion, no Sturm und Drang. "Itzik" Manger appears to be the only young Jew to have become a writer, poet, painter, or composer without ever leaving home.

Romania was the birthplace of the Yiddish theater, founded there by Abraham Goldfaden in 1877. "My childhood years," writes Manger, "were filled with theater. I frequented Avrom Axelrod's Yiddish-German Theater. For the privilege of being allowed to stand behind the curtain during the performance I lugged chairs and set them out and ran errands for the actors."[4] In those years, he tells us, he stood behind the flats and followed the action on stage as he held a copy of the play in his hands, breathing in the theatrical atmosphere, learning to evaluate texts for their theatricality. The Yiddish theater became his Gymnasium. "A fine Gymnasium for someone who was head-over-heels in love with the Yiddish theater."[5]

Luckily for young Itzik-Yitskhok, the outbreak of world war forced him and his family to move to Jassy. (At last, one biographical fiction with a basis in fact!) Otherwise he might never have known his ancestral eastern Galician (later Romanian) landscape and, what's worse, might never have found himself as a Yiddish troubadour. Jassy was a godsend for a young romantic poet in search of inspiration. Here, in "the old city with secluded crooked streets," one could hear a young maiden singing Yiddish love songs from her window, and one could still commune with the spirit of those "nocturnal vagabonds," "hungry, pale, and joyous," who raised their cups and voices in song. Most famous among the latter was Velvl Zbarzher (1826–1883), easily recognized "By his lively large eyes, / By his dusty, dark green cape, / His head rakishly bent to one side." This inspiring figure was "Drunk from the stars, wine, night, and wind." Where the "song and sorrow" of troubadours once blossomed, where their living memory still glimmered from every window, lulling the passer-by with longing, here was a place that a budding Yiddish poet could call his own.[6]

Poet, playwright, and parodist—all this supposedly nurtured on native ground. The most detailed account that Manger gave of his poetic beginnings was on the occasion of his sixtieth birthday. To an aging but adoring audience at the Waldorf Astoria Hotel in New York, Manger described an epiphany that had occurred, aptly enough, in a tavern late one night, his Muse appearing as a drunken old man, the last of a generation of beer hall singers.

> I was sitting one night in a tavern in Bucharest. A guest from Berlin was with me—Dr. Israel Rubin. Long past midnight an old man of some seventy years dropped in. He was well and truly drunk. This man was old Ludvig, the last of the Brody Singers.
>
> We invited him to our table. He poured himself a large glass of wine, made a sort of Yiddishized kiddush, then later he began to sing [songs] from his Brody repertoire.
>
> When he had finished singing Velvl Zbarzher's song "The Tombstone Engraver," he improvised a stanza of his own:

Here lie Velvl Zbarzher and Abraham Goldfaden
Our brothers whose sweet songs could unsadden
So many; and now there they lie
With their heads, which they held once so high
As they thought noble thoughts, but see how
Empty those fine heads are now.
My ending will be just the same,
Lying in the dust with no name.

My eyes lighted up: This! This was it! The shapes of the Brody Singers glowed in my mind. All the wedding jesters, rhymesters, and Purim players that had amused generations of Jews came alive. I will become one of them; one of "Our brothers." Perhaps what they created and sang was primitive, and not lofty poetry; but they themselves were poetry.

I remembered the lovely folksongs I had heard in my father's workshop. What an orgy of color and sound. What a heritage lay there abandoned. Gold being trodden underfoot. And I paid attention and gazed.[7]

The image of that drunken wandering minstrel with the wineglass in his hand over which he recited a Yiddishized blessing never entirely left Manger. In the course of his life he would create other aspects of himself, but the one he clung to until his dying day was that he was of the race of shabby-cloaked wandering minstrels thirsty for wine, tips, and applause. Just recently, a former *landsman* of Manger's recorded a heretofore unknown song called "Manger's Testament," which ends as follows:

Don't carve out upon my tombstone
All those dates, the wheres and whos,
Just carve out in great big letters
That Manger used to love his booze.[8]

In short, a folk poet, an admirer and re-creator of oral literature, of the ballad, the folktale, the Purim play. In short, a romantic poet for whom the Gypsy with his homelessness, his rootlessness, and his music was an attractive figure.

A closer look, however, at Manger's epiphany in the Bucharest tavern belies this myth of humble origins. The late-night setting relived by

Manger those many years later bespeaks death, as does the grotesque figure of the ancient rhymester. Would any self-respecting poet mimic this doggerel? Would anyone who had once been drawn to Goethe's "Erlkönig" and "The Loyal Eckardt" and to Heine's "Zwei Grena-dieren," later, to Rainer Maria Rilke and Edgar Allan Poe, find anything in the Yiddish "folk legacy" worth salvaging? What was it, then, that tore open the poet's eyes and ears to the orgy of color and sound? That now drew him to the popular Yiddish performers who "unsadden so many" with their "sweet songs"?

To begin with, they were a native—and therefore, welcome—source of revelry and sentiment. The primitive verse of Velvl Zbarzher and Abraham Goldfaden, in turn, reminded the modern poet of his own discarded past, the very folksongs he had once heard in his father's workshop. Precisely because that past lay buried and abandoned it could now be unearthed anew. Anyone could try to mimic Goethe and Heine; any artist of a certain age could rhapsodize on the theme of death. What the Yiddish literary and theatrical tradition offered Man-ger was something else. It challenged him to search (long and hard, if necessary) for indigenous sources of poetic inspiration, to relearn the art of simplicity, to recloak his modern—and modernist—sensibilities within a folksy, Jewish garb. In a way, Manger's poetic pedigree did derive from Berlin via Romania. And in a way, the tattered present recloaked as the seamless past was just the kind of thing that tailors did to eke out a living. Like father, like son, like brother.

◆ ◆ ◆

It was easier, Manger discovered, to pass oneself off as a born minstrel and wastrel than to make a real living at it. Recently demobilized from the Eighth Fusilier Regiment of the newly established Romanian army and situated back in his native Czernowitz, Manger refused a job clerk-ing in a store. He would live from Yiddish or not at all. Aside from two notebooks of unpublished poems, including a great many ballads, housed today in the Manger Archive at the Jewish National Library in Jerusalem, the formative postwar decade in Manger's life (1918–1927) has left a scant paper trail. According to Reisen's *Lexicon*, Manger moved to Bucharest, where he was one of the leaders of the "radical Yiddishist movement in Greater Romania," wrote for the local Yiddish press, and did the lecture circuit, speaking on the ballad, on Spanish, Romanian, and Gypsy folklore. "The most important improviser of Romanian folksong is the shepherd," he informed his audience. "He has, in his flute, captured the subtle, silken tremor of the evening wind, the hot anguished trill of the nightingale, and the silver rhythm of the clouds that hang over his hut, over his hills and over his steppe."[9] Having exhausted what Romania had to offer, Manger headed next for Warsaw, the capital of Yiddish culture.

He was twenty-seven when he arrived in Warsaw as a Romanian poet with thick, disheveled flowing hair, blazing eyes, and a lighted cigarette perpetually dangling from his lips. To the Yiddish literary scene in Warsaw, Manger was an exotic newcomer. He would call this period "my most beautiful decade." It was by far the most productive.[10]

Warsaw between the two world wars was the largest and most polarized Jewish community in Europe. Each of the major political parties—the socialist Bund, the Zionists, and the orthodox Agudas Yisroel—sustained its own network of schools, libraries, newspapers, publishing houses, social services, youth movements, and soccer teams. Linguistically, too, the community was divided. The poor Hasidim, the working class, and the underworld spoke Yiddish. The merchant and professional classes spoke Polish, and a smattering of intellectuals spoke Hebrew. Everyone hated the Litvaks, those know-it-alls from the northeast with their funny accents.

Few were the neutral venues within this fiercely divided landscape. Depending on the bill, merchants and workers and their spouses could meet in the Yiddish theater, though the cabarets, with their antireligious and off-color fare, catered only to the fashionable. Then there was the Yiddish Writers' Club on Tlomackie 13, right next door to the Great Synagogue. The buffet was kosher, and on consecutive nights you could hear writers from across the political and aesthetic spectrum—and from across the Yiddish-speaking world. Melekh Ravitch, the club's secretary, remained steadfastly apolitical and tried to maintain calm when the public programs got out of hand. Finally, for the chosen few, there was the rarefied ambience of the Yiddish PEN Club. The four youngest initiates, elected in January 1930, were Israel Rabon, I. Papiernikov, Yitskhok Bashevis, and Itzik Manger.[11]

Bashevis, in time to become known to the whole world as I. B. Singer, represented the last—and broken—link in the chain of rabbinic culture. Like his father, Pinchas Menachem Singer, of 10 and later 12 Krochmalna Street, Bashevis was fit only for intellectual pursuits. Both father and son were self-absorbed, impractical, and vastly overqualified for their lowly and low-paying jobs. The father was a run-of-the-mill rabbinical judge, the son a proofreader at a Yiddish literary weekly. The father spent his days dreaming about God and his messiah. The son spent his nights dreaming of women and omniscient narrators. Because for Bashevis there could be no reconciling religion and art, piety and profanity, that split became the sum and substance of his career. In a breakaway journal immodestly titled *Globus* (The Globe), Bashevis railed against modernism, politics, and stylistic mediocrity. To make ends meet, he translated European classics and ghostwrote sensational potboilers. In the Yiddish Writer's Club, he sat alone.

Itzik Manger, by contrast, burst onto the literary scene in person and in print. He granted interviews and published articles in the *Literarishe bleter,* the same weekly where the young Bashevis first worked as proofreader, gave readings at the Writer's Club, where he recited all his poetry by heart; published *Stars on the Roof* (Bucharest, 1929), a meticulously edited volume of his verse; put out twelve issues of his own four-page literary journal called *Chosen Words* (Czernowitz-Kraków-Riga, 1929–1930), filled mostly with his own manifestos, poems, and literary musings; invented a new genre, which he called *Bible Poems* (Warsaw, 1935); rewrote the Purim *Megillah* (Warsaw, 1936); penned a personalized history of Yiddish literature from the eighteenth to the early twentieth century (*Intimate Portraits;* Warsaw, 1938); published three more volumes of verse, *Lantern in the Wind* (Warsaw, 1933), *Velvl Zbarzher Writes Letters to Malkele the Beautiful* (Warsaw, 1937), and *Twilight in the Mirror* (Warsaw, 1937), an anthology of European folksongs (Warsaw, 1936), and a fictional autobiography in prose (Warsaw, 1939); witnessed the production of his *Hotsmakh Play* (1936–1937), loosely based on Goldfaden; composed lyrics for the Yiddish cabaret and the fledgling Yiddish movie industry; crisscrossed Poland without knowing more than five words of Polish; and got involved with women.

Manger in love—a sordid chapter, to say the least. What Manger needed was a mother more than a wife, someone who would iron his shirts, pack his bags, clean up after him, and forgive him his transgressions. Such a woman was Rokhl Auerbach (1903–1976), a noted Yiddish and Polish journalist, who suffered physical abuse from Manger, inspired some of his finest poems, remained in Warsaw in September 1939, among other reasons, to save Manger's archive, and was reunited with him in London after the war. Manger, who had since taken up with another woman, and who never fully regained his psychic balance, greeted Auerbach with such a barrage of invective that she fainted dead away. They were not to see each other ever again.[12]

◆ ◆ ◆

But we get ahead of our story. As a Romanian national and otherwise superfluous Jew, Manger left Warsaw in 1938 and headed for Paris, the Mecca of expatriates, where he eked out a living by lecturing on French literature to Yiddish-speaking audiences. Being on French soil reawakened his interest in the nineteenth-century poet Paul Verlaine. On a visit to Metz, Verlaine's birthplace, Manger had himself photographed beside a statue of the poet.[13] Northern France then fell to the Germans and Paris was no longer a safe haven, so in 1940, Manger moved south to Marseilles, where for a while he lived in a shelter for emigrants. There he slept on a bare mattress with only his coat for a blanket. His sleep was troubled by dreams in which he saw "Goethe with a rubber truncheon in his hand, Immanuel Kant wearing an S.S. uniform, Faust wearing a swastika on his right arm, and blood, blood—Jewish blood . . . dreadful dreams."[14] Manger's hope, in Marseilles, was that by working his way on a ship he might get to Palestine, but he lacked the necessary documents.

One version of the story has Manger sitting one day in a tavern in Marseilles nursing a glass of wine when a ship's captain happened to walk in. What follows next is typical of Manger, who all his life, by looking helpless, poverty-stricken, or abandoned, could rouse in other people the impulse to look after him. Manger in the tavern was, just then, looking as dejected as the man in Picasso's *Frugal Repast*. The ship's captain, a gunrunner, noticed the gaunt and vacant-eyed look on Manger's face and asked him, "Why are you looking so bewildered?"

The upshot of the encounter was that the captain took Manger aboard his ship, which after some North African wandering deposited him in Gibraltar. There Manger was found by another ship's captain, this time a Scot, who took a very sick Manger to Liverpool, where Manger was hospitalized. It was then Christmastime. The Yiddish-speaking Manger woke in the Liverpool hospital on Christmas Day to find his bed filled with presents. The nurses, who had clubbed together to buy him the presents, lied delicately to him saying that a rabbi had brought the gifts.[15]

According to another, more prosaic, version, Manger was hospitalized in July, not December, 1940, and the ship's captain who brought Manger to Liverpool was French.[16]

Manger eventually became a British citizen and later traveled with a British passport, but he would characterize his ten years in England as the worst period of his life. "He felt as if he was imprisoned," recalls the Anglo-Jewish writer Joseph Leftwich, "far from the effervescent Yiddish folk-life in whose midst he had been in Eastern Europe. [His] environment was too restricted. He wrote marvelous poems, published them in books. But, as he told me, the poems in the book *The Journeyman Tailor Notte Manger Sings* were written in London in spite of the bad Jewish atmosphere."[17]

Manger was not only writing in those years, he also acquired a reading and speaking knowledge of English. He immersed himself in English classical poetry, reading Christopher Marlowe, Ben Jonson, John Bunyan, Jonathan Swift, and William Blake. He dreamed of editing a book of Yiddish translations of English poetry. One way or another, he acquired Jewish and non-Jewish friends, among them Arthur Waley, the expert in Chinese poetry. And he was writing essays, stories and poems. A collection of poems, *Clouds over the Roof*, appeared in 1942.

Then began his friendship with Margaret Waterhouse.

Margaret Waterhouse, said to be a descendant of the poet Percy Bysshe Shelley, owned a bookstore in London. The romantic story goes that, one rainy day, Itzik Manger was standing looking hungrily into the window of her bookshop in Swiss Cottage. Waterhouse invited him to come in out of the rain. With that gentle beginning a relationship was formed that lasted some years. As the New Zealand poet Dan Davin writes, "by all accounts only the term 'ministering angel'—angels were not just clichés in Itzik's world—suffices for the part she played in his life during his London years. At their first meeting she had discerned his special quality and thereafter did her best to look after him and dissuade him from ruining his health through drinking and smoking too much and allowing his irascibility to spoil his prospects with people who wished him well."[18]

That Manger was productive does nothing to contradict his assertion that he was unhappy in his years in England. From the time he got there his hope, and his focus, was on finding the means to get to New York, where there was still an active Yiddish literary community and where he felt he belonged. He and various of his friends made effort after effort to get him the necessary documents and the money he would need to make the move, but for a long time their endeavors were unsuccessful.

In June 1941, Manger, harassed by poverty and the disaster that had overwhelmed the Jews in Poland, sent a strange letter to H. Leivick, at that time the most famous Yiddish poet living in New York. The letter, part prose and part verse, is a document written in despair. In the verse part of the letter Manger announces,

I am weary—ah, good night,
For my eyelids have grown heavy;
Life and thought and love
Have flown, have vanished like a dream.
I am weary—ah, good night,
For my eyelids have grown heavy.

Half awake and halfway dozing,
I prattle now my final poem;
See a great bird flying off
From the earth to heaven.
Half awake and halfway dozing,
I prattle now my final poem.

A dream it was that once I brought you,
It was the dream you thrust away
And when darkness fell, you turned me
Out and sent me on my way.
It was a dream that once I brought you,
It was the dream you thrust away.[19]

The letter continues in prose that is a mixture of self-pity and accusation. "Where am I? Tattered, abandoned, wandering among strangers. Harried, depressed, unhelped by anyone in any of my needs, I curse the unfortunate trance that led me into Yiddish literature. I have grown sober now, but it is too late. I've lost everything that was precious and dear to me. I am a cadger of cigarettes, and nothing more."[20]

Leivick, faced with so much agony, reacted with unforgivable tactlessness. First, he had Manger's letter published in the Yiddish daily *Der tog* of July 10, 1941. Then, on subsequent days, he published his rejoinder. His intent, he says, is to help Manger find his way out of his present anguish and despair. "Because," he writes, "what essentially is your verse-letter to me if not a desperate game with yourself." Leivick does not shrink from accusing Manger of egocentricity, and this at a time when "our entire people is in deadly peril and when the whole world lies under a hail of fire and disaster."[21]

The two letters are accurate reflections of their authors: Manger desperate, self-pitying, Leivick condescending, Olympian, self-satisfied, and pompous. The exchange of letters produced between the two men a breach that lasted eight years, in the course of which time Manger grew convinced that there existed in New York a cabal of writers that included Joseph Opatoshu, H. Leivick, and Aaron Glantz-Leyeles, who wished him ill.

At this great distance from the anguish that prompted Manger's letter and the defensiveness that provoked Leivick's reply, the entire exchange feels very much too bad: an expense of spirit in a waste of shame. Manger was intemperate, Leivick insensitive. History was harassing them both.

In March 1951, after having first been feted in Paris on his fiftieth birthday, Manger was on his way to Montreal. The God who looks after brilliant but hapless poets finally took a hand in Manger's life. Later that year, with the help of the poet Mani Leyb and the critic Abraham Tabachnik, Manger finally made it to New York. "Manger came like a ghost from the land of the dead," writes Ruth Wisse.

> Haggard, always with a cigarette at the corner of his mouth and a performer's talent sharpened by years in the Yiddish theater, he looked and played the part of the ruined troubadour. Through his brokenness he evoked the Jewish tailor shops of Romania where he had worked as a boy and the Jewish cabarets of Poland for which he had traded them in as an adult, granting audiences a posthumous glimpse of their liveliness. No one could remain indifferent to Manger or his poetry.[22]

Or, for that matter, to his heavy drinking. The surviving Yiddishists either condemned Manger or assiduously turned a blind eye. At least one patron of the arts refused Manger entry to her literary salon.[23] Dan Davin took a more compassionate view.

> During the time I knew him, one would not have described Itzik as temperate. Not that he was an alcoholic either. But he was at all times excitable, and alcohol made him more so; he had rather a weak head and so got drunk on what would have affected others comparatively little; and he enjoyed the company of drinkers and the social pleasures that go with drinking. I suspect also that, like other imaginative writers who have passed their first lyric spontaneity, he valued the stimulus alcohol can give to the imagination, the access to paradox, unexpected simile, dislocated association. And he may also have needed it for escape from his often acute consciousness of a past and a people utterly destroyed.[24]

Davin first met Manger in August 1950 at a PEN International conference in Edinburgh. The two men cut out from the conference and made their way, amid talk of Shakespeare and Marlowe, to a pub called the Bell Inn. Davin, with his poet's sensibility, intuited at once that his new friend was "a natural lord of language whose metaphors and figures were strange, simultaneously evoking the Bible, the farmyards of my childhood, and the idiom of surrealism so remote from either of these." He was drawn to Manger by a presence "that suggested a power, a force, not a power of the world but a power within the self." In the days that followed, Manger and Davin became habitués of the Bell Inn, where the Yiddish poet ingratiated himself to the Scots in the pub by quoting Robert Burns in his Yiddish accent. Eventually his fellow drinkers made him an "honorary Scot and christened him Mac Manger."[25]

♦ ♦ ♦

Let us stop for a moment and try to imagine Itzik Manger reciting Burns's famous poem "A Red, Red Rose" to his newfound *landslayt* (countrymen) in the Bell Inn:

> O my Luve's like a red, red rose,
> That's newly sprung in June;
> O my Luve's like a melodie
> That's sweetly played in tune.
>
> As fair as thou, my bonie lass,
> So deep in luve am I;
> And I will love thee still, my Dear,
> Till a' the seas gang dry.

The studied simplicity of this poem would certainly have appealed to Manger, as would the word "melodie," the non-Yiddish word that he injected into his own verse on more than one occasion, and used it in precisely the way that Burns (1759–1796) was here playing the local Scottish dialect off against the official, neoclassical diction of British high society. Behind the regular beat and monosyllabic rhyme, behind the naive folk-facade stood a champion of natural verse, natural speech, natural love.

Like Burns, Manger used his vernacular to counteract what in academic circles nowadays are called the "hegemonic claims" of the majority culture. British English was to Burns as German was to Manger. Growing up in Czernowitz, Manger was surrounded by upwardly mobile Jews who tried to "pass" by speaking German, just as Burns must have known any number of Scots who used the King's English to get ahead in life.[26] In a wonderful spoof, Manger called the child-protagonist of his *Book of Paradise* Shmuel-Aba Abervo, borrowing his surname from the German expression commonly used by the Jews of Czernowitz: "*Aber-vo*, Come off it! What nonsense!" Like Burns, Manger tried to fashion the uncouth "jargon" into a vehicle of high culture and, therefore, of national self-determination. Unlike Burns, however, and the whole romantic school of which he was a part, Manger rose to the status of folk poet only after arriving in Warsaw and becoming part of its urban mosaic.

True to the Yiddish folk imagination, Manger returned to "nature" through the ancient biblical landscape learned by rote and the reimagined byways of the shtetl, the Jewish market town. Paradise, in Manger's book, was an eastern Galician shtetl at the turn of the century, surrounded, to be sure, by forests and fields, but laid out in boulevards and back alleys, an urban grid divided along social, ethnic, and religious lines. Folklore, Manger proclaimed in 1939, even urban folklore, was the last repository of myth, as the Bible was the eternal and untapped source of drama ("Folklore and Literature"). Through the Yiddish language, once considered the handmaiden of Hebrew and treated in more recent years like the Cinderella of European tongues, Manger set out to reunite folklore and the Bible on native soil—in the shtetl of God.

Having come to English poetry late in life, Manger surely did not learn the subversive art of simplicity from Robert Burns. He learned it, rather, from Sholem Aleichem, from the Yiddish ballad revival in New York, and from Eliezer Steinbarg.

A lifelong admirer of Sholem Aleichem and especially of his stories for children (see, in this book, "Sholem Aleichem, the One and Only"), Manger credited the great master with launching the "grotesque-realistic school" of Yiddish literature. Almost alone among the next generation of Yiddish writers, Manger captured the radical innocence of childhood, whether as paradise lost or as a rustic life protected by birds and inebriated geese.

The ballad, surprisingly, was being revived in the urban maelstrom of faraway New York by the Yiddish poets who were known collectively as *Di yunge*, the Youngsters. One of them, Mani Leyb, dedicated one volume of his 1918 poetic trilogy to the lyrical ballad. In response, the raucous and rambunctious Moyshe-Leyb Halpern used the ballad structure to play form against content, revealing in *The Golden Peacock*

(1924) the absurdity of the human condition, while Zishe Landau, the chief theoretician of the group, rendered the English, Scottish, and American ballad repertoire into Yiddish.[27] Mani Leyb would live long enough not only to welcome his Old World disciple to New York but also to chair the Itzik Manger Jubilee Committee that would produce the beautiful edition of Manger's *Song and Ballad* (1952).

Manger's first published poem, "Meydl portret" (Portrait of a Maiden), appeared in 1921 in *Kultur* edited by Steinberg, whose verse fables were widely known and admired. They circulated for decades by word of mouth before they ever appeared in print. From Steinberg, Manger learned how to enliven dialogue through the use of dialect; how to manipulate ancient forms to produce both a lyric and satiric effect; how to make rivers, birds, and inanimate objects speak idiomatic Yiddish; how to use anachronism to shift temporal boundaries.[28] This and more Manger put to brilliant use in *Medresh Itsik* (Itzik's Midrash), his bold and zany retelling of the Bible.

◆ ◆ ◆

What makes Manger's versions of the beloved Bible stories so audacious is that he has plucked the biblical personages out of their mythic past and set them down in a time and place much closer to home. "The experienced reader," Manger counsels us, "will catch on to the fact that the landscape in which the biblical characters move is Slavic rather than Canaanitish. I was thinking of eastern Galicia." Manger's Bible folk, moreover, are weighed down not only with the heavy burden of their present lives but also with the knowledge of the roles that they play in the biblical versions of their life stories. Manger has done more than redirect our view of the biblical world from above to below. He compels us to recognize that below is where, even in the Bible, those God-struck folk had always been.

Revealed in Manger's Midrash are those poignant moments when the humanity of the biblical characters is openly displayed. Right from the start in Eden there is the lost struggle against temptation; there is Cain and Abel's disastrous quarrel; Lot's drunkenness; his seduction by his daughters; the story of Jacob cheating his brother Esau out of his blessing; Jacob's meeting Rachel at the well; Joseph's petty sadism as he torments his brothers in Egypt by charging them with the "theft" of his silver cup; old Jesse's exultation that his son David will eventually inherit the throne.

What Manger has done is to zoom in on his biblical cast of characters; then, by making use of his acute theatrical instincts, his lyricism, and his comic genius, he has invested his characters with the sort of ordinariness that links them to our own lives. It is a trick Charles Dickens would have admired. Manger's biblical folk, by having their ordinariness intensified, manage to become extraordinary. Not heroic and, above all, not holy, but down-to-earth real persons capable, in the work of literature they inhabit, of being at once themselves and the allegorical figures that their lives imply.

In "Cain and Abel," for instance, Manger is not interested in how Cain, after committing the world's first murder, feels about Abel. Instead, we find his Cain, who has never seen violence or death, meditating over the curiously lovely body of his dead brother:

"Does the beauty lie in my ax
Or is it perhaps in thee?
Before the day has passed,
Speak, answer me."

When we come to Manger's "Abraham Scolds Lot" we find the patriarch suffering the social anxiety of a respectable man whose kinsman is bringing shame to the family by his drunken behavior:

"Lot—it's disgusting—it's got to be said—
You and your nightly carouse—
Yesterday in the Golden Hart . . .
What a terrible scandal that was.

Manger the tailor can do such things,
But it simply won't do for you.
You've a couple of daughters to raise, you're rich—
Praise God!—and besides, you're a Jew."

In "Abraham Takes Itzik to the Sacrifice," Jewish pride and stubborn obedience are fully played out. Bitterly serene, the poem follows its three persons from the time they leave Abraham's house until they reach a point near the place of sacrifice. Here, Abraham is the rich shtetl Jew, this time obeying an insane command from his God; his servant, Eliezer, in turn knows that something bad is about to happen, but he will make no choice except to be dutiful; and finally, there is the child, Isaac, whose thin, sleepy questions early on a grim morning hauntingly suggest that he knows the purpose of the trip. To the boy's question, "Daddy, where are we going now?" the father offers the pathetic lie: "To Lashkev—to the fair . . . [to buy] A soldier made of porcelain, / A trumpet and a drum." His soul scalded by the lie, the father mumurs bitterly to himself, "To Lashkev . . . the fair . . . some fair."

Then there is Manger's story of Hagar, the handmaiden who is about to be driven from Abraham's house because of Sarah's jealousy. In "Hagar's Last Night in Abraham's House" we find Hagar sweeping the kitchen floor, scouring the copper pan, remembering the presents Abraham gave her when he was courting her, and wondering where in the world she will go with her bastard child in her arms.

> She takes the kitchen broom up,
> She sweeps the kitchen floor.
> Under her blouse, her heart says,
> "I love him." She sweeps some more.

Like sea-worn glass, bright gleams of humor are strewn throughout the poems in *Medresh Itsik,* but this humor is often edged with satire or lightly moistened with tears. "The Patriarch Abraham Gets a Letter" has a little of both. The first three stanzas of the poem, which is sharply divided into two parts, focus on young Isaac, who is moved to tears when he sees a butterfly perching on a cornflower. In the last four stanzas we overhear Isaac's father, Abraham, chatting with the postman, then reading the letter Abraham's servant, Eliezer, has sent reporting on his search for a bride for young Isaac. Naturally, we wonder why the butterfly-cornflower event brings tears to Isaac's eyes and what that has to do with the bride-to-be's ability to cook fish. The answer to the riddle is that Manger has given us a single snapshot of two men experiencing different kinds of love. Isaac, sexually innocent and repressed, weeps because he reads the butterfly's perching on the cornflower as an erotic event and, thinking no doubt of his own dream life, concludes that the world is filled with sin. The homely detail about cooking in the second part of the snapshot is Manger's shorthand for the bittersweet love that Abraham over the years has cherished for his lost Sarah.

When we come to "Jacob Teaches the Story of Joseph to His Sons," anachronism is the chief source of pleasure the poem can give. The implied frame is *The Selling of Joseph,* the most popular Purim play in the Yiddish folk repertoire. Mimicking these amateur theatrics, we can expect broad humor, bathos, or doggerel rhyme—or all three, which is what we get, in the small space of the poem. But we also get the comic pathos of the bewildered sons who must suffer simultaneously in the present and in the past as they ready themselves to perform the Purim play about themselves. Manger's grieving wit sets time-present swirling into time-past and future as Jacob pontificates, telling his favorite son, Joseph, how in the play he should behave:

> "And when they throw you in the pit,
> Weep, but not for long.
> It's not for the first time that you act
> This play out, my dear son."

As he prattles, Jacob resembles the old Polonius, talking past the perceptions of his children. He bumbles on, sliding from fatuousness to tenderness as he advises Joseph:

> "But when you pass your mother's grave
> That stands beside the way,
> Be sure you shed a real tear
> And softly, gently, say
>
> That gladly would old Jacob serve
> Another seventh year
> If once, before his death, he might
> Again caress her hair."

In the traditional *Selling of Joseph,* the two set-pieces were, in fact, Joseph's lament from inside the snake pit and the scene of him passing by Rachel's tomb on his way to Egyptian captivity. Not only, then, did

Manger succeed in rescuing the nobility and vulnerability of his Bible folk. He also reanimated the hackneyed repertoire associated with their lives, replacing the accumulated weight of the generations with his modern Midrash for all seasons. And to ensure that his Midrash traveled more lightly, Manger eliminated the Bible's major player: Moses the Lawgiver. Gone from his secular humanistic rereading are all three pillars of biblical theology: Creation, Revelation, and Redemption. There is no primordial chaos, no Flood, no Exodus, no theophany at Sinai, no Golden Calf, not even Balaam's comical run-in with the talking ass. Manger effectively replaced the Torah with *literatoyre*.

When it came to foretelling the Scroll of Esther, however, Manger was on native ground. For one thing, God's name appears nowhere in the Scroll. All events get played out on the field of human desire and deceit. Jewish historical experience, for another thing, recapitulated the contemporary relevance of the story: whenever a Jewish community was rescued from destruction, the date was marked by the celebration of a local Purim and the writing of a new Megillah, specifically recounting the abyss they had been rescued from. Furthermore, when Yiddish folk theater was finally born, at the end of the seventeenth century, the palace intrigue of the Persian king Ahasuerus, Vashti, his queen, the Jew, Mordecai, his young cousin and ward, Esther, and the king's favorite, Haman, was tailor-made for amateur theatrics. Some of the shtick was so ribald that the printed version was sometimes confiscated and burned by the city fathers. With such a rich menu, what was left for Manger to do?[29]

On the most obvious level, Manger has modernized and complicated the narrative by weaving into it a romantic subplot that predates Esther's life as Ahasuerus's queen. In Manger's tale, Esther's lover is Fastrigosso, a journeyman tailor with whom Esther is planning to elope—to Vienna! Fastrigosso (his mock-Aramaic name means "a basting stitcher") is a schlemiel antihero worthy of Sholem Aleichem. At once hapless and loveable, Fastrigosso is a member in good standing of the radical tailors' union. When Esther becomes the queen, thus shattering his dream of marriage to her, he goes berserk and tries to assassinate the king. Possessing nothing but a penknife, the desperate young lover is comically foiled.

At this point, the political realities facing Manger's audience move to the foreground. Who is Fastrigosso if not a reincarnation of the shoe-maker Hirsh Lekert, a member of the Jewish Labor Bund, who on May 5, 1902, tried and failed to assassinate a Vilna governor in retaliation for the brutal flogging of a group of workers? "Haman," then as now, uses the assassination attempt as proof of Jewish disloyalty, phones his son, Vayzosse, editor of the local antisemitic ragsheet, and tells him to run an inflammatory headline against the Zhids in the morning edition. When Fastrigosso is tried and hanged, and the president of the Society of Needles and Scissors delivers a eulogy for the Jewish martyr, the balance between laughter and tears has decidedly shifted. "At the edge of the abyss," Manger was to write a few years later, "even laughter becomes desperate."[30]

What ever happened to the victorious Jews, to the timeless parable of Jewish salvation? These Manger relegates to the hoary and laughable past. In the bleak Polish-Jewish present, there are only ordinary working-class heroes. Haman, of course, will get his just deserts, as tradition dictates, but Manger's version will provide a truer ending to the story. Fastrigosso's mother lights a memorial candle on the anniversary of her son's death and curses Esther the harlot, who didn't even send her tailor-lover a note during his final days in prison. "This bittersweet ending, devoid of salvation," writes Ruth Wisse, "implies that the biblical fairy-tale is almost an insult to East European Jews, who cannot, despite their best efforts, stave off their political enemies. Like a wealthy relative who comes round once a year to grace his impoverished family, the biblical story reminds the Jews of their weakness, even as it tries to offer them a moment of forgetful relief."[31]

In the prefatory verse to his *Songs of the Megillah*, Manger promises that the reader will find "wonders dark and deep / to make you laugh or weep." To make good on the promise, he peoples the new improved version of the Esther story with a gallery of very human characters, each with her and his own inner life, dreams, and disappointments. Manger deftly juggles the two sides of Purim—the epic-heroic drama of the Hebrew original and the grotesque spectacle of the *Purim-shpil,* where all roles are played for laughs, especially the female roles played (as in Elizabethan times) by men. Whereas the biblical Esther is beautiful, obedient, and, for a moment, brave, her Purim play incarnation is "green," and appears on stage wearing galoshes. For Manger, Esther is a complex figure with a rich inner life. Part loving Juliet, part treacherous Cressida, part whore, she becomes a poignant figure who, for the sake of her people, pays a grim price as the sexual toy of a drunken king, meanwhile suffering all the agonies of love—guilt, above all, for having been so pliable.

> Esther always does everything
> That Mordecai commands
>
> As she betrayed the tailor's lad
> Because it was Mordecai's will:
> Yet Fastrigosso, the tailor's lad,
> Was a treasure, a perfect jewel.

Mordecai, in turn, is portrayed both as the buffoon-hunchback of the Purim play and as a wheeler-dealer of socialist agit-prop. As in the folk theater, a clown (here called a Runner) introduces the whole laughable cast of characters and to strengthen the genetic link, Manger provides a rhymed prologue written in mock–Old Yiddish.[32] This ancient scroll turned into folk farce turned into melodrama is a three-ring circus, with the balance between pathos and parody maintained through the juxtaposition of lively, jolly acts with more episodes of great poignancy. Sometimes Manger mixes them up in the same scene, as he does, most brilliantly, in "Vashti's Song of Grief."

Above all, what drives Manger's *Songs of the Megillah* is its theatricality. It was a script crying out to be staged. Thirty years later, in the mid-1960s, *Songs of the Megillah* starring the Bursztyn Family of actors became the longest-running play in the Tel Aviv equivalent of off Broadway. Set to sing-along tunes by the Israeli composer Dov Seltzer, this cabaret-style production established a place for Yiddish theater in the Jewish state. Twenty years later still, Manger's *Megillah* made its debut in the English translation that appears here in print for the first time.

♦ ♦ ♦

More than any other work, *Songs of the Megillah* lays bare Manger's lifelong campaign to fuse and confuse incompatible realms. As we proceed, in reverse chronological order, to his first great literary love, the ballad, we can see the degree of his self-awareness as a poet and crafts-man, and the precise position that Manger wished to occupy in the modern pantheon. The ballad genre, we learn from literary history, "sought to impress by the vivid representation of a single event, to bring home to the hearer its wonder, its pathos, its fatefulness, or its horror."[33] Two of those elements, the pathos and the horror, clearly affected the young Manger: the pathos because it was so very Yiddish, and the horror because it expressed the postwar perception of reality.

From Manger's programmatic essay "The Ballad: The Vision of Blood" (1929), we learn just how grandiose was his sense of that genre's importance in the history of world literature.

> Imprecision stirs at the edge of the horizon. Silhouettes darkly emerge. Trees, houses, lanterns. Old hunchbacked beggars. The blood begins to seethe, swallowing silhouetted panoramas. There is noise, intoxication. And through the union of silhouette and the sound of blood the balladic transformation emerges. The silhouetted beggars, with their heavy drag-ging tread, carry balladic question marks. And they incise the question marks on the night's stars. Stumbling figures inquire. Lost shapes search. The night is silent, makes no excuse. Does not restore the lost. Now the great bacchanalia begins. The withered hands of the beggars ignite sinful red moons. In the background of the night, and in a wild ecstasy, the wan-ton deed is born. The befuddled aimless laughter of human despair. The great mystical vision of our blood—ballad.

This seething, hallucinatory prose is of a piece with the expressionist manifestos of the 1910s and early 1920s. The staccato rhythm, jagged images, and above all, the apocalyptic temper, reveal Manger at his most universalistic.

At the same time, the ballad's "vision" was primeval. Like the En-glish ballads, the classical German ballads Manger memorized in the Gymnasium touched on the full range of human passion: death, rape, incest, dishonor, betrayal, torture, family quarrels, as well as on a wide spectrum of human encounters with sprites, goblins, witches, and demons; dark themes that are rooted in the darker manifestations of behavior, in the unconscious, and in nightmare. Returning to the ballad as a practicing poet, Manger discovered "the black fantastic crown of poetry, demonic and dark, that floats through our thought and spirit carrying in its dark light endless revelations—fearful bacchanalias" ("The Ballad: The Vision of Blood").

From the German ballad revival, Manger learned to emulate the traditional theme of Death and the Maiden, which Gottfried August Bürger, a staple of the German school curriculum, had immortalized in his "Lenore." In Manger's exquisite "Ballad of the White Glow," for example, the young woman who sees a radiance in the fan of the night recognizes at once what it means. She tells her mother, "my heart, in that cool glow / Is throbbing with desire," then adds later, that "the white glow calling me / Calls from the beyond." The meaning of the white glow is unspecified to the end. Is it some erotic fulfillment in a desirable elsewhere that draws the young woman out in the snow, or is it eros-interrupting Death? The aura of imprecision coupled with the melodic diction give the poem its own mysterious glow.

Clearly modeled on Goethe's "Erlkönig," Manger's "Ballad of the Man Riding to the Fair" rocks along on its tetrameter couplets that mimic the trotting of the horses. The doggerel measure and rhyme intensify the pity that is building as the tale races toward its climax. Though there is no maiden visible in the poem and all we ever see is the father riding to the fair, her non-presence looms so large that, when the last of the ghosts scatters with ashes "the face of the wind," we do not need to be told her fate.

"The Ballad of the Necklace of Stars" is perhaps Manger's finest in this traditional form. As in his biblical poems, time-present and time-past coexist, and just as, in those poems, Manger sustained a dynamic tension between two contending elements, so here, in "The Ballad of the Necklace of Stars," there are two contending elements: the real world of Jassy and the fabulous world of myth.

In the real town of Jassy, we are told, lived a pious old Jew named Mekhele Blatt who is anxious to see his daughter well married. That much is real. But almost at once, the tale veers off into the fabulous. We do not see mortal suitors coming to visit the daughter who is "slim / As a pine tree in the wind." Instead Spring comes with a lilac branch; then Summer brings cranberry blossoms; and Autumn follows, banging on the door. The old man hears the marching rain "Singing the song of departed youth / That flies, like a bird, away." When we see the "necklace of stars in the window pane" and "the thin, dark girl" wearing the crown and the shirt that were brought to her in a dream, we know that a story that began in the day-daily real world has become an allegory of lost chances, the fleeting nature of youth, and the ever-near presence of that permanent wooer, Death.

But sometimes Manger drops the mask of studied simplicity. Sometimes he abandons the patriarchal setting of the shtetl, the familiar cast of characters, and the landscape of eternal longing. Despite his promise, in his Introduction to *Poem and Ballad,* to

> . . . sing simply, directly and plain
> Of all that's familiar and dear.
> Of agéd beggars who curse at the frost
> And of mothers blessing the fire.

despite his uncanny ability to impersonate the folk voice, Manger does, on occasion, exploit the ballad form to reveal an alternative vision, grotesque and difficult, which places him among a very different pantheon. In "Hospital Ballad," "The Ballad of the Blue Pitchers," and "Erotic Ballad," to name only those included in this volume, and such occasional poems as "In the Train," "With Silent Steps," and "November," Manger reveals the profound influence of the French symbolist poets Paul Verlaine, Arthur Rimbaud, and Stéphane Mallarmé.[34]

Rimbaud would have recognized the symbolic narrative technique that Manger uses in such poems as "November" and "The Ballad of the Blue Pitchers." Focused more on feelings than on narrative, they produce their effect through a combination of surreal imagery and rigidly formal poetic structure.

"November" is durable nightmare, firmly and steadily composed, gathering in its stanzas the stuff of madness and sexual repression:

> An infected wind weeps in our garden;
> Before our house, a scarlet lantern glows;
> Death's silver razors play, like fiddle bows,
> White music on the throats of pious calves.

In the nursery, cradles rock themselves;
And mother's gone—her chaste still music dies,
A guiltless sacrifice of lullabies.

The poem is muscular, dense, unsafe, filled with glimpses of hallucination, yet the lines are beguilingly melodic.

In "Erotic Ballad," a black monk and a blue soldier exchange laments of dismay, as they "Throttle the night on their lonesome way." From each of their bodies there emanates an odor of "sweat and of grief." The soldier complains because he got only "love's glare," and the monk, because his prayers were interrupted by temptation so that he "fondled her breast" and "toyed with her shame." The interplay between the language of passion and the language of grief makes it clear that for each of the speakers the erotic experience, charged with guilt, has been disastrous.

In the best of these poems, such as the "Ballad of the Blue Pitchers," the degree of "difficulty" hardly obscures the visual and musical quality. Here, a feeling that resembles free-floating anxiety is embodied in the dream-narrative of the white-clad women carrying blue pitchers,

With small blue pitchers in their weary hands,
White mothers to the dark well drift.
It may be they will find their golden fortune
Hidden in its silent depth. . . .
But pitchers tremble in their weary hands.

This tone poem, on the theme of turmoil and personal sorrow, ends with a resounding, stately, flourish:

The silent mothers through the village passed
And caused a silver grief in me to sound,
As did the pitchers, weeping on the ground.

◆ ◆ ◆

If anything, the balancing act between pathos and horror became even harder for Manger to sustain in his prose fiction than in his poetry. This is because he turned to writing prose on the eve of the Second World War. One part of Manger's agenda was clearly restorative. In

Noente geshtaltn (1938), Manger assembled an "Intimate Portrait Gallery" of Yiddish poets, playwrights, and prose writers, both men and women, both real and fantastical, from the late Middle Ages until the late nineteenth century—a usable Yiddish past for his overwhelmingly secular and working-class readership. He dedicated this book to the children of the Yiddish secular schools in Poland.[35] Then Manger proceeded to reimagine Paradise as a very *heymish* place where all the generations meet and speak Yiddish. Alas, however, he could not but confront the condition of his people in European exile. In *The Book of Paradise* (1939), Shmuel-Aba Abervo, Manger's great child-protagonist, comes face-to-face with the Jewish historical experience. The work was published on the eve of the German invasion, the whole first edition was destroyed, and only a few review copies reached the United States. Mendl Reif, the artist who illustrated the book, was killed; killed, too, were the vast majority of Manger's readers.

The premise of Manger's plot is cheery enough. A roguish ten- or twelve-year-old angel named Shmuel-Aba Abervo is sent down from Eden to earth to be born as a mortal child. But Shimon-Ber, the angel who is supposed to deliver him to earth, gets so drunk that he fails to notice that the boy has stuck a clay nose over his real one. As a result, the fillip Shimon-Ber makes against the boy's nose, intended to take away the memory of his previous existence in Eden, fails to take effect and Shmuel-Aba is born into an earthly family with his memory intact. Born on a Friday night, he immediately reveals to his parents his miraculous condition and asks that three local dignitaries be invited to the house so that he can describe to them his former life in Eden. (They bear a striking, if comical, resemblance to the Three Magi in Bethlehem contemplating the Baby Jesus.) This, then, is the framing device. The rest of the novel consists of Shmuel-Aba's vivid flashbacks of paradise lost.

With the innocent candor of youth, Shmuel-Aba reveals a highly unorthodox picture. The biblical patriarchs, for example, do not live in perfect harmony either among themselves or with the more recent arrivals, the great Hasidic masters from the Ukraine and Galicia. The cruel round of mortal life as it is experienced on earth is played out in Eden as well. The patriarchs, the kings David and Solomon, and the most venerated saints are the privileged rulers over a mass of poverty-stricken angel-toilers. "Whatever the day hides or blinds with its sunlight, the night reveals." So says Shmuel-Aba's best friend, the boy-angel Pisherl (whose name means Little Pisser). "It lifts the veil of things and you get to look into the abyss."

One thing makes life in Eden different from how it is lived on earth: the citizens of Eden are immortal. But Manger makes of even that reality an occasion for acerbic comment. When two angels fall in love with the grocer's daughter and one of them, in despair, tries to commit suicide, he must, after dangling many hours in the noose with which he tried to hang himself, give up the project and resume his miserable daily life.

On one side of the Paradise ledger, then, are exemplars of love: the friendship between Shmuel-Aba and Pisherl; the ever-compassionate Elijah the Prophet; and Pisherl's innocent love for Anyella, the Christian girl-angel who lives in the Christian Eden to which Pisherl and Shmuel-Aba have been sent on an important mission. On the other side—greed and gratuitous cruelty. Our selection ends with the viciously antisemitic angel Dmitri (who speaks Ukrainian in Manger's original) forcing our young innocents to dance the obsequious Mayofes Dance and to eat forbidden swine. Saintly (Russian-speaking) Saint Peter cannot help them here. The borders are closely guarded. Getting out of the Jewish Eden is easy enough. Getting back in can cost you your soul.

Manger planned still another fiction project, a collection of stories modeled structurally on Bocaccio's *Decameron*. In the projected volume, ten Jews, each from a different part of Eastern Europe, are hiding in a bunker. Aboveground, the slaughter continues unabated. To combat their fear, each surviving Jew tells another tale. Only two of those tales were written: "The Tales of Hershel Summerwind" and "The Story of the Nobleman's Mustaches," both included in this book.

Grounded in early childhood memories (see "At Grandmother Taube's in Stopchet"), "The Tales of Hershel Summerwind" turn fact into fancy. As in the folktale, a wicked stepmother mistreats an orphan. More comical than cruel, she paves the way for other misadventures, including the mock-mythic battle between Hershel and the stepmother's beloved rooster and culminating in Hershel's flight through the air drawn by a flock of drunken birds. Has there ever been a folktale hero who did battle against greater odds?

"The Story of the Nobleman's Mustaches," by contrast, is Manger's darkest fiction. "The Polish nobleman," Manger reminds us, "is a sort of bogeyman figure both in Jewish history and in Jewish folklore: the old nobleman with his wild caprices because of his drinking; the old nobleman with his fierce Polish mustaches and his even more ferocious dogs; the young nobleman attracted to lovely Jewish daughters."[36] Manger's story, a cross between I. L. Peretz and Edgar Allan Poe, retells the well-worn plot of a cruel Polish squire who torments an innocent Jew. To complicate the polarity between Gentile and Jew, however, we glimpse the marital misery of both: while the Jewish barber Mottl Parnas endures his hell with Red Feygele in silence, the nobleman's sexual unhappiness, more openly dealt with than Mottl's, drives him to murder.

The demonic and macabre elements in an otherwise sprightly and almost playful narrative are designed to signal the story's allegorical meaning, which is tied to Mottl's profession and the nobleman's mustaches. In the real world, there is no recourse when a mad despot with a mustache vents his murderous rage against a defenseless Jew. Only in a world still governed by divine retribution does such evil get exposed and punished. Red Feygele's curse speaks for all the bereaved widows, for all Jewish women everywhere.

Luckily for us, no storytelling round is complete without at least one comic tale about that most famous of fools' towns, Chelm. Who doesn't remember what happened one night when the inhabitants of Chelm did not see a moon in the sky? Why, they sent out messengers to buy the town another moon! Where the naive reader sees only hijinks and stupidity, Manger, the lifelong student of Jewish folklore, discovers a "red kernel of tragedy." "Chelm," he writes, "is child. Child with beard and ear-locks, helpless and naive. And from all of its experiences and sorrows there emanates the aroma of the cross. It is where the golden childish naïveté is crucified on the poles of the world's sly refined perversions."[37]

For Manger, the Chelmites are a people whose destiny it is to act out the limitless stupidities of which humankind is capable. They are, then, heroes of disaster and deserve compassion. He thinks of them as Everyman with a duncecap. Holy missionaries who, like Manger himself, are doomed to search for God in the wrong places. From this profound insight comes Manger's jewel, "The Rabbi of Chelm: May His Memory Be Blessed."

The story's ending is especially noteworthy. After we have had our laugh at Chelm stupidity, Manger luxuriates for a few paragraphs on the rebbe bent over his book, in the course of which two things happen: we confront the spiritual heroism of the rebbe, and we achieve a deeper understanding of the Book of Job or of any comparable text in which the nature of divine as opposed to human justice is examined. Thus the simple tale of Chelm that promised nothing more than a moment of humorous condescension has flooded our minds with near-mystical clarity. No wonder the rebbe and his shadow dance.

◆ ◆ ◆

The same impulse that turned Manger into a champion of the folk and that inspired his multiple myths of origin—Berlin, Brody, Jassy, a train compartment—also directed his restless spirit toward a desired goal. At his most romantic, he presents himself as a simple folk poet; the tailor-lad with a mouthful of rhymes who sings of the joys and sorrows of ordinary folk; the troubadour, the wandering, shabbily clad, wine-bibbing minstrel, who is familiar with the open road; a latter-day François Villon, the impractical poet with a head dazzled by metaphors and music. Then there is Manger, a despairing mystic on his pilgrimage to God. Manger the pilgrim, like Manger the folksinger, is a solitary figure, devoted though not devout, for whom the vision of God, like the vision of poetic perfection, is distant before his eyes. "Come with me," he writes in "Evening,"

Hushed, to the edge of the night.
I know that at midnight we'll find
The ultimate light.

Enfolded in lightning
God made his way through my nights,

His footstep moving through me
Resounded with music and light.

And the stars lighted up,
Gleamed on my face and my hair.
If God exists in a dream,
He exists everywhere.

Unlike the vast majority of modern poets, however, Manger's pil-
grimage did come to an end. In 1958, on the eve of departure for Israel,
he composed his own Song of Zion. Echoing the words of the great
twelfth-century Hebrew poet Judah Halevi, our Yiddish poet-pilgrim
had this to say in "For Years I Wallowed":

I'll not kiss your dust as that great poet did,
Though my heart, like his, is filled with song and grief.
How can I kiss your dust? I *am* your dust.
And how, I ask you, can I kiss myself?

And indeed, it was in Israel that Manger finally settled, where he
found a new mass audience and where, for several years before he died,
a Manger Festival was held at which the best actors and singers de-
claimed his verse and performed his songs, in Yiddish and in Hebrew.
On October 31, 1968, the Itzik Manger Prize was established in Israel
at a banquet attended by, among others, Prime Minister Golda Meir,
and President Zalman Shazar.

Manger died in April 1969. His funeral in Tel Aviv, attended by hun-
dreds of mourners, including the translator of this volume, took place
on a hot, sun-drenched day. Throughout the ceremony, some kind of
industrial machinery in the neighborhood tried to invade the grief of
the occasion with a rhythmic metallic noise like the beating of a steel
heart.

Manger, in his own way, would have appreciated the moment. In
Sholem Aleichem's work, Manger had written, "two elements, the
bizarre and the spectral, are vividly present: the intimately idyllic and
the bizarrely grotesque. That romantic expedition into the spectral-
bizarre is, incidentally, characteristic of all the great humorists of world
literature" (see "Sholem Aleichem, the One and Only"). Among them,

François Villon, Charles Dickens, Anton Chekhov, Nikolai Gogol, Sholem Aleichem, and now the Wallachian tailor lad, Itzik Manger.

NOTES

1. Itzik Manger, Foreword to his *Hotsmakh-shpil: a Goldfadn-motiv in 3 aktn*, reprinted in Manger, *Shriftn in proze*, ed. Shloyme Shvaytser (Tel Aviv: Y. L. Perets, 1980), 343.

2. "A shmues mit Yitskhok Manger," *Literarishe bleter* (January 1929), reprinted in Manger, *Shriftn in proze*, 283.

3. Yankl Yakir, "Itsik Manger un zayn yikhes-briv," *Sovetish heymland* (November 1969), 140.

4. Manger, Foreword to *Hotsmakh-shpil*, 343.

5. Ibid. Manger's fullest treatment of the Yiddish theatrical legacy is his Introduction to *Der yidisher teater tsvishn di tsvey velt-milkhomes* (1968), reprinted in Manger, *Shriftn in proze*, 347–359.

6. David G. Roskies, "The Last of the Purim Players: Itzik Manger," in *A Bridge of Longing: The Lost Art of Yiddish Storytelling* (Cambridge, Mass.: Harvard University Press, 1995), 234. This chapter attempts to chart Manger's self-transformation into a folk-bard.

7. Manger, "Mayn veg in der yidisher literatur" (1961), reprinted in Manger, *Shriftn in proze*, 364–365.

8. "Mangers tsavoe," in Arkady Gendler, *My Hometown Soroke: Yiddish Songs of the Ukraine*, notes and introduction by Michael Alpert and Mark Slobin; translated by Jeanette Lewicki (Berkeley, Calif.: Berkeley-Richmond Jewish Community Center, 2001), CD, band 5.

9. Manger, "Dos rumenishe folkslid" (1929), reprinted in Manger, *Shriftn in proze*, 289.

10. See Chaim S. Kazdan, "Itsik Manger in Varshe," *Itsik Manger* (New York: CYCO, 1968), 24–30.

11. See Ruth R. Wisse, Introduction to Isaac Bashevis Singer, *Satan in Goray*, translated by Jacob Sloan (New York: Farrar, Straus and Giroux, 1996), vii–xviii.

12. See Roskies, *Bridge of Longing*, 262–263. Manger's Yiddish biographers, including Rachel Auerbach herself, rarely recorded Manger's misdeeds.

13. Chaim S. Kazdan, *Di letste tkufe in Itsik Mangers lebn un shafn (1939–1969)* (Mexico City: Mendelson Fund, 1973), 12.

14. Ibid., 16, from two letters to Jacob Glatstein dated April 28 and May 6, 1940, printed in *Tog morgn zhurnal*, March 12, 1969.

15. Dan Davin, *Closing Times* (New York: Oxford University Press, 1975), 162.

16. See Kazdan, *Di letste tkufe*, 44. Manger would say later that he arrived in London in 1941 "with one pair of shoes, the shirt on my back, carrying a stick in my hand" (51).

17. Joseph Leftwich, "Epizodn inem lebn fun Itsik Manger," in Itzik Manger, *Oysgeklibene shriftn*, ed. Shmuel Rozhansky (Buenos Aires: Ateneo Literario en el Iwo, 1970), 377.

18. Davin, *Closing Times*, 169.

19. Untitled poem in the Epilogue to Itzik Manger, *Lid un balade* (New York: Itsik Manger Committee, 1952), 479.

20. Reprinted in Kazdan, *Di letste tkufe*, 23.

21. Ibid., 25, from *Der tog*, July 12, 19, 1941.

22. Ruth R. Wisse, *A Little Love in Big Manhattan: Two Yiddish Poets* (Cambridge, Mass.: Harvard University Press, 1988), 229.

23. First, in Czernowitz, c. 1938, then some twenty years later in Montreal, Masha Roskies refused to fete Manger on account of his uncivilized behavior.

24. Davin, *Closing Times*, 155.

25. Ibid., 160.

26. For a bitter exposé of Jewish assimilation in Czernowitz, see the novels of Aharon Appelfeld, beginning with *Baddenheim, 1939*.

27. On Di Yunge, see Wisse, *Little Love in Big Manhattan*.

28. For a sampling of Steinbarg's fables, see Leonard Wolf's translations in *The Penguin Book of Modern Yiddish Verse*, ed. Irving Howe, Ruth R. Wisse, and Khone Shmeruk, 2d rev. ed. (New York, 1989), 113–122.

29. The major scholarly source on the *Purim-shpil* is Chone Shmeruk, *Maḥazot mikrai'im beyidish, 1697–1750* (Jerusalem: Israel Academy of Science and Humanities, 1979). The earliest studies of the *Purim-shpil*, well known to Manger, were by the Polish-Jewish historian Isaac Schipper.

30. Itzik Manger, Foreword to *The Book of Paradise: The Wonderful Adventures of Shmuel-Aba Abervo*, trans. Leonard Wolf (New York: Hill and Wang, 1965), v.

31. Ruth R. Wisse, "1935/6—A Year in the Life of Yiddish Literature," *Studies in Jewish Culture in Honour of Chone Shmeruk*, ed. Israel Bartal et al. (Jerusalem: Zalman Shazar Center, 1993), English section, 99.

32. For a thorough analysis of Manger's classical and modern literary sources, see Chone Shmeruk, "*Medresh Itzik* and the Problem of Its Literary Traditions," Introduction to *Medresh Itzik*, ed., Chone Shmeruk, 3d rev. ed. (Jerusalem: Magnes, 1984), v–xxix.

33. T. F. Henderson, *The Ballad in Literature* (New York: G. P. Putnam's Sons, 1912), 8. See also Gordon Hall Gerould's classic, *The Ballad of Tradition* (Oxford: Clarendon, 1932).

34. For Manger's debt to Verlaine in particular, see "First Letter to X.Y." (1929), translated in this volume.

35. *Noente geshtaltn* is reprinted in Manger's *Shriftn in proze*, 11–134.

36. Itzik Manger, "A zeltener poylisher porits" (1955), reprinted in Manger, *Shriftn in proze*, 472.

37. Itzik Manger, "Di khelmer mayses" (1929), reprinted in Manger, *Shriftn in proze*, 317.

Poetry

INTRODUCTION

A Gift to My Father, the Splendid and Excellent Master Tailor, Hillel, Son of Abraham Manger

The poems gathered in this book are a sort of mischievous toying with the gray beards of the Patriarchs and the head-shawl corners of the Matriarchs.

A sort of intermezzo on the way to an elevated balladic vision.

The alert reader will recognize that the landscape in which these biblical figures move is not Canaanitish but Slavic. I was thinking of eastern Galicia.

That landscape, with its roadside willows, its vineyards, and its strange hushed twilights, has vibrated in my mind from the time of my earliest childhood. It was framed in that landscape that my father, as a wandering journeyman tailor, wrote his Purim plays and acted them out with his comrades.

As I wrote this book, the rogue's cap of the Yiddish Purim play hovered always before my eyes.

As well as the lyric-pious pantomime of my mother bent over her Yiddish Pentateuch.

A propos the landscape:

Once, long ago, on a vacation to my grandfather, away from Czernowitz. In the wagon of my grandfather, the wagon-driver, Abraham Manger, dusk was descending. Darkening. The clouds were not properly clouds at all but rather strange creatures that hung over and lay upon the willows beside the road, frightening to a child's mind.

A sweet terror in a child's mind! Whether my grandfather was driving me to the sacrifice?

My grandfather had sorrowful eyes. His whip had a red tassle. And a piece of the hide of the horse that was harnessed on the right side had been rubbed smooth.

THE SACRIFICE OF ITZIK

Rock me, blind fate, rock me
As I dream with open eyes
Of a bird with silver wings
Crossing the sea as it flies.

What does the silver bird bring me?
Only God in his Heaven can tell.
Sweet wine in my grandfather's cup*
From the Land of Israel?

But who has mentioned my grandfather's name,
That wagoner from Stopchet?
He says, as he strides toward me,
"The sacrifice is set."

Blazing at me are his eyes
Like two bright autumn stars;
His beard, disheveled by the wind,
Is moist with seven great tears.

Over cities, towns, and graves
He leads me by the hand.
The towns are large, the cities small
As we stride over them.

He says, "Do you remember
Itzik, those years gone by
When the angel revealed himself
And, Itzik, you survived?

Our old God regrets that now
And wants his sacrifice,
Though I've lived many lifetimes
And many times have died.

Enough! Who needs His mercy?
He'd better not think, up there . . .
It's well for her, your mother's dead—
At least she's spared more tears."

Over cities, towns, and graves
He leads me by the hand.
The towns are large, the cities small
As we stride over them.

I PRAISE THEE LORD in Heaven, I praise / Thee God for
strengthening my days. / I thank Thee that with hand so weak /
I've finished just the same this work. / Diligence and care I've
taken / And the Patriarchs I've wakened / From holy texts and
silver dust / That hardened on them like a crust. / Here they stand,
prepared to give / You proof that they are now alive; / To greet, dear
readers, each of you / With a cheerful, "Howdy-do?" / They with
their holy mouths will tell / Of many wonders, all so still. / And he
who worked to make this book, / Days and hours and days he took.
/ Itzik Manger's is the hand, / The tailor from Wallachian land.

EVE AND THE APPLE TREE

She stands before the apple tree
While the red sun sets.
Mother Eve, what do you know,
What do you know of death?

Death, ah death's the apple tree
Whose weary limbs bend down,
It is the bird upon the branch
Singing an evensong.

Adam's to the wild wood gone
At dawn into the wood.
Adam says, "The wood is wild
And all that's wild is good."

But Eve is frightened of the wood,
Prefers the apple tree,
And when she does not go to it,
It comes to her in dreams.

It rustles; it leans over her;
It says, "Beloved Eve,
Not every warning Word God speaks
Has to be believed."

In love, she plucks an apple—
She feels strangely light.
Round and round the tree she goes
Like a butterfly in flight.

And God Himself who warned her
Says, "The tree *is* fair."
And keeps the sunset lingering
Another moment more.

This is what she dreams each night,
But what's the truth? A tear
Shed by the weeping apple tree
That falls into her hair.

"Lovely apple tree, don't weep,
I am your melody.
I know that you are stronger
Than the Word that's warning me."

Eve enfolds the apple tree,
She clasps it in her arms
While overhead, the pious stars
Tremble with alarm.

EVE BRINGS ADAM THE APPLE

The first man, Adam, lies in the grass,
And spits at a passing cloud,
Humbly, the cloud says, "Adam,
"Please, would you cut that out."

But Adam sticks out his tongue
And says to the cloud, "Too bad,"
Then spits a slender stream of spit
And says, "There's more of that."

Wiping the spittle with his sleeve
The cloud grumbles angrily,
"That's what comes of nothing to do,
And lying about all day."

The first man, Adam, laughs and laughs,
His teeth make a fine display
Just as Mother Eve comes back
From her walk in the apple allée.

"Where have you been, oh Eve, my wife,
My dear, where have you been?"
"Strolling about in the plum allée
And chatting with the wind."

"You haven't been to the plum allée,
It's a lie; you've not been there.
Your body smells of ripe apples
And there's apple smell in your hair."

"It's true, I've been in the apple allée—
What a poor memory I have;
You've guessed it at once, my dear husband,
God bless you, my darling love."

"What did you do in the apple allée,
My dear, where have you been?"
"I was chatting with the serpent
About a blessed-sin."

The apple trembles in her hand,
Gleaming scarlet red,
Foreshadowing, as she holds it,
Twilight and passion and death.

The first man, Adam, is puzzled by
The sweetness in her voice.
And he simply cannot understand
Her strange new loveliness.

Trembling, he puts his hand out—
"Stop, Adam. You're making me blush."
The night extinguishes their shapes—
H, U, S, H spells "Hush."

ABRAHAM SCOLDS LOT

Lot—it's disgusting—it's got to be said—
You and your nightly carouse—
Yesterday, in the Golden Hart . . .
What a terrible scandal that was.

Manger the tailor can do such things,
But it simply won't do for you.
You've a couple of daughters to raise, you're rich—
Knock wood—and besides, you're a Jew.

You've cattle and sheep and flocks of goats—
Take my advice—fear God.
Already, a swilling Gentile is said
To be "As drunk as Lot."

I know how it is, on a Friday night,
To drink a cup or two
Of wine with the fish, while the Sabbath lights
Shed their holy glow.

But how can one go on drinking
Day in, day out—like you?
It's all right for Havrillah, the Sabbath-goy,*
But certainly not for a Jew.

Consider what will be said one day—
That the Patriarch Abraham's kin
Was worse than a convert—steeped in wine
And other kinds of sin.

They're saying already—Listen to me!
My God, don't you care what they think?
And you're a father . . . the matchmaker
Avoids your house like a stink.

Even the humblest tailor's lad
Considers himself too fine
To marry your daughters—Shall their braids
Turn gray—for the sake of wine?

Lot—it's disgusting—it's got to be said—
You and your nightly carouse—
Yesterday, in the Golden Hart . . .
What a terrible scandal that was.

Manger the tailor can do such things,
But it simply won't do for you.
You've a couple of daughters to raise, you're rich—
Praise God!—and besides, you're a Jew.

Lot's daughters sit in the kitchen
Whispering among themselves.
One of them plucks a new-killed goose,
The other one mends a dress.

The first one says, "A week ago
It was my fortieth year.
Today when I looked in the mirror,
I saw my first gray hair.

Father carouses in taverns
And the years pass swiftly by.
My bridal shoes in the closet
Lie waiting, hopelessly."

The second lets her needle drop
And sits engrossed in thought.
"Sister," she says, "my bedclothes
At night grow feverish hot."

She says, her breathing parched, "I dreamed
A blue-clad soldier came
And slept all night between my breasts . . .
It was a lovely dream.

And then he left the dream and me—
He does not reappear—
As if no troops were garrisoned
Among us any more."

The first one says, "Now listen,
Because I have a plan.
If bridegrooms will not come to us—
A father is also a man."

Her cheeks are flushed, her breath is hot,
Her voice unsteady, dim:
"Sister, on this very night
I mean to lie with him.

Tomorrow, you. Why should we wait?
Our father is drunk as Lot.
And mother, in that cursed town
Of Sodom turned to salt."

They're both inflamed. Around their lamp
Beats a tardy butterfly . . .
"Sister, get ready. Our father comes
Stumbling heavily."

ABRAHAM AND SARAH

"Abraham, when will we have a child?
We're not getting younger, you know.
Other women my age would have had
Eighteen children by now."

The Patriarch Abraham puffs at his pipe
And waits, then he says with a smile,
"A broomstick, my dear, can be made to shoot
If the Lord thinks it's worthwhile."

"Abraham, love, each night I hear
My body sobbing for life . . .
Hagar is only your handmaiden
While I am your own true wife.

Often, it seems to me that the star
That gleams in the windowpane
Is the soul of my child that's wandering
Among shadows and wind and rain."

The Patriarch Abraham puffs at his pipe
And waits, then he says with a smile,
"A broomstick, my dear, can be made to shoot
If the Lord thinks it's worthwhile."

"When I see Hagar's son playing
With sunbeams in the sand
I find myself caressing him
And grief overwhelms my hand.

And when I take him in my lap
His smile's so bright and sweet,
I feel my blood turn strangely cold
And then my eyes are wet.

Abraham, when will we have a child?
We're not getting younger, you know.
Other women my age would have had
Eighteen children by now."

The Patriarch Abraham puffs at his pipe
And waits, then he says with a smile,
"A broomstick, my dear, can be made to shoot
If the Lord thinks it's worthwhile."

HAGAR'S LAST NIGHT IN ABRAHAM'S HOUSE

Hagar, the servant, sits in the kitchen;
A smoking oil lamp spills
The shapes of shadowy cats and dogs
To flicker on the walls.

She weeps because her master
Fired her today.
"Beat it, you bitch," he told her.
"Can't you let me be?"

It was Sarah who egged him on,
That proper deaconess,
Saying, "You get rid of the girl
Or give me a divorce."

Hagar takes out of her trunk
A summer hat of straw;
She takes her green silk apron
And her bloodred beads of coral.

These were the gifts he gave her
Once upon a day
When they strolled the meadow
By the railroad right-of-way.

"How like the smoke of a chimney,
How like the smoke of a train
Is the love of a man, dear mother,
The love of any man.

God knows where we will run to,
Myself and his bastard child,
Unless in some alien kitchen
We are allowed to hide."

She takes the kitchen broom up,
She sweeps the kitchen floor.
Under her blouse, her heart says,
"I love him." She sweeps some more.

Again, she does the dishes,
She scours the copper pan.
"How like the smoke from a chimney
Is the love of any man."

HAGAR LEAVES ABRAHAM'S HOUSE

The dawn is blue at the window,
Three times the rooster crowed.
Outside the horse is neighing,
Impatient for the road.

Hagar is worn with weeping;
Her child lies in her arms:
Once more she casts her eyes around
The gray, familiar room.

Outdoors, the teamster haggles
For his fare with Abraham:
"All right, six dollars, even,
For hauling both of them."

The pony scrapes the gravel
As if it were saying, "Come on!
Give me a chance to show you
How to make the highway tame."

"This is our portion, Ishmael;
Darling, dry your tears.
This is the way of the Fathers
With their long and reverend beards."

She foresees herself abandoned
In a railroad waiting hall
In a foreign country and she sobs
Into her Turkish shawl.

"Hagar, stop that sniveling—
Woman, do you hear me or no?"
Hagar takes her bundle,
Hagar turns to go.

He stands with his silken cap on,
The pious Abraham—
"Dear mother, tell me, does he feel
My heart's defeated pain?"

The whistle blows; they've started.
She sees, through tear-rimmed eyes,
The village houses slowly
Scrape backward in a haze.

She takes the earth and heaven
To be her witnesses:
This is the way of the Fathers
With their long and reverend beards.

HAGAR ON HER JOURNEY

Hagar, worn with weeping,
Sits on a highway stone.
She asks of every passing wind
The way that she must go.

One says, "Hagar, take the east."
Another, "West, that's where."
A third wind is a prankster
And plays among her hair.

Hagar asks the passing birds
Flying through the air.
One whispers, "You go north."
Another, "South, that's where."

She weeps, "For years, O God,
I served him faithfully.
See now how any bird or wind
Can make a fool of me?"

Hagar lifts her head
And sees a caravan
Led by the Turkish sultan
With a mantle all of green.

Nearer, he comes, and nearer,
Then speaks. His voice is firm:
"Tell me, are you Hagar,
Servant to Ibrahim?

And your little baby boy,
Is Ishmael his name?
We have heard our prophet say
That we descend from him."

The sultan falls before her,
He kneels down in the dust.
"Our lineage finds its honor.
Allah, O Allah be praised."

Not knowing what the truth is,
She can only stare
While the moon is a silver crescent
Glistening in her hair.

ABRAHAM TAKES ITZIK TO THE SACRIFICE

The gray light of the dawning
Touches the earth with dawn.
Eliezer, the loyal servant, puts
The black team's harness on.

Taking the child up in his arms,
Old Abraham shuts the door.
Over his ancient roof, there gleams
A blue and pious star.

"Up, Eliezer"—the whip rings out,
The road has a silvery look.
"Sad and lovely," the poet says,
"Are the roads of the Holy Book."

The graying willows on the way
Run to the house again
To see if his mother stands beside
The cradle of her son.

"Daddy, where are we going now?"
"To Lashkev—to the fair."
"Daddy, what are you going to buy
At Lashkev—at the fair?"

"A soldier made of porcelain,
A trumpet, and a drum;
A piece of satin to make a dress
For mother, who waits at home."

Abraham feels his eyes grow moist
And the steel knife pressing, where
It scalds the flesh beneath his shirt . . .
"To Lashkev . . . the fair . . . some fair."

"Eliezer, stop at the water mill.
Stop for a while and wait.
Isaac, my son, and I will go
On from there on foot."

Eliezer sits and grumbles, and casts
Down the road an anxious look.
"Sad and lovely," the poet says,
"Are the roads of the Holy Book."

THE PATRIARCH ABRAHAM GETS A LETTER

The Patriarch Isaac walks in the field,
Serious, solemn, and grave,
And sees a butterfly perching on
A cornflower, where it waves.

A moment, two, and it's gone—
Far, far, without remorse—
Ah, has the charlatan at least
Given the flower a divorce?

In Isaac's eye there gleams a tear—
"The world is filled with sin."
Then slowly, gravely, Isaac goes
To his father Abraham's tent.

The Patriarch Abraham on the sill
Chats there with the postman,
Who has brought a letter, sealed,
For Abraham, Terah's son.

"The bride's well-dowered, lovely, too,
And everything's *all right.**
Very soon I'll bring her home,"
True Eliezer writes.

"Yes, very soon, I'll bring her home
With camels, jewels, and cash.
Her name is Rivke, and she's famed
For the way that she cooks fish."

Abraham smiles and gives
The postman some baksheesh.
Ah, since his dear wife, Sarah, died,
Abraham's not tasted fish.

He shuts his eyes—Ah, he feels good
To hear the melody.
Of the Gemara* Yitshok sings—
He'll grow in piety.

*Amar Abai,** how sweet it is.
The old man nods and smiles.
In his beard a sunset ray
Plays, trembling, for a while.

Rachel stands at the mirror and braids
The strands of her long, black hair;
She hears the sound of her father's cough—
His wheezing on the stair.

Swiftly, she runs to the alcove,
"Quick, Leah—it's Daddy, come."
Leah hides her *True Romance*
And slowly leaves her room.

Her face is weary, pale, and wan;
Her eyes red-rimmed with grief.
"Leah, you're ruining your eyes;
Haven't you read enough?"

Rachel takes the water jar
And starts off to the well.
The evening's enough to make you weep—
So pale . . . so beautiful.

She passes through the darkling field.
A hare goes darting, quick
As lightning . . . a little *lamed-vov**
Chirps in the grass—*Tshirik.*

A golden earring in the sky
Gives off a shimmering gleam.
"How I'd want them—ah, how much—
Were there but two of them."

Nearby, a piper's piping,
"Tri-li, tri-li, tri-li."
In the breath of every sheep and cow
Is the smell of dusk and hay.

She runs. It's late. The Bible says
A guest waits at the well;
Today, the cat has washed itself;*
Rachel is fasting still.

She runs, and the golden earring casts
Above her its bright gleam.
Ah, how she would want those rings
Were there but two of them.

THE PATRIARCH JACOB MEETS RACHEL

It's late in the evening. Weary,
The Patriarch plods his way.
"There's the well, the one to the left.
That's it, certainly."

He checks his pocket Bible.
"Of course, of course, right there!"
In that case, what's the reason
That the girl is not yet here?

She comes! The pitcher in her hand.
She runs. "Ah, what a girl.
More lovely than the Bible says.
She is a perfect jewel.

Bon soir, my pretty *mademoiselle.*
I am an *étranger.*
That is . . . perhaps . . . *vous comprenez*
I mean . . . I'm not from here.

However, Miss, know that I have
An uncle hereabouts.
It may be he's well known to you.
Vous comprenez, sans doute.

His name is Lavun. *C'est a dire,*
He's not just anyone.
He's said to be a millionaire
By all the folks back home."

"Laban Harami is, young man,
No one but *mon pappa.*"
"Then, *mademoiselle,* unless I'm wrong,
You must be cousin Ra . . . "

"And you are Jacob, *mon cousin.*"
She's ember red with shame
As Jacob, in his secret heart
Thinks, "Wow, oh what a dame."

Each takes the other by the hand.
A cooling evening wind
Swirls them in a firm embrace
One moment and is gone.

LEAH BRINGS MANDRAKES FROM THE FIELD

A handful of mandrakes* in her hand,
Leah makes her way
Across the field. The evening sprinkles
Gold on a hut of clay.

Running to greet her, a slender wind
Calls out breathlessly,
"Leah, your children are weeping
Behind the green nut-tree."

"A mother's troubles—" Leah runs,
Her dress stirred by the wind,
Passing the windmill on the hill
That stands with her outstretched vanes.

As if she, also, somewhere had
A Jacob and children of gold
Weeping behind a green nut-tree . . .
As if she, too, were called.

Past Dudyeh's roadside bar, she runs,
Where the evening's first lamp burns.
And here's the little chapel green,
And here, the courthouse stands.

A moment's pause as she breathes deep.
She sees her sister go—
In Rachel's hand, an infant's shirt
Of silk, sewn long ago.

Leah calls, "Dear Rachel, see
The mandrakes that I've brought.
Set them under your pillow
When you go to bed tonight.

God willing, when nine months are gone,
Then, sister—wait and see . . . "
The poet hears them whispering
But not the words they say.

He turns his head discreetly.
Though he can't hear a word,
He knows it is a whispering
Eternal as the earth.

JACOB TEACHES THE STORY OF JOSEPH TO HIS SONS

"What makes you all so silent,
Reuben, my oldest son?"
"Our Purim play, dear father,
Is ready to begin."

"Come, put on your silken shirt,
Joseph, my best-loved son.
Your brothers need to sell you
To strangers once again.

When they throw you in the pit,
Weep, but not for long.
It's not the first time that you act
This play out, my dear son.

But when you pass your mother's grave
That stands beside the way,
Be sure you shed a real tear
And softly, gently say

That gladly would old Jacob serve
Another seventh year
If once before his death he might
Again caress her hair.

By now, you know the rest by heart—
Your exits, cues, and bows.
Again, in Pharaoh's dream there graze
His seven fattened cows.

Unriddle his dreams without a fault,
As truly as before;
And don't forget, in Heaven's name,
To send me a sack of flour.

And one thing more, in Heaven's name,
Be virtuous, my dear . . .
Look out for the wiles of Pharaoh's wife,
For she is young and fair.

Hey, now, my sons, why do you stand
Without a word to say?"
"Because, Father Jacob, you yourself
Have spoiled the Purim play."

Bathsheba looks at the brilliant ring
She's slipped onto her hand.
It isn't the ring he sent that counts,
But the king who rules the land.

Ah, not the ring but the note he sent,
The note that makes her weep.
"Your face, your walk, your graceful ways
Have robbed me of my sleep."

Bathsheba looks in the mirror and sees
She's lovely. That much is true,
But how can a faithful woman like her
Go to a rendezvous?

What of her aged father-in-law,
And her husband, the general?
And what about God? What will He say—
The Guardian of Israel?

Again, she reads the note. He writes,
"Your beauty is all I see.
As for God, we've worked things out.
I do what pleases me.

If I sing him a psalm from time to time,
He forgives me all of my sins.
As for your husband . . . trust me, dear,
I'll take good care of him."

A curtain rustles. "What's that? What's that?"
It's only the wind at play.
She hides the ring; she hides the note
And slowly makes her way

Into the garden. Her slow steps
Are muffled by yellow sands;
But all at once, at the garden gate,
A scarlet moonbeam lands.

One final twinge of shame and then
She opens the door with her hand.
It isn't the ring, the ring that counts,
But the king who rules the land.

KING DAVID AND ABISHAG

King David leafs his book of psalms;
(It's the middle of the night).
Outside, a soldier stands his watch
Before the palace gate.

Murmurs the king, "All-powerful God,
I know that you are here
Within me and my book of psalms
Each second of each hour."

He rises. That's enough for now,
This talk with blessed God.
Like a shadow, he drags himself
Slowly toward his bed.

Abishag sleeps gently
And talks out of her sleep.
From her dream there drifts the scent
Of a meadow with its sheep,

Of a river and a stand of pines
And a village moon that glows,
Of an ancient, pious linden tree
That guards her mother's house,

Of longing, and the gnawing pain
Of grief that leads away
Both from the king and from his psalms
To its own melody.

King David thinks—"How strange it is.
She sleeps in her nightgown
Beside me close enough to touch
Yet distant and alone."

The old king bends his head to kiss
The village that she breathes,
And kisses the old linden tree
That guards her mother's house.

Back to his study desk he goes
With weary, silent tread.
He leafs the book of psalms again
And sighs and strokes his beard.

ABISHAG WRITES A LETTER HOME

Abishag writes a letter home—
Sends wishes to the farm and sheep;
She sits in her alcove and she writes—
Her sighs are long and deep.

Best wishes to her mother dear,
To the ancient linden tree—
In her dreams, her parents both
Appear quite frequently.

Best wishes to the handsome boy
Who labors in the mill—
And to the shepherd Oyzer for
His piping song so shrill.

David, the king, is pious and old—
As for her, life isn't bad . . .
She is the royal warming-flask
And warms the old man's bed.

She had supposed—such notions as
A country girl conceives.
Often at night, she sees her fate,
And silently, she grieves.

The wise men say that she does well,
And well they speak of it;
And they have even promised her
A line in holy writ.

One line, because her body's young,
And for her years of youth.
A line in ink on dry parchment
For an entire truth.

Abishag puts aside her pen;
Her heart is heavy, strange.
From her welling eye, there falls
A tear upon the page.

The tear erases "Mother dear."
It wipes out "linden tree."
The maiden-dream in the alcove
Is sobbing, silently.

CAIN AND ABEL

Dost thou sleep, my brother Abel,
That thou art so fair?
Never have I seen thee
As beautiful before.

> Does the beauty lie in my ax,
> Or is it perhaps in thee?
> Before the day is done,
> Speak, answer me.

Thou art still, my brother Abel,
As the heavens and the earth.
Such pensive silence, until now,
In thee I never heard.

    Does the stillness lie in my ax,
    Or is it perhaps in thee?
    Before the day is done,
    Speak, answer me.

I stand beside thee, here,
And see thee, so alone.
Never hast thou been
So strangely alien.

    Does the strangeness lie in my ax,
    Or is it perhaps in thee?
    Before the day is done,
    Speak, answer me.

Come, Mother Eve, see how
My brother Abel lies still.
He never slept so bemused,
In his cradle, for all of thy skill.

    Does the stillness lie in my ax,
    Or does it come from thee?
    Before the day is done,
    Speak, answer me.

Come, Father Adam, and look
At the scarlet ribbon of blood
That wriggles along the earth
And smells so sad and good.

    Does the sorrow lie in my ax,
    Or is it perhaps in thee?
    Before the day is done,
    Speak, answer me.

London, 1941

Even in the king's window, the sun dies.
The king is old; he is as white as snow.
Still to his harp, his wandering glances go.
Even in the king's window, the sun dies.

Death, his echo, waits behind his back,
A smiling Lord of Lords. Upon his head
He wears a crown that is suffused with red;
He stands enfolded in a gold-trimmed cloak.

The king leans on his harp and starts to doze.
Death gently murmurs, "Now, I will enclose
The king within his final nightly grief . . .

Lo, him . . . who was believing as a child,
Sinful as gods, and like the wind, as wild,
And fair, as dreams are fair—past all belief."

◆ ◆ ◆ *Songs of the Megillah*

This Little Book Is Dedicated to My Brother, the Journeyman Tailor, Notte Manger, My Very Best Friend from My Earliest Childhood Days

PROLOGUE

The poems gathered in this little book are once again a kind of mischief-making on the model of Purim* players in every age.

In this little book is retold the lovely old story of Queen Esther, who, together with her uncle Mordecai, set themselves energetically against wicked Haman, whom, finally, they vanquished. May their merit sustain us, now and forever, *amen, selah.*

True, the story is told here a bit differently. The official authors of the Megillah,* for example, have kept silent about the existence of such a significant figure as the tailor lad Fastrigosso, though his despairing love for Queen Esther and his attempt to assassinate King Ahasuerus were crucial elements on several important occasions.

The official chroniclers have kept silent even about the pious old Master Tailor Fonfosso. It would seem that they did not want to weaken the Persian court legend with such crude liveliness.

The reader will conclude that, evidently, they have falsified historical truth, and the reader would be right. But they, the chroniclers, have been lying with stubbornly clenched teeth so long in the earth with their bottoms pointed to the stars that you can call them anything you like, until the coming of the Messiah.

The author of the Megillah Songs has worked diligently to rediscover the personages that have been thus overlooked. He spent years doing research in all sorts of archives, until he succeeded in finding the journeyman tailor Fastrigosso and his old master, Fonfosso.

Was all that work worth it? The author thinks that it was. First of all, he corrected the injustice done by the ancient chroniclers to the two knights of the Society of Needle and Shear. And second:

This work enabled him to approach the comedy of which he had been dreaming for a considerable number of years.

INVOCATION

For this book, no thought was stinted / That would make it nicely printed / And it was made for everyone / For women, and for men / It's filled with wonders dark and deep / To make you laugh or weep / With sayings that they used to say / In dear Queen Esther's day / Then hurry come and look / From crannies, and from nooks, / Come buy this lovely book / So that the vagabond / Who comes from Wallach land / Itzik Manger named / Can pay for his carousing / And, while our Itzik's sousing, / Our God, for Itzik's sake, / Will send away bad luck / As quickly as the wind, / And may the Lord soon send / Messiah ben David down / Amen, selah.

THE SONG OF THE RUNNER

Quiet, people. Stop your din
And let the Purim play begin.

A Purim play in rhyme,
So great you'll love each line.

A play for eyes and ears,
That makes you laugh through tears.

There they go, so still—ah,
The heroes of the Megillah.

Ahasuerus, the drunkard king
Who drinks. Drinks anything.

Esther, the innocent queen,
And Vashti in crinoline.

Mordecai, bilious and wise,
And Haman, the crook, damn his eyes.

And Zeresh, the cursing witch;
Plague take the ugly bitch.

There's Vayzosse, the crashing bore,
The chatterbox edit-or.

And Fastrigosso, with a sigh,
Letting the grander folk go by.

He'll tell you himself what haunts him,
What joy, what sorrow taunts him.

In short, there's plenty of stuff
To cry over—and laugh.

It's all in the play. You'll see,
If you watch carefully.

And if I've told you a lie—
Shut up and watch the play.

HOW THE BLESSED MORDECAI FOUND FAVOR IN THE EYES OF THE KING

"Who's that man at the king's gate
With a knapsack on his back;
The sneaky fellow who sidles up
To eavesdrop when people talk?"

"You mean to say that you don't know
His name? You little fool—ah,
That's the Blessed Mordecai,
The hero of the Megillah.

He found favor with our king—
Our king who's always drinking;
Whose shiny nose is always red,
Whose breath is always stinking."

"How was it he found favor with
Our king who's always drinking;
Whose shiny nose is always red,
Whose breath is always stinking?"

"It happened this way, dear. One night
When he went by, eavesdropping,
He heard Bigthan and Teresh say,
'To hell with our drunken king.

He is a tyrant, he's a boor—
No drink will ever slake him.
Let's put poison in his cup
And let the devil take him.'

The plotters agreed and then
Away they went, so still—ah.
And Mordecai squealed on them
In the accents of the Megillah.

Oh, the king was furious
And punished those poisonous fellows.
The rebels dangled side by side
On two adjoining gallows.

The king rewarded Mordecai,
With a permanent right to sell
Shoelaces, almonds, and kosher soap
For sending those rebels to hell."

The evening turns blue as a prayer,
The child and its mother are still—ah . . .
Quietly, the flies on the wall
Hum the music of the Megillah.

QUEEN VASHTI

Wearing her nightshirt, Queen Vashti sits—
The morning is bright and fair;
She dandles a sunbeam on her knee
Then lets it play in her hair.

Vashti's embarrassed and she says,
"Go away, you impudent thing,
Play with the kitchen servant girls,
But stay away from the queen."

Pretending he doesn't understand,
The sunbeam, that little flirt,
Slips for an instant down her neck
And gambols about in her shirt.

"Ah, you," she trembles—and dreads to think
What her husband, that simpleton,
Would do if he knew that she, the queen,
Had toyed with a common man.

The thought of her husband turns her pale—
A fool and a drunkard, too,
God knows what dangerous things a man
Like that in a rage can do.

She looks at herself in the mirror.
An aging general
Killed himself because of her
In the yard of the arsenal.

"Much good my beauty . . . " the question is,
Is the banquet set for tonight?
Music, lieutenants, champagne, ballet,
Much laughter and delight.

As for Haman, let him sit at home,
That rascal, that parvenu.
God, how she hates his guts—she knows
That Haman hates her, too.

"Zoschye!" The chambermaid comes in,
"Give me the gorgeous dress."
Vashti's unable to hear the sob
Of her inward loneliness.

THE KING'S BANQUET

The king is drunk, as he talks
There's a glistening tear in his eye,
"Vashti my queen is more beautiful
Than the morning star in the sky.

Her braids reach to her knees,
And her body's snowy white,
And her eyes will turn you dizzy,
They are so dazzling bright."

Then, Haman slyly says,
"Why not let Vashti the queen
Come naked before us, here,
So her beauty may be seen?

Then all these noble lords,
By whom you are surrounded,
Can see her loveliness
And stare, astounded."

Then says the drunken king,
"Good thought . . . thus I decree . . .
Let Vashti the queen come naked
Here . . . so they all can see . . . "

The messengers run swiftly,
Come swiftly running back,
"Vashti, the queen can't come.
She says that her teeth ache."

Then slyly Haman smiles,
"Those teeth, my lord—excuses
That wouldn't fool a child—
One of her female ruses."

Then says the drunken king,
"She'll come when I command her
Or else I'll have her shot,
And then I'll hang her."

The messengers run swiftly
And return with baited breath,
With chattering teeth and trembling limbs
Because they're scared to death:

"The queen has barred her door," they say
"With seven bands of steel,
And the message she sends the king:
'I will not do his will.

The king's a sorry drunkard,
And more than that, a lout.
If he wants to make a fool of himself,
Why should I help him out?'"

———————————————

One lord to a second says,
"Time to be getting home,
The old woman must be grumbling,
Lying in bed alone."

A third takes out his watch
And holds it to the light—
They put their stovepipe hats on
And file into the night.

VASHTI'S SONG OF GRIEF

Vashti the royal queen
Is weeping bitterly
Because, young though she is,
She is condemned to die.

"My father was a mighty
Nobleman, a *pan*,*
Whatever made me marry
A drinking man?

Oh, my father warned me,
'Vashti, daughter. Don't.
You'll do better to marry
That Lithuanian count.'

I chose not to listen—
And now I wish I had.
In just a little while,
Queen Vashti will be dead.

I chose not to listen,
Now see my punishment—
Oh you hills and valleys
Pay heed to my lament.

I filled up countless jars
With jellies and with jams;
And now I've got to leave
My spacious rooms.

To leave my spacious rooms,
My bedsteads made of brass,
My silk and satin clothes,
And my designer hats.

Young and beautiful
The king's new wife will be;
While the worms gnaw a young corpse
As beautiful as she.

Back, hangman, back.
Don't come quite so soon.
Let me stand another moment
Grieving here alone.

Give me one more moment
To see my last sun set.
An instant more to feel
A last pang of regret.

How lovely was my life,
My youthful years, how fair—
My rings were all of gold,
And golden was my hair.

Back, hangman, back,
Hold back the night a while,
Give me one more moment
To smile a final smile."

Thus, Vashti, the queen,
Weeps bitterly
Because, young though she is,
She is condemned to die.

"D'you see, Tsippl, through *that* street
Queen Vashti will be led.
Poor thing, the king's condemned her
To a bitter death.

And well deserved. If the king calls
Ought not the queen to go?
You! Had you been in her place,
Would you have gone, or no?"

"Rivke, dear, have you gone mad?
I'd have flown there like a bird.
Mother naked I'd have stood
Before that noble crowd.

I'd have said to Ahasuerus
Just this, word for word:
'You called me—here I am,
My king, my destined lord.'

The king would have enfolded me
In his royal mantle red
And with no cause for anger,
Would not have wished me dead."

"Tfoo! Dvoyre. It isn't nice
To talk so nastily.
My grandpa says that any girl
Who talks like that may be . . . "

"Make way, make way." They lead the queen
To her execution.
Above her young and lovely head
Wheels a youthful falcon.

She walks along with measured tread,
Her eyes brimful of meaning,
Before the sad and silent crowd
Of tailor lads and maidens.

"I leave you now forever,
Forever and a day,
Speak kindly of me please
When you play the Purim play."

"Make way, make way." They lead the queen
To her execution.
Above her young and lovely head
Wheels a youthful falcon.

ESTHER GETTING READY FOR THE KING

Slim Esther stands at her mirror
In her blue velvet dress.
It's dusk, and at her throat
Her pearls are luminous.

She murmurs, "The Purim players
Mock me and say I'm 'green.'
Enough! I know I'm beautiful—
I wonder what they mean?"

Night falls. At Esther's window
An aged walnut tree
Says, "Esther, where is your uncle?
Esther, where can he be?"

Esther blushes, "My uncle's gone
To the courtyard of the king,
Where maidens fair and their matchmakers
Are gathering.

Ah, walnut tree, in a little while
I, too, will be going there.
Tell me, dearest walnut tree,
Can one be green and fair?"

Steps. Mordecai and his umbrella
Make shadows that seem to crawl,
Like versions of his thin hunched back,
Slowly across the wall.

Scratching his beard, he says,
"Are you ready, are you done?
God bless you. Ah, how fine you look
In that blue velvet gown.

Esther, as I live and breathe,
The king, when he sees you—
You'll knock him absolutely dead.
I give you my word, as a Jew.

Well, best foot forward, Esther dear."
They go off, hushed and still,
The humpbacked little uncle
And Esther, slim and tall.

MORDECAI LEAVING ESTHER'S WEDDING

It's dawn and old Reb Mordecai
Leaves the wedding, tipsy.
The wind toys with his beard
And earlocks like a Gypsy.

What's old Mordecai to do?
Chase him? What the hell!
He's old and tired. Who wants to fight
With a windy ne'er-do-well?

What matters is that Esther,
Thank the Lord, is queen,
And that she's inherited
Vashti's golden crown.

Mordecai imagines himself
In the study house surrounded
By bright-eyed Jews with trembling beards
Whose happiness is unbounded.

"Well, what if Esther's no daughter of mine—
In fact, she's only a cousin.
Still, think of the favors she will do
For me and the Jewish nation."

And Mordecai hears Reb Godl saying,
"Here's how it was. When I
Made my annual Succoth* trip
To 'him,'* Reb Mordecai.

God bless him! I heard him say,
'Who knows the good Lord's mind?
But I think if He means to save the Jews
It'll be by a woman's hand.'"

He prattles on, but though the words
At first seem very near,
They slip away from Mordecai
As to a distant star.

It's dawn, and old Reb Mordecai
Leaves the wedding, tipsy.
The wind toys with his beard
And earlocks like a Gypsy.

What's old Mordecai to do?
Chase him? What the hell!
He's old and tired. Who wants to fight
With a windy ne'er-do-well?

Under Queen Esther's window stands
Fastrigosso, the tailor's lad.
"Ah, Esther, do you remember?
'I love you. I love you,' you said.

Don't you remember, Esther dear?
I know what it was I heard.
Esther, why have you deceived me?
Say something, a phrase—a word.

Remember, remember that rainy night
At the gate when we clung together,
And I whispered a secret in your ear
And we did not mind the weather?

I whispered, 'Esther, marry me,
Let's elope to Vienna.'
You were wearing a calico dress
And beads the color of henna.

'But there's my uncle Mordecai,'
You said, 'We can't forget him.
He'll be awfully mad.' You blushed
And said, 'Alright, then, let him.'

Holding each other's hands,
Each of us plighted our troth
And vowed we would be married
On the Saturday after Shavuoth.*

But see what you've let your uncle do!
You're a queen surrounded by guards.
And I hold the wreck of my youth in my hands
Like a gambler who holds bad cards.

Yes, I've thought of drowning myself,
And I've hurried down to the river;
But then I worried that even dead
I would yearn for you forever.

And I have thought of wandering
The world's highways and byways.
But then I thought, 'Wherever I go
Your image will greet me, always.'

And you'll tell me again that you love me—
I know what it was I heard.
Esther, why have you deceived me?
Say something . . . a phrase . . . a word."

QUEEN ESTHER CAN'T SLEEP

The king's asleep. Queen Esther lies
Sleepless in her bed.
She stares at the shadows on the wall
And her eyes are wet.

Pale Fastrigosso's in her thoughts—
The tailor's journeyman.
He loved her truly. Now his love's
Forbidden to the queen.

His latest letter's on her shelf.
Written with tears, not ink.
He writes that he means to kill himself.
What's she supposed to think?

It's true, he's made that very threat
A hundred times or more,
And nothing came of it,
For which she thanks the Lord.

But when he writes that he wanders about
And can't find peace of mind,
Then she grows sad and feels herself
On the verge of losing her mind.

She sees him standing before her with
That puppy-dog look in his eyes,
Singing that song for the thousandth time
Of the golden peacock that flies.

But what's accomplished by her tears,
What good's her sorrow for him?
She is the queen through whom will come
The miracle of Purim.

She prays: "Ah, Fastrigosso, go,
My love, my one desire.
It's true that your needle gleams with gold
But the crown draws me with fire."

And Fastrigosso goes. His head
Is bowed. He walks alone,
Singing to himself the song
Of the peacock that has flown.

And tomorrow another letter will be
Slipped somehow onto her shelf,
A letter threatening, once again,
That he means to kill himself.

FASTRIGOSSO DREAMING

Fastrigosso smiles in his sleep, he sees
Esther, all loveliness,
Walking as he remembers her
In her simple calico dress.

Barefoot, devout and slender, she smiles
And the breeze is in her tresses
And her body is fragrant with spring rain
And it smells of fresh-cut grasses.

Bending over him, she says,
"Please forgive me, dear.
Love is not a trivial toy—
It burns like a blazing fire."

And he—he smiles and is content,
"Ah, my darling bride.
You know, I longed for you so much
I thought of suicide.

Come, dear Esther, let's elope
To Vienna as fast as we can;
I'll be a master tailor there
And have three journeymen.

And you will wear a velvet dress
And bake and cook our food;
And I will rock our little child;
And I will chop the wood."

He sees them already mounted on
A horse as fleet as the wind.
Fastrigosso sits behind Esther,
Who holds the reins in her hand.

"Giddap—oh, Esther, I'm falling . . . help!"
But she doesn't see him fall;
She doesn't see his bloody head
Or his bloody nose at all.

He gets to his feet, he runs, he tries
To catch her, but she's gone;
She's disappeared into the east,
Where now there's a rising sun.

Fastrigosso groans deeply in his sleep,
"I've lost her again, my Esther.
And the golden peacock, once again,
Has lost a golden feather."

Mordecai's weary, but still they beg
For favors, large and small.
"Esther the queen, Reb Mordecai,
Is a relative, after all.

She is the darling of the king,
As anyone can see.
For love of her he will annul
His very own decree."

Mordecai groans. They call from their shops
In their thousands, and each is a Jew.
"They've banned us from the marketplace,
Dear Lord! What shall we do?"

And on top of that, his old rabbi and he
Have just ended another discussion:
About decrees and more decrees—
There's no end to the repression.

In the bathhouse they say that What's-his-name,
Haman, the Wicked, is planning
Trouble for us, but Esther the queen
Can undo all of his cunning.

Reb Mordecai smiles. Our enemies
Are self-important asses.
Not a thousand troops have the power that lies
In one of Queen Esther's blouses.

He sets his watch. Tomorrow he'll be
At her back door in the morning.
And, God willing, he means to give
His niece a few words of warning.

She'll wind the king round her finger
Till he does what she wants, you'll see.
For love of her he will annul
His very own decree.

Reb Mordecai pulls off his boots,
He muses a while, and hears
Off in the distance, a pack of dogs
Who bark at the autumn stars.

THE QUEEN COMES TO THE KING

Surely you know that the king
When he sleeps, doesn't sleep alone.
Into his royal bed
Comes Esther in her nightgown.

She creeps under the covers;
She cuddles up to him;
She blows in his ear and whispers
As she tickles him,

"Daddykins, sweetie, my Lord,
Do you really think that it's right
To make that Wicked Haman
A Panjandrum of the State?

And, darling, my dear, if it's true
That you really love me best,
Then you'll do me this tiny favor—
I'll tickle you if you resist."

The king embraces Esther.
"Stop, sweetheart. You cut that out.
I promise you that Haman
Will have an ugly fate.

I'll hang him one fine morning,
Esther, just wait and see.
But darling, stop that tickling.
Esther . . . tee, hee, hee!"

Outside, a wind is blowing,
Outside there is a rain.
If that wind were clever,
If it had half a brain,

It would carry the news to Mordecai
And it would let him know—
To Mordecai the hunchback
Who has a singed eyebrow.

The king whispers to Esther,
"Will you do . . . that thing . . . that I want?"
She cuddles close, and closer:
"I'm yours, Lord, to command."

Until the clock strikes two,
They hug and kiss and play
Then, sadly, Esther falls asleep:

"*Vayhi . . . vayhi bimey.*"*

FASTRIGOSSO HAS THE BIRDS CARRY A GREETING TO ESTHER

Fly, little birds, fly my darlings,
You know how my heart aches.
Sing, sing at Queen Esther's window,
Sing her this song till she wakes.

Tell her that you have met me
Wandering about on the road.
And tell her the loaf in my knapsack
Is all of the wealth that I own.

And ask her—and tell her—my darlings,
Fly to her roof, fly away.
And sing, along with the breezes,
The words that I've taught you to say:

If the loaf of bread in my knapsack
And the needle in my lapel
Were all that I owned—*and* Queen Esther,
I'd heed the world not at all.

What was it my master, Fonfosso,
Said—he said it so well?
Ah, yes, a man who is yearning
Is stronger than iron and steel.

How right he is, my old master.
A pearl each word that he says.
Isn't it yearning that drove me—
And drives me—from place to place?

Fly little birds, fly my darlings.
You know how my heart aches.
Sing, sing at Queen Esther's window,
Sing her this song till she wakes.

And if you should chance, my darlings
To see the queen shedding a tear,
Catch it up on a wingtip
And bring it to me here.

The tear of a distant lover
Is wealth of a sort, one might say,
Making it easier and harder
To keep wandering day after day.

HAMAN TELEPHONES VAYZOSSE, THE EDITOR, AT HIS OFFICE

"My son! God damn it to hell,
I have news that you never will guess—
An item for your *Daily Fool*
So hot it will stop the press.

The king—long may he live—
Went last night to the market to hunt.
As usual, he caught nine flies—
Then ten, his usual stint.

There among Jew butcher shops,
Suddenly a wild young man is
Who wields a dagger and shouts,
"*Sic semper,* o King, *tyrannis.*

Give me my Esther at once—
Or your days on earth are done.
You think you're a king. Not at all—
You're a bastard, a charlatan."

The king's in the hospital now
And they've jailed the wild young man.
Now, Vayzosse, be smart, spread the news
As widely and quick as you can.

Say it's a dastardly plot
A dreadful intrigue of the Jews.
And when the king gets well,
I'll tell you what else I will do.

"Kill the Jews, my Lord," I will say,
"They're immigrant scum . . . who knows . . .
Lithuanians, Russians, or Poles . . .
And all of them wear funny clothes."

Ah, Vayzosse, my son, you'll see,
The revenge I will take will be good.
This year, the kikes will have
Quite a Purim—a Purim of blood."

Vayzosse smiles. "Yes, yes, yes.
We'll play 'Run, rabbit, run.'
And laugh as they round the kikes up.
And laugh when they're all dead and gone."

Vayzosse at his desk sits and writes;
He laughs, he talks to himself,
As the portrait of the king
Looks benignly down from its shelf.

FONFOSSO, THE MASTER TAILOR, DELIVERS A EULOGY ON FASTRIGOSSO

A crowd of tailors sits in the tavern,
Members of Needle and Shear.
Fonfosso, the Master Tailor, stands
And wipes away a tear.

"I knew Fastrigosso well—
A fine young journeyman.
A decent lad with a heart of gold
And gold in the touch of his hand.

He was quick, very quick with his needle,
Much quicker indeed than the wind.
Many's the time that I offered
To give him my daughter's hand.

I mean my dear Hannah-Dvoyre,
The oldest daughter I have—
A woman as meek and as mild
And true as a turtledove.

But the boy always said, 'My master,
That wedding's not meant to be.
There's only one woman, Queen Esther,
Who's destined to marry me.'

He went on, 'We'll run off to Vienna
And there we'll be married soon.'
It was easy to see that the lad
Was crazier than a loon.

But that he'd make use of a penknife—
My gift—to attack the king
There in the public market . . .
Who could predict such a thing?

Surely you know that rebellion
Is punished by death, to this day.
It's a crime for which Fastrigosso
On the gallows, in chains, had to pay . . .

All the while the poor fellow was singing
Of Esther the beautiful queen,
And that other song of the peacock
That flies on golden wings.

He had bad luck from the outset—
Fastrigosso, the poor journeyman,
Here's to him and pray that his fortunes
Improve where he lies underground."

Thus spoke the old Master Tailor
To the members of Needle and Shear,
And dabbed with his sleeve at his old eyes
To wipe off a second tear.

THE KING AHASUERUS AFTER THE ASSASSINATION ATTEMPT

The king in his underpants looks out
At the sparkling summer night.
He thinks, "How plentiful the stars . . .
How marvelous their light."

He takes a breath, "How sweet it is
To be alive; to shout;
To guzzle wine and fornicate
And wave my sword about.

Just think what might have happened—
Just think what might have been,
If that crazy young tailor had killed me,
What would have happened then?

They'd have stuck me ten feet under,
And there I would have lain
Where birdsong never reaches
And starlight's never seen.

Who knows? Perhaps my Esther
Would mourn for me a year?
If that. Good Lord, what if
She has a love affair?

While I, underground, meet Vashti,
Who cries, 'So it's you, little man—oh!
Tell me, how does my canary,
And who's playing on my grand piano?'"

He shudders. "That Haman is right.
Get rid of them all this time.
Tomorrow I'll send off the letters
At a quarter after nine.

Let the kikes understand that I mean it.
It's not just a Purim play."
Slowly, he closes the window
Against the cool damp of the day.

He sits at his desk. He spits in
The inkwell and takes a deep breath.
Then signs, page by page, the decree
That will send the Jews to their death.

It's night, Queen Esther patches
The king's shirt in her hand.
Once she was only an orphan,
Estranged in a strange land.

But her mother's soul interceded
And her uncle, the go-between.
Now the fool of a king is her husband
And she is his proper queen.

And Esther can have what she wants—
The king's true and faithful to her . . .
She can bathe both in milk and in wine.
Who could ask for anything more?

Knock, knock. There's a knock at the door.
Slowly, Mordecai comes in.
"Esther, I've brought you some news.
And I'm glad that I find you alone."

She says, "Perhaps my dear uncle
Would like a nice cup of tea?
It's been raining and snowing outdoors—
Storming the livelong day."

"As for that," Uncle Mordecai sighs,
"Things, Esther, are really not good.
On the fourteenth of Adar*—that's Purim—
Blood will be shed. Jewish blood."

Esther is silent. She knows
How angry the king has been
Since he was attacked in the street
By the tailor journeyman.

And she knows that Haman is whispering,
"Jews this . . . and Jews that, and Jews do . . . ,"
Reminding the king that the man
Who attacked him was also a Jew.

Softly, old Mordecai says,
"Esther, prepare your great fast.
Satan and I've made a deal
And he's promised to do his best."

He whispers a word in her ear,
"Do you know what I mean or not?
This Purim, with God's help, and yours,
We'll have something to celebrate."

Esther turns feverish, the shirt
She holds falls out of her hand.
Again, she feels like an orphan
Estranged in a strange land.

WICKED HAMAN CAN'T SLEEP

"Haman, what's wrong? Why can't you sleep?"
"I can't, my dear. It's true.
The minute I doze, old Mordecai
Appears in my dream—that Jew.

'Haman,' he says, 'What news, old boy?'
Then he sticks out his tongue.
'I see I've got you climbing the walls:
And your nose . . . good Lord, it's long.'

Then he utters a curse and laughs, 'Ha, ha!'
And he eats a *hamantash**
And takes a drink from my bedside flask—
Jack Daniels, sour mash.

'Haman,' he says, 'To your defeat!
That's what I drink to you.'
Then he hums through his crooked nose some tunes
From *The Essential Jew.**

'Beat it, you kike,' I cry. He says,
'Like hell,' or something worse.
'Who led whom through the market square
Astride the king's own horse?'"

"Plague take you, my love. You're a man of rank . . .
Remember that you once said
To my father you had a knack for power,
That you had a prime minister's head.

And here you let some scabby Jew
Lead you around by the nose.
Dear jackass, we ought to start feeding you
Oats and chaff and grass."

"Zeresh, my wife, enough, enough.
Spare me your woman's speeches.
Tell me what I'm supposed to do
When the queen wears the royal breeches."

"Do? The thing is to flatter her.
To wind her about, like a thread.
Praise her, Haman, my darling oaf,
And turn her foolish head."

"You're right, as always, Zeresh dear.
And it's true, I'm a simpleton.
Now hand me my trousers, Zeresh, my love . . .
Ah, flattery—that's the plan."

Haman smiles, "I'll fix you, you kike.
Do you hear what I have to say?"
In the garden, a thousand sparrows
Sing to greet the day.

Peter, the royal watchman,
Is sweeping up the dirt
When he sees wicked Haman
In the yard of the king's court.

Peter thinks as he scratches his neck,
"Lord Haman looks a fright;
You can tell from the bags he has under his eyes
That he hasn't slept all night."

"Good morning, Sir Haman," Peter says,
And then he doffs his hat.
"We had one terrible time last night
Because of Queen Esther's cat.

You know her. Well, Mitzi died—
God spare us both. And the queen—
Such weeping and wailing . . . I tell you, Sir,
'Twas like nothing you've ever seen."

Haman twisting his black moustache
Says, "Beat it," and utters a curse;
Then he strides across the palace court
Jingling his sword and spurs.

And Haman sees the queen herself
Where, at the window, she stands
Emptying her silver chamber pot
With her royal hands.

"I thank you, my queen," he says aloud,
"For the favor I've been shown."
Then mutters softly, "Can you believe
The Jewess sleeps in her crown."

"Good morning, Lord Haman," Esther says,
The silver pot in her hands.
"I'd like to invite you, Haman, Sir . . ."
Confused and perplexed, she stands,

And then goes on, "Next Saturday night
I'm giving a great masked ball.
And you're invited, Haman, Sir,
It'll be in the royal hall."

Esther closes the window
And Haman laughs with delight,
"Well, my beautiful Esther, well,
Just wait until Saturday night."

FONFOSSO AND HIS APPRENTICES SEW A UNIFORM FOR HAMAN

Fonfosso, the chalk in his hand, says,
"Better to cut the sleeves short.
Or else," continues the tailor,
"The risk is, we'll run out of cloth."

He says, "Now, apprentices, listen,
You've done fine, and the work's well begun,
But we only have till tomorrow
To get Haman's new uniform done."

Their needles fly, and they're singing,
And the time's just past two A.M.
Fonfosso finds himself musing—
"Merely the thought makes me sick.

Haman—who issues his edicts
As if edicts are all he can do.
If it makes even converts uneasy,
Don't ask what it does to a Jew."

Tall Lozer sings, "A tailor's lad
Saw the queen in a mirror one day
And the beautiful Esther stole
The young man's heart away.

So he said to her, 'Esther, my dear,
Let's elope to Vienna, my queen.
We'll pawn what we own and we'll buy
A Singer sewing machine.'"

Fonfosso sighs, "That song was the one
His union comrades made,
Remembering poor Fastrigosso,
Who worked at the tailor's trade."

Their needles fly, they glitter;
And the hands of the clock show four.
The work has to be done by tomorrow,
Haman's new uniform.

Outside, in the court, the apprentice
Waves the iron he has filled with hot coal,
Sending up showers of sparks
Scorching the night as they fall.

PIOUS MORDECAI WAITS FOR SATAN

Mordecai thinks, "Where's the devil—
May his name be blotted out—
Can it be that the fellow's deceived me
Or merely that Satan is late?"

Mordecai's meeting in secret
Tonight with the devil, who said
He would teach him a trick to push Haman
Straight into Queen Esther's bed.

Where she, God bless her, Queen Esther,
Will be lying, apparently sick.
Mordecai, who loves the idea,
Is pleased at this part of the trick.

The king, seeing Haman in bed
With Esther will set up a shout,
"Haman, God damn you, Haman,
What the hell is this all about?

Making a pass at the queen, eh?
I'll see you six feet underground."
Then turning to Mordecai, he'll say,
"It beats all. I don't understand."

And Haman—here, Mordecai's certain—
Will have a most miserable end.
He sees him strung up on the gallows,
The villain will swing in the wind.

He can hear the excited old rabbi,
"Hey, bring your noisemakers out.
Louder, much louder, the villain
Is dead, beyond any doubt."

But quietly, Mordecai will say—
His voice dignified and genteel,
"I praise the miraculous hand
Of the Lord, who has turned fortune's wheel."

But damn it to hell, where's the devil?
May his name be blotted out.
Can it be that the fellow's deceived him
Or merely that Satan is late?

Mordecai's meeting in secret
Tonight with the devil, who said
He would teach him a trick to push Haman
Straight into Queen Esther's bed.

The master tailor, Fonfosso,
Sits at his sewing machine;
And sad and dark are the thoughts
That are racing through his brain.

Today, Reb Gedaliah, the rabbi
Read out Queen Esther's decree;
And the rabbi wept as he read it,
It was pitiful to see.

"Jews," thus Esther has written,
"Hear me and obey
All of you, rich or poor,
Shall eat no food today.

The merit of your fast
Will fling bad Haman down.
And pious Jews will get
To keep their beards unshorn

And Jews henceforth will eat
Poppy-seed hamantashn.
And Purim plays each year
Will be in fashion."

The old master tailor sighs,
"The apprentices say they refuse
To fast. They've hidden their needles
And not a one of them sews,

'No, master, no. We won't fast.
No, no, and ten times no.
And if the tyrants come,
We'll break a bone or two.'"

The master tailor Fonfosso
Sits at his sewing machine,
Sad and dark are the thoughts
That are racing through his brain:

He thinks of his wife, Sarah-Gitl,
It's been years since she died.
And of Hannah-Dvoyre, his daughter,
Who's becoming an old maid.

And of his apprentice tailors
Who are plotting some foolish scheme—
And now the master tailor
Sheds tears on his sewing machine.

QUEEN ESTHER, FASTING

Esther, the queen, is weary and pale,
And trembles as if she had fever.
"Soon—in forty-five minutes, thank God,
The fast day will be over."

The king, when he saw her, said, "Dear,
What makes you look so pale?
Tell me what makes you so wan
On a day this beautiful."

How to the foolish king can she say,
"My Lord, I'm pale, it's true . . .
It's Esther's fast and I must fast
Because Mordecai told me to?"

May the fast bring Haman down, Lord,
Him and his flattery . . .
That charlatan, that crashing bore,
That sly old debauchee.

"The light of the sun and the moon and the stars
Compared with you are dim."
Each hypocrite word he utters is false,
But she has to put up with him.

It's what her uncle wants. He says,
"Let him bark on to the end.
Every word of a villain like that
Is a spume that blows in the wind.

The Megillah," her uncle says,
"Has prophesied of him
That Haman one day will be a thing
Of scorn to kith and kin."

That's what her uncle Mordecai says,
And Mordecai understands.
And Esther always does everything
That Mordecai commands.

As she betrayed the tailor's lad
Because it was Mordecai's will:
Yet Fastrigosso, the tailor's lad,
Was a treasure, a perfect jewel.

And here, she's been fasting ever since dawn
At Mordecai's command;
Her uncle's a wise old Jew—
And Mordecai understands.

HAMAN GETS READY FOR THE MASKED BALL

Nervously, Haman paces.
It's almost eight o'clock
And still the uniform's not here—
Damn the tailor kike.

Zeresh, Haman's wife, says, "Dear,
The banquet's not until ten.
No use your getting yourself upset;
You've plenty of time until then.

What matters—pay attention, dear—
The market women say
That the queen is inflamed with desire
And lustful in every way.

They say that on Friday nights
She has a rendezvous
With Satan—and what they say
Is absolutely true.

What more do you need? I myself
Saw you last night in my dream.
You were beside her bed,
Then you disappeared, unseen.

I said to my fortune-teller,
'Interpret the dream,' but he sighed,
'I saw a widow upon a stone
Who lamented and moaned and cried.'

I said to him, 'Uncle, I told you my dream.
Now tell me, interpret, explain.'
He muttered, 'I can't; you'll have to wait
For a while till I know what it means.'"

Haman nervously paces,
"Ah, Zeresh, my wife, be still.
You follow my every step and your mouth
Grinds on and on, like a mill.

And the masked ball takes place today,
And the queen is waiting there.
And today is also the Judgment Day
That I've been so eager for.

There's the bell. My dear, open the door.
No doubt it's the tailor's man."
And Haman hears as Fonfosso says,
"I kiss your hand, Madame."

The king is snuffling—a certain sign
That he is hopping mad—
He mutters, "Who ever would have guessed
That Haman would turn out bad?

But there it is, the man I chose
To be prime minister
Is a crazy pervert who treats the queen
As if she were his whore.

Lucky for me that Mordecai
Came rushing in today—
Dusty and panting and sweating—
And said what he came to say:

'Your majesty, watch Haman tonight.
I think you'll find there's more
To Haman than the plaster saint
Your majesty takes him for.

I've seen him—it's true—as I wish to see
The messiah on his white horse—
Leap into Esther's bed . . . she screamed
And drove him away, of course.'"

The king is snuffling—a certain sign
That he is hopping mad.
He mutters, "Who ever would have guessed
That Haman would turn out bad?"

Then the king remembers a certain night
When Esther in her nightgown
Came (like a dream from far away)
To his bed, where she lay down.

He remembers that he promised her,
"My darling . . . hee, hee, hee, hee . . .
Haman will hang one fine morning,
Esther, my dearest, you'll see."

And Esther the queen had smiled
And given herself to him.
He remembers the perfume in her hair
And his tongue still remembers her skin.

The king folds his hands on his belly—a sign
That he's thinking with all of his might:
"Is it better to hang the fellow by day,
Or would it be better at night?"

HAMAN BEING TAKEN TO THE GALLOWS

Open the windows,
Fling the doors wide.
Through the streets of the town
Wicked Haman is led.

He's being led
To the square where a throng
Surrounds the gallows
Where he will be hung.

"Hangman, Hangman,
You know who I am,
Can't I see my sons
To take my leave of them?"

"Your sons, your sons . . .
Soon someone will bring them
And then when I have done
With you I'll hang them."

"Hangman, Hangman,
See my dismal fate.
I who drove in hansom cabs
Now stumble on my feet.

I am dragged from place to place
And haul a heavy chain.
Hangman: can you tell me why?
Perhaps you can explain.

Never mind, Hangman.
I see the gallows
Dancing toward me,
Behind, the mob follows.

I hear the ravens,
The gallows I see.
In the old graveyard,
Please bury me.

But plug up my ears
To spare me the shame
Of the noisemakers drowning
Out Haman's name."

Thus the villain complains
As the women and children
With laughter and insults
Flock to revile him.

THE MASTER TAILOR, FONFOSSO, PRESIDES OVER A BANQUET

Fonfosso wipes his glasses
And is ready to begin
In his gentle fashion
His speech to his journeymen.

"I gather that wicked Haman
Is now a guest of hell.
They're boiling the villain in asphalt,
And it suits the fellow well.

Two pockmarked demon sextons
With scarlet side-curls and beards
Whip him the way a post-horse
Gets the whip on his rear.

That's what comes of his picking
On Jews and their God. More pitch.
Punish him well, he deserves
What he gets, that son of a bitch."

Fonfosso wipes his glasses
And gets ready to speak again . . .
This time to Hannah, his daughter,
And not to his journeymen.

"Well, Hannah-Dvoyre, my daughter,
It's time to set out the food:
Poppy-seed hamantashn . . .
And fish. Ah, that fish is good.

What are you waiting for, fellows?
Drink up, it's time to begin.
Let's get the Purim play ready,"
He says to his journeymen.

The cups resound and they glisten:
"Long life to Needle and Shears.
We drink to the innocent Esther,
To the king, that simpleton-bear."

But Hannah-Dvoyre, the daughter,
Stands looking out at the night:
"I wonder how many stars it takes
To shed so much Purim light?"

Fastrigosso's old mother
Has hot tears on her face
As she lights the memorial candle
And puts it back in its place.

"A year, a year has passed
And still the stars shine on . . .
While I, the ancient raven,
Am here, and my son is gone.

It seems only yesterday
That they led him away in chains
To the gallows. A sight so dreadful
It should have moved the stones

To see how at the last moment
He uttered Queen Esther's name—
You'd have to search the world over
To find such another gem.

You may search the wide world over
And still you will not find
A jewel such as Fastrigosso was,
A diamond—one of a kind.

'Was'! Ah, Father in heaven!
Was and is gone . . . and is gone.
While I, the ancient raven,
Live, and the stars shine on.

I wish she was dead and buried
That whore, that Esther, that queen!
All the while that he lay in prison
She never inquired about him.

What if she presides over Purim?
A desolate Purim to her
And to Mordecai, her uncle,
The rich man, the entrepreneur."

Fastrigosso's old mother
Has hot tears on her face
As she lights the memorial candle
And puts it back in its place.

◆ ◆ ◆ *Ballads*

THE BALLAD OF THE WHITE GLOW

"You've grieved enough, my daughter dear,
You've mourned enough, your woe."
"Mother, see, in the depth of night—
A cool, white glow."

"It's a will-o'-the-wisp, my daughter,
A will-o'-the-wisp, be sure.
May it always wander the empty fields
And come here nevermore."

"It cannot be a will-o'-the-wisp,
It may not be false fire,
Because my heart, in that cool glow,
Is throbbing with desire."

"Say your prayer, my daughter.
I cannot understand—"
"Mother, the white glow calling me
Calls from the beyond.

What shall I say to my urgent heart?
Shall I refuse to go?
If it's my heart that's calling,
Shall I answer, 'No'?"

The storm is blowing out of doors,
Outside there whirls the snow.
"Wait one moment more, white light.
One moment and I'll go."

Quickly, quickly, she takes up
Her little crimson shawl.
Her own red blood is a brighter red—
The look of death is pale.

Long, long at the windowpane,
Her mother sees her go,
Until the virgin silhouette
Fades in the pallid glow.

THE BALLAD OF THE CRUCIFIED AND THE VERMINOUS MAN

On the darkening road, stands the verminous man
Who rouses from sleep the crucified one.

"Tell me, O Jesus, where did you hear
That your crown is holier than my tear?

Jesus, tell me, who says that your crown
Is holier than all my pain?"

King Jesus stammers, "I'm only a child
Whose home is the wind where I'm crucified."

King Jesus stammers, "Woe and thrice woe
To my scarlet spring amid fallen snow."

Feverish, the verminous man says, "My home
Is cobwebs and night and wind and loam.

Forever a stranger, wherever I go,
Lice flicker like stars in my shirt—they glow.

You are rocked on the wind by two women so mild.
One murmurs, 'Beloved,' the other says, 'Child.'

There are pitying lips for each of your wounds;
They hallow your flesh, O crucified man,

While I am like shadows or dogs that bark
Or howl, abandoned on roads after dark."

King Jesus stammers, "O wretch, I believe
Your dust is more holy, more holy your grief."

From the crucified trickles a thin, silver cry;
Smiling, the verminous man turns away

With heavy step toward the evening town
For a loaf of bread and a pitcher of wine.

OLD-FASHIONED BALLAD

The song is old, but no matter
If it's sung from time to time,
Especially at firesides in winter
Where poor folk try to keep warm.
And willows tremble beside the cool river.

A musician there was with two children,
Two daughters, ah lovely they were.
One problem: each of them thought
She was destined to reach for the stars.
And willows tremble beside the cool river.

One longed for a silver castle
And a count to go with it—insane.
Ah when a Jewish maiden
Goes mad, there is nothing but pain.
And willows tremble beside the cool river.

The second, what did she long for?
Her wish—a Bohemian king.
Now how can a Jewish musician
Give his daughters any such thing.
And willows tremble beside the cool river.

A week and a year and then years
Flit by, the musician grows gray;
And now, and now any minute
Feels death is coming his way.
And willows tremble beside the cool river.

On the stoop his daughters still sitting
Eyes fixed on the passing road,
Still waiting for golden stars
To fall from their roof of wood.
And willows tremble beside the cool river.

"What is it you see, tell me, Mindl?
A cloud?" "No, a flock of sheep."
"You're wrong. I see two riders.
Dear old musician, sleep."
And willows tremble beside the cool river.

"Two riders?" "Indeed, I see them
Riding, two of them, yes.
One of them's waving a kerchief
The other—can you see who he is?"
And willows tremble beside the cool river.

"See, Malke, I now see his features.
He's dressed like a hunter in green.
It's the count of the castle of silver
In the greenest green ever seen."
And willows tremble beside the cool river.

"See, Mindl, I now see his features,
It's the king of Bohemian land;
His royal signet-ring's sparkling
And twinkling on his hand."
And willows tremble beside the cool river.

"A net of the finest gold thread
Reaches from there to here.
But Mindl, I can see nothing
Else beside my own tear."
And willows tremble beside the cool river.

"A bridge of most precious stones
Reaches from there to here.
But Malke, I can see nothing
Else beside my own tear."
And willows tremble beside the cool river.

At night on the stoop made of wood,
They bow heads now crowned with white hair,
Wearily rocking in shadow
As a Gypsy boy plays on the stair.
And willows tremble beside the cool river.

The song is old, but no matter
If it's sung from time to time.
Especially at firesides in winter
Where poor folk try to keep warm.
And willows tremble beside the cool river.

HOSPITAL BALLAD

The hospital lights go out on the hill,
Seven beech trees gleam in the vale.

Madman, softer! You hear them go,
Descending the hill, as if joyfully now.

Two nurses leaving the hospital
Fluttering down like birds into the vale.

There's a moment's pause; then says the first one,
"How amazing to be alone."

The second one stammers, "I am not me;
Instead I'm a silver melody

An old Gypsy thought up for sheer delight
When leaves fell on a September night."

The first one stammers, "I have been
A spider all blue that could spin and spin.

Of Zanzibar, now, I am the queen
And whip my fool until he bleeds

Because, when his mouth filled with happiness
He made a spot on my silken dress."

The hospital douses its light on the hill.
Seven beech trees glisten and glow in the vale.

Madman, softer! You hear them go,
Descending the hill, as if joyfully now.

Someone naked, in shoes that are worn,
Is stammering to himself as he runs:

"I'm a solar eclipse that has been mislaid;
I've no father, no mother to come to my aid.

Wherever I go; wherever I stand,
I'm always alone, alone like the rain."

"Solar eclipse," says the first nurse, "Come!
Embrace me, take me in your arms.

At your cradle's side, whether late or soon,
I rocked you and rocking you, I was the tune."

"Solar eclipse," says the second nurse, "Come!
Embrace me now, take me in your arms.

I'm the enchanted child's smile and then
The tiniest sister of the September wind."

The naked one weeps, "Wherever I stand
I'm always alone, alone, like the rain."

The hospital lights now glow on the hill
And the light of the beech trees goes out in the vale.

THE BALLAD OF THE MAN RIDING TO THE FAIR

Three times the man cracks his whip in the air,
"Giddyap, horses. We're off to the fair."

Contented and joyful, he strokes his small beard:
The bride is all ready; her dowry prepared.

"Giddyap, horses, my horses so fine.
We're off to buy bride-clothes and sweet raisin wine."

The horses run fleetly; a cry of deep woe
Chases the wagon, "No, Father, no."

As if he heard nothing, the man merely smiles,
Behind him unwind, like a ribbon, the miles.

A brook . . . and a bridge . . . and a sapling go by.
The man sings his song, "Tam, deri, dai."

The horses run fleetly; there blows a chill breeze
That mingles the night with the whisper of trees.

A brook . . . and a bridge . . . and a sapling go by.
The man sings his song, "Tam, deri, dai."

The horses run fleetly, the night's breath is cold;
It sends the first specter his eyes will behold.

"Merchant my dear; merchant so fine,
See, I have brought thee a pitcher of wine."

The specter is gone; a second appears,
Pale as a willow, as bent as its tears.

"I have, for thy daughter, stitched stitches and sewn
Of silk and of samite a long wedding gown."

The specter is gone; a third one now stands
Sadly before him, an urn in her hands.

"Merchant my dear, merchant so fine,
Where didst thou leave that daughter of thine?

The brook has a water that's doleful and clear;
There she went washing her soft golden hair.

The brook has a water that's doleful and sweet,
There she went washing her lily-white feet."

Before the third specter was gone, with her hand
She sprinkled with ashes the face of the wind.

"Giddyap horses! Up mourners mine—
We ride after bride-clothes and sweet raisin wine."

BALLAD

September, the thin woman in green
On the sidewalk goes fluttering by.

She knows that the cherry tree blossomed
And that—ah, once it was May.

On the steps of the church mad Vasil
Lies, his white beard disheveled by wind.

He breathes deeply; his soul has the smell
Of blackberries, blacker than ink.

"Come, brother, come walk with me,"
Says the thin woman in green.

Overhead, the street lanterns tremble
And each of them trembles alone.

Smiles the madman: "Sister, you see
How the forest is suddenly here,

And I am the ancient great dark
That has been here a million years."

Stammers the woman in green,
"Indeed, the forest is here—

And you are the ancient dark
That has been here a million years.

And you" (she sobs like a flute),
"You . . . Who am I? I'm afraid . . . "

"You . . . are the one I imagined
Wearing gold shoes and black braids."

"But to what end? Let me go—
Back to the town where I've been."

Laughed the madman, "There is no such town
Nor on earth has it ever been seen.

Only I and the woods and the wolves
All converging on you, as you see."

Says the feverish woman, "Yes,
There are wolves converging on me."

She falls to her knees. "Lord, forgive
Me for all of my sins.

For the cherry tree that's in bloom,
And the insulted springtime wind."

———————————————

On the church steps lies madman Vasil,
Nearby weeps the woman in green.

On wet rooftops over the way
Creeps an ugly old spider, the dawn.

With small blue pitchers in their weary hands,
White mothers to the dark well drift.
It may be they will find their golden fortune
Hidden in its silent depth . . .
But pitchers tremble in their weary hands.

Above them comes a white bird flying.
Round and round their three white heads it swoops:
"On a staircase, gilded nine times nine,
Fortune, in a marble castle sleeps."
But pitchers tremble in their weary hands.

Then there comes a gray bird flying:
"Fortune, by a stepmother tormented,
Weeps inside a dreary hut—
While father squanders it—by cards demented."
But pitchers tremble in their weary hands.

Then there comes a black bird flying
To the well and perches on the brim:
"Fortune sleeps inside a certain field
All by itself, beneath a marble stone."
But pitchers tremble in their weary hands.

The first of the three mothers gently speaks:
"Our golden fortune waits for us nearby.
Let's go and take it home. It's ours by grace
Of June, and evening, and the reddening sky."
But pitchers tremble in their weary hands.

The second of the mothers softly says:
"Perhaps by grace of the first evening star
Whose blazing light our eyes have lived to see . . . "
In her handkerchief, she sheds her tears.
But pitchers tremble in their weary hands.

The third of the three mothers gently speaks:
"Our grandchildren have golden hair . . .
By grace, it may be, of that loveliness
Our dream will suddenly as truth appear."
But pitchers tremble in their weary hands.

Carrying blue pitchers in their weary hands,
Pale and frightened, the white mothers move . . .
As if, in stockinged feet, through the dark town
A row of mourners walked at Tisha b'Av.*
The pitchers tremble in their weary hands.

Behind them fades the river and the town.
Compelled to answer, which of them today
Can tell where rocks the cradle she once rocked—
(They only know their need to get away).
The pitchers tremble in their weary hands.

The pitchers tremble in their weary hands . . .
Behind them fades the bridge and fades the mill.
(They only know their need to get away.)
Compelled to answer, which of them can tell
Where and in what garden, first love bloomed,
Or in what corner stood the cherry tree?
The pitchers tremble in their weary hands.

Farther and faster, till they come at last
To the first gravestone. In a tree, there cries
The owl on his dark branch. He bids them pace
The wedding dance. They dance with glittering eyes.
The pitchers tremble in their weary hands.

Pale, the mothers dance, both pale and mute . . .
Like princesses long lost in distant towns
Who find their way back to their father's tower—
His crown shines in their eyes like seven suns.
But pitchers tremble in their weary hands.

Faster and faster, until midnight whispers
A secret: "Time to sleep"—each mother lies
Down when she has heard it and with soft,
Weary, samite fingers shuts her eyes.
The pitchers fall out of their weary hands.

The moon goes up—is gone—the morning star
Marks in the sky a bright new day.
White mothers, lying tired and fast asleep,
Drift like smoke into the night, away.
The pitchers weep after their weary hands.

And I myself, who made this very song,
Hardly know what thing it is I made.
The silent mothers through the village passed
And caused a silver grief in me to sound,
As did the pitchers, weeping on the ground.

THE BALLAD OF THE NECKLACE OF STARS

—*in memory of Anna Margolin*

Gentlemen, I'll sing you a song,
A song of sorrowing luck—
The kind that flutters by like a bird
But never comes fluttering back.

"In beautiful Jassy, that peaceful town,
Enhanced by ancient schools—"
So it is written, I read it myself
Once, with my very own eyes,

"There lived an old and pious man—
Mekhele Blatt his name;
He had one only daughter dear,
This old and pious man.

A year goes by, the second comes,
Comes and goes and is gone;
The daughter grows quickly. She grows slim
As a pine tree in the wind.

How he smiled, that good old man,
When there came a knock at his door,
And there was Spring with a lilac branch
That he had plucked for her.

And how he smiled, that good old man,
When the king of Summer brought
Cranberry blossoms to her bed
Late on a dark blue night.

But he shuddered when Autumn banged on the door
And he heard the marching rain
Singing the song of departed youth
That flies, like a bird, away.

A year goes by, the second comes,
Comes and goes and is gone.
The daughter grows quickly. She grows slim
As a pine tree in the wind.

But once, upon a pale, pale night,
In her dream, a messenger
Came and laid a silken shirt
On the narrow bed for her.

And when the old man sprang awake
Just after dawn to pray
A necklace of stars in the windowpane hung
Like a silver melody.

Before her mirror, the slender girl
Stood, wearing the silken shirt—
Strange and quiet, with staring eyes,
Her hands crossed over her heart.

A day is gone. On the second night,
Again the messenger
Draws near and puts a golden crown
On the narrow bed for her.

And when the old man wakened up
Just after dawn to pray,
There hung a necklace of stars in the pane
Like a silver melody.

Before her mirror, the thin, dark girl
Stood wearing the crown and shirt—
Strange and quiet, with staring eyes,
Her hands crossed over her heart.

Soon, the old man understood—
The dream and his child were gone . . .
His child—sole wonder of his flesh . . .
He tore his clothes and mourned.

He scattered ashes on his head
And piously he prayed.
Stars in the window paler turned
As dawn crept on toward day.

Across the white snow, bare-footed,
Wearing the shirt and the crown,
His daughter went with silent steps . . .
Grieving and strange—alone.

EROTIC BALLAD

The monk who is black and the soldier who's blue
Throttle the night on their lonesome way.

The blue soldier's stammer is heavy and fierce
And his whole body reeks of sweat and of grief.

"So still and so wan you've come, and I see
That love's glare is all that you've brought me,

The sound a girl's fluttering blouse has made
Over a town that's both foreign and sad."

The black monk's stammer is heavy and fierce
And his whole body reeks of sweat and of grief.

"You came hot and wild, you came bringing tears,
Diffusing, like smoke, my sorrow-filled prayers.

Her sketch in my hand turned alive in its frame;
I fondled her breasts; I toyed with her shame.

In the middle of the road, abandoned I stand
Counting hours, counting days as if they were wounds."

The monk who is black and the soldier who's blue
Throttle the night on their lonesome way.

They throttle, they sob, they feel where they stand
How blood, wind, and sorrow seep through their hands.

And over them both, there hangs a red bloom—
It's the moon whose smile is profound and long.

THE BALLAD OF THE MAN WHO WENT FROM GRAY TO BLUE

Barefoot and gray, in the courtyard
Dawn knocks at the shabby pane;

The poor Jew, waking from sleep,
Gets up, puts on gray clothes.

Settling his sack on his shoulders,
His gray stick in his hand,

He makes his way with measured step
Together with the road.

And as he walks, the gray becomes
Thick and heavy as lead,

Making him so sad, a tear
Wells up in his eye.

The tear is large, and softly rolls
Down into his beard.

The silver, tenuous, bright tear
Brightens his gray beard.

But how long may a tear endure—
A moment and it's gone?

He stops beside a graying tree
And says a prayer aloud:

"Lord of the World, erase the gray
From all my ways and let

My wandering journeys through the world
Be bright and clear, at least."

When he has done, his heart grows light,
His prayer, a butterfly,

Flutters before him, a dot of blue
In a landscape of gray on gray.

The poor man travels farther on
Until he sees appear

An inn of gray and on the porch
A woman fair, in blue.

His eyes grow thirsty, they grow large,
They drink the blueness up.

"Good afternoon," the woman says,
"No doubt you're travel-worn,

Come in. Stay with us for a while,
We have both bread and wine."

He parts the doors with weary hands;
The room is painted blue;

In a corner sits the husband,
His young son in his lap,

And tells of a kingdom all of blue
Girt round by a river of blue.

The traveler listens, fatigued with blue,
And dozes, fatigued with blue,

And his dream spins a road, and the road is blue,
His stick is blue, and his sack is blue,

And the bird that flutters by is blue,
And the field and the wood and the river are blue;

The innkeeper gapes, and his wife gapes, too,
At the way the traveler gushes blue

That fills the room and streams outdoors
Enfolding all of the house in blue.

Who's crying? Do you hear? Outside
The gray road's weeping like a child,

"Why has he left me all alone,
Outdoors, abandoned to the wind?"

The innkeeper wakes him, "Up. Get up.
The highway outside is waiting for you."

The sleeping dreamer smiles. In his dream
He's just at the gate of the kingdom of blue;

In a moment, he'll open the gate and see
In the valley the first three cities of blue.

The innkeeper gapes, and his wife gapes, too,
At the way the traveler gushes blue

That fills the room and streams outdoors,
Enfolding all of the house in blue,

And the blue becomes murmur and stammer and flight
And whisper and song from afar.

It turns leaf and twig and branch and tree
And cloud and forest and dream on dream,

And the blue turns waves and river and sea,
Mysterious inkling and holy rhyme,

Turns tread and stamp and dance and joy,
Turns joy after joy and eternity.

Turns glitter and shimmer, and beam and light,
Turns shade and flesh and features, too;

The innkeeper gapes, and his wife gapes, too,
At the way the traveler gushes blue

That fills the room and streams outdoors,
Enfolding all of the house in blue,

And . . .

IN THE TRAIN

The train is hounded, like an exile's heart.
In the fields, a harvest of white snow.
Red eyes glisten, glow, and are extinguished,
But brighter, clearer is the field of snow.
All roads are bright; only the heart is dark
As it goes stumbling through the ripened white.
Tired and hushed, I say and hear the blue
Of your name. I say it to the night—
Your blue name to the whiteness of the night.

When the train is hounded, then its spark
Flies back, as if it had turned to longing
That wavered, searching for the right way back,
Only to perish in an infant's cry.
All my yearning's crucified on wind;
It waves about, like dangling spider's thread
Enclosing everything my sorrows spun
Long ago, and all I then conceived.
Now, you are all I know, and the white night.
Now, you are all I know, and the white night.

The train is hounded, like an exile's heart—
In the fields, there blossoms the white snow.
Would that my soul might be as bright and clear
As the clarity of white-spread snow.
The night is bright; only the heart is dark
As it goes stumbling through the ripened white.
Tired and hushed, I say and hear the blue
Of your name. I say it to the night—
Your blue name to the whiteness of the night.

BAAL SHEM*

At the edge of the village, stands the Baal Shem,
Sees evening winding the veils of the dark.
Over the peat land he sees a spark
That becomes a vision that glows in him.

The golden gleam on the banner of night
Is holy, thrice holy. He falls to his knees
And drinks the night's essence, the melody
Snatched by the wind from the steppes in its flight . . .

Drunk with colors, with magic and song,
He stands in the dark a bit longer, alone.
His features, suffused by prayer, now glow.

Ecstatic, he runs to the village and cries
As he pounds the dark walls announcing the news
That "the world is thrice lovely, and sanctifies."

SATAN'S PRAYER

How many eons have I fought
Against Thee, O great Lord of Light?
Now, with my scorched wings, I stand
Before Thy blazing sight.

So be it! There my kingdom lies
Shattered beneath Thy feet . . .
While every nerve in Thee declares
The joy of victory is sweet.

So be it—my black crown burns out
Into a thousand sickly stars.
Lilith, meanwhile, crucifies
Herself upon her tears.

Accept the grief of one who ran
With crimson torches through the night
And shook her tresses to the wind
Like serpents—O Thou Lord of Light.

Accept the grief of one who could
Blaspheme and yet believe in Thee;
Who, in the sisterhood of Hell,
Looked up toward Thee, longingly.

I bow before Thee, Lord of Light;
But she, my wild one, may not bow.
O quench the sorrows of her hair
And rest Thy smile upon her now.

Kindle pleasure in her eyes—
Those eyes that darkly, darkly grieve;
A boon—a boon. Grant me Thy boon;
Give my wild one, Lord, Thy Love.

O Lord of Light, from Thy great realm
Whence holy icons shine upon us,
Set your crown of Song of Songs
On her, most sinful of Madonnas.

Evening on the rooftops—
A weave of the lucid and dark.
On my face and hair, stars gleam
Like blue and golden sparks.

My footsteps are hushed.
The moment lights up, then dies down,
And the resonance of grief in me grows
With walking through dust and through wind.

Come with me,
Hushed, to the edge of the night.
I know that at midnight we'll find
The ultimate light.

Enfolded in lightning
God made his way through my nights,
His footsteps moving through me
Resounded with music and light.

And the stars lighted up,
Gleamed on my face and my hair.
If God exists in a dream,
He exists everywhere.

The way to him
Is through midnight, dust, and wind
We all intuit his light—
The child and the old man who's blind.

Come with me,
Hushed to the edge of the night.
I know that at midnight we'll find
The ultimate light.

Almost midnight. The Baal Shem sits
In his quiet alcove, lost in thought.
The night is holy, lovely, deep.
Even a man with barefoot step
Moving alone through a foreign land
Can feel himself in God's blue hand.

The Baal Shem rises; then suddenly
There sounds at the window a tremulous cry.
"Who grieves at night; who is it weeps
When the bird, the wind, and the hut all sleep,
And the forest sleeps along with them?
Who drives the gold away from his dream?
Listen," the Baal Shem says, and turns
To the exiled grief, "Come sleep in my hands."

But the cry at the window is tremulous, fine
As a spider's web or a violin
Or the gasp of a dying child, turned thin
While the child's head writhes against the wind.

The Baal Shem opens the door and tries
To discover what creature disturbs the joys—
The joys and dreams of all the world.
The river dozes and there the town
Is dozing and the field as well.
Who's weeping now
When the bird, the wind, and the hut all sleep
And the forest sleeps along with them?
Who drives the gold away from his dream?
"Listen," the Baal Shem says, and turns
To the exiled grief, "Come sleep in my hands."

But the cry at the window is tremulous, fine
As a spider's web or a violin
Or the gasp of a dying child, turned thin
While the child's head writhes against the wind.

Then, he raises his clear eyes . . .
To heaven raises his clear eyes
And sees a gray cloud pass before
A single star, and then
The Baal Shem stands a moment by,
Attentive to its silver cry.

He raises to heaven his brilliant hand . . .
To heaven raises his brilliant hand
And wipes the cloud away. The star
Begins to flutter. Relieved of fear
It flutters and shimmers, sparkles and rings
Through the air like the sound of gold rings.
The Baal Shem smiles and says, "You scamp,
See how you've shaken the world awake?"

With silent steps, he makes his way
Home to his hut of brick and clay.
Seating himself beside the sill,
He waits for the birds' first morning trill.
He waits for the first gleam of the sun—
For the first golden gleam of the sun—
Before the dawn becomes the day,
Softly, to himself, he says:

"The cry of the earthworm or the hare,
The cry of a blade of grass or star
Can shake the world into alarm.
Father! Keep them safe from harm."

Then, to his hand a bright drop falls
And downward to his garment rolls.

LIKE A MURDERER

Like a murderer, with knife in hand,
Ambushing his victim late at night,
I listen for your steps, O Lord, I wait;
I, from whom you hide your smiling light;
I, the grandson of Iscariot.

I'm ready to do penance with my blood—
Your prophet's blood still burns my fingertips . . .
Although a shepherd, in the midst of spring,
Is fluting silver magic with his lips
And no one calls me to account for anything.

To see you! Just to see you once.
To know with certainty there is a You;
To know you really crown a saint with light;
To know with certainty, your sky is blue . . .
And then, to hide forever from your sight.

I'll fling the thirty silver coins
To be confounded with a careless wind;
And, barefoot, Lord, I'll make my way to you
To weep before you, like a child returned
Whose head is heavy with the crown of sin.

Like a murderer, with knife in hand,
Ambushing his victim late at night,
I listen for your steps, O Lord, I wait;
I, from whom you hide your smiling light;
I, the grandson of Iscariot.

WITH SILENT STEPS

With silent steps in yellow sand,
I, a king, walk through the land
In my clothing howls the wind
Red-tongued, howling like a hound.

The soldier, shop man, and the wife
Hoarsely groan the word "betrayal."
My foe as sharp as a sharp knife
Will be encountered without fail.

Every fence is broken now—
I am a wind, I am a dream,
And at sunset shed my pain
The way a serpent sheds its skin.

What say you, Brother Notte, eh?
Caw, caw is always the crow's sound?
It's the nature of that sort of fellow
Even when he sees a crown.

On a thousand spears the war was fought,
The soldier, citizen, and crow
Hoarsely groan the word "betrayal,"
And victory, like an apple, rots.

The cripple limps upon his grief,
The famous killer walks alone,
His foeman, like a whetted knife,
Will, as he should, encounter him.

NOVEMBER

Seven ancient women croak—"November."
All through the town, the clocks begin their ringing.
My body, here beside you, burns, Anyella.
Listen! How beautifully sick owls are singing.
One by one, the funerals take flight;
The graves are young and ready, and they wait.

An infected wind weeps in our garden;
Before our house, a scarlet lantern glows;
Death's silver razors play, like fiddle bows,
White music on the throats of pious calves.
In the nursery, cradles rock themselves;
And mother's gone—her chaste still music dies,
A guiltless sacrifice of lullabies.

November: young and slender brides are weeping,
"Where are you, loveliest and golden one?"
But pimps glide to their windows to peer in,
Fooling their aged fathers into thinking,
"Good fortune flies like that when fortune flies,"
And they suspect the proof of their old eyes.

The watchman, gray and grumbling, stands before
His lamp and asks, "Are you my destiny?
Too bad!" A nurse is bandaging a star
That only lately fell out of the sky.
Trains in the distance go and come again.
Deserted wives at stations wait their men.

Stumbling on the roads, moon walkers yearn
To find the moon; they search with tender hands
And feel about, but only touch the rain.
They sob, "Oh, woe is us. The night erases
From our memories familiar traces;
It wipes our shadows out, and all our homes;
And there is no one left who knows our names."

The youthful murderer in prison waits
The coming of the dawn that is to bring
The moment of delight when he will hang
And twitch. Upon the wall, his shadow burns.
The young man asks, "How could you?" of his hands,
But gets no answer he can understand.

Seven ancient women croak—"November."
All through the town the clocks begin their ringing.
My body, here beside you, burns, Anyella.
Hear how beautifully sick birds are singing.
One by one, the funerals take flight;
The graves are young and ready, and they wait.

AT THE KOLOMEY STATION

At the station Kolomey,
In the middle of a crowd,
My grandpa and my grandma—
Stand like shadows bowed.

"Shaindl, listen," Grandpa says,
And his eyes are glowing,
"Our grandson's coming, tell me how
We'll be sure to know him.

Because, you know, when Khove rocked
His cradle, we lay dead
Beneath the wind-stirred grasses
On the far side of the road."

Grandma smiles and in her hands
A bunch of flowers trembles.
"Silly fool, what made you bring
That stuff?" my grandpa grumbles.

"Itzik, dear, I gathered them
In the field as we were passing.
It's the custom nowadays
To greet guests in this fashion."

Then she is still. An engine shrieks,
"Where is he? When's he coming?"
In my grandma's withered hands
The bunch of flowers is trembling.

"Oh, my—they say our grandson is
Some kind of big-shot poet.
It's his mother's weeping soul
Throbs in his rhymes—the verses show it."

Grandma turns her head away
By something overpowered.
Then she weeps; and in her hands
Trembles the bunch of flowers.

TWILIGHT

Chatters away the mad monk
To the ailing November wood,
"The great twilight is on her way now
Who is an eternity old.
She folds and enfolds and then stills
The woman, the forest, the wine.

She walks with the silentest tread
Because she is silent herself.
She rejects the gold of good luck
And transforms all things into grief;
She has faith just in sleep and in rest,
And the weariest eyelids that close.

Come out to welcome her in
With heads that are weary and bowed.
She, with a magical spell,
Will wipe away the blue stairs
The lead up and then up and then up
Through dream and through space and through God.

Me she anointed a seer
Of the seventh order of dream—
What is the sound of the sun
High in the apple tree's crown
Compared with her silent tread,
Compared to the depth of her sight?

Sound and sparkle and throb
Make sleepy then lull one to sleep;
The murmur of child and of wind
Softly moved into stillness itself.
Throb and tremble and twitch
Tremble, pulsate—and enough.

The flutter of birds in flight,
The roar and hum from the wood.
The great twilight is on her way now
Who is an eternity old.
She folds and enfolds and then stills
The woman, the forest, the wine

An instant or two, then she will
Reveal that kingdom of hers—
The white islands of rest
Eternally yearning toward you—
Who have, for an age, been prepared
With a joy that is frigid and pure.

Come out to welcome then—
Those white islands of rest.
Go prudently barefoot and blind
And to each other say, 'You!'
As lightning flares, and then sleeps
Like the woman, the forest, the wine."

THE WORDS OF THE JOURNEYMAN TAILOR NOTTE MANGER
TO THE POET

With closed eyes
You hear the sea is near.
With feverish fingers,
You feel a rhyme appear.

The golden peacock
In its flight is discerned.
And yearning's more lovely
When it's for the beyond.

And fatigue's more weary
At the house's sill.
And God's greatness more sharply
Felt when you kneel.

What has made God great,
If one may speak of him so,
Is not his thunder in heaven
But his sobs here below.

Well is it for him
Who that sobbing can hear.
That fate has been yours—
It resounds in your ear.

And there was a tear
That when it fell down
Entered your soul
And blossomed to song.

THERE IS A TREE THAT STANDS

There is a tree whose branches
Bend across the road.
All its birds have flown away
Leaving not a bird.

The tree, abandoned to the storm,
Stands there all alone:
Three birds east and three birds west—
The rest have southward flown.

I say to my mother,
"If you won't meddle, please,
I'll turn myself into a bird
Before your very eyes.

I'll sit all winter on the tree
And sing it lullabies.
I'll rock it and console it
With lovely melodies."

Tearfully, my mother says,
"Don't take any chances.
God forbid, up in the tree
You'll freeze among the branches."

"Mother, please don't cry," I say,
"Ah, Mother, don't be sad."
But on the instant I transform
Myself into a bird.

My mother says, "Oh, Itzik, love . . .
In the name of God
Take a little scarf with you
To keep from catching cold.

And dear, put your galoshes on.
The winter's cold and aching.
Be sure to wear your fleece-lined cap.
Woe's me, my heart is breaking.

And, pretty fool, be sure to take
Your woolen underwear
And put in on, unless you mean
To lie a corpse somewhere."

I try to fly, but I can't move . . .
Too many, many things
My mother's piled on her weak bird
And loaded down my wings.

I look into my mother's eyes
And, sadly, then I see
The love that won't let me become
The bird I want to be.

RABENU TAM*

Let us sing the lovely song
Haydl, didl, di,
Of the golden peacock and its flight
Across the darkened sea
Carrying a billet-doux
A lovely, lovely billet-doux
For Rabbi Simpleton.

Who was it wrote the billet-doux?
Haydl, didl, di,
She who wrote the billet-doux—
Was empress of Turkey.
The letter, written with red ink,
Was sealed with teardrops three.

What was in that billet-doux?
Haydl, didl, del,
"I love you Rabbi Simpleton.
Why don't you speak up? Well?
I do not eat, nor drink nor rest.
My longing heart is sure to burst."
Said that billet-doux.

Then what does the rabbi do?
Haydl, didl, deh,
He strokes an earlock and his beard
And three times murmurs, "Feh!"
And the kid inside his stall,
That pure white little kid,
In counterpoint bleats, "Meh."

Well, what of her, the rabbi's wife?
Haydl, didl, des,
She thwacks him with her rolling pin
And this is what she says,
"You've got *shikses** on your mind?
And me, then what am I?
If not your well-loved wife?"

Try to guess who wrote this song.
Haydl, didl, don,
A tailor lad to honor him,
That Rabbi Simpleton.
But Saturday, twixt night and day,
A laughing prankster found a way
To sneak his own rhymes in.

REB LEVI YITSKHOK*

Reb Levi Yitskhok, in prayer shawl and *tfiln,**
Is rooted where he stands
Before the altar, with prayer book open,
But refuses to utter a sound.

He imagines the ghetto: like so many pictures
Of agony, trouble, and pain.
Silent and stubborn, the old man quarrels
With his old God again.

SINCE YESTERDAY

I've lived since yesterday upon this star
And taken only love and song with me.
I do not mourn my withered cherry tree.
Naked at my glass, I shed no tear.

My one desire: listening, listening, listening
To the rhythm of all that breathes or swoops in air.
A minor Hasid* at the cosmic fair.
My magic lantern, too, is glistening.

Who knows where I was cradled or was born;
My mind's familiar address book is torn.
I live with love and song upon this star.

My one desire: listening, listening, listening
To resonant, colliding, distant stars—
A minor Hasid at the cosmic fair.

FOR YEARS I WALLOWED

For years I wallowed about in the world,
Now I'm going home to wallow there.
With a pair of shoes and the shirt on my back,
And the stick in my hand that goes with me everywhere.

I'll not kiss your dust as that great poet did,
Though my heart, like his, is filled with song and grief.
How can I kiss your dust? I *am* your dust.
And how, I ask you, can I kiss myself?

Still dressed in my shabby clothes
I'll stand and gape at the blue Kinneret
Like a roving prince who has found his blue
Though blue was in his dream when he first started.

I'll not kiss your blue, I'll merely stand
Silent as a *Shimenesre** prayer myself.
How can I kiss your blue? I *am* your blue.
And how, I ask you, can I kiss myself?

Musing, I'll stand before your great desert,
And hear the camels' ancient tread as they
Sway with trade and Torah on their humps.
I'll hear the age-old hovering wander-song
That trembles over glowing sand and dies,
And then recalls itself and does not disappear.
I'll not kiss your sand. No, and ten times no.
How can I kiss your sand? I *am* your sand.
And how, I ask you, can I kiss myself?

Mousie, micey, mouse
I can sing no more,
Though I whistle at your groschen,
Don't throw me out the door.

I'll go out myself,
But where shall I be gone?
Here I am a stranger
As lonely as a stone.

The night is winter cold,
The tavern's shut its door—
May your luck be better
Than mine for I am poor.

So, I give a whistle
To God in heaven above,
Who's dozing in the infinite—
"Your stalk is ripe enough.

With bread and need and grief
Earth nourished me so long.
And so I gave my tears
To her with my song.

Now we are both quit.
The earth has heard me sing,
And at last your stalk
Is ripe for harvesting."

Micey, mousie, mouse
And cat without a tail.
I pipe my final tune
And gladly leave. That's all.

Prose

♦ ♦ ♦ *Autobiographical Episodes*

CHILDHOOD YEARS IN KOLOMEY

We lived for some little time in Kolomey. I can't remember how long. But I have many memories of those early years. Much of what I remember has been turned into verse. And certain specific memories have been transformed into tales. Kolomey, for me, was always a town of poetic magic.

It was in Kolomey that I bought a whip with a red tassel on it. It never occurred to me to buy a horse. Every stick, every broom became an instant horse for me. And even the garden bench that could not be budged from its place was a horse—and what a horse!—all it needed was a whip. A real whip with a red tassel. A whip that would let the garden bench know—and feel—that it was a horse; that when I cracked the whip that horse must be off and running, just like my grandfather's horses that ran between Stopchet and Kolomey.

But without a whip, the garden bench refused to budge from its place. No matter how much I urged it or goaded it on, it stood fast and ignored me. All of my gee-ups and giddyaps were wasted.

One day, when I was sitting on that bench—on that stubborn horse of mine—I looked down and saw something glittering on the ground. I picked it up. It was a coin that someone had lost. I knew that it was money, but I did not know what it was worth. But it occurred to me that I might be able to buy a whip with it.

I ran to the little shop, where among other things, whips were sold. I held out my hand with the coin in it. The woman shopkeeper, evidently, knew the value of the coin. She handed me a long whip that had a red tassel at its tip and gave me a piece of candy into the bargain. Now the garden bench would get a taste of my whip with the red tassel on it and would fly like an eagle. Meanwhile, it was getting late. Almost time for dinner. Tomorrow, all of Kolomey would be astonished to see a boy mounted on his garden bench as he zoomed by in a cloud of dust cracking his long whip with the tassel on it.

My mother was puzzled when she saw me with my whip (it was four times longer than I was tall). She knew that it was not possible that Elijah the Prophet had revealed himself on an ordinary summer evening to a small Jewish boy to present him with a whip. (I would guess that Jewish mothers in Kolomey had never even heard of Santa Claus.)

She began to question me. Reluctantly, I told her about the coin I had found and about the transaction I had made. From what I said, she was unable to determine whether the coin I had found was a crown or a gulden because I did not know the difference between the two. She took my hand, and together with the whip, we went off to the woman who had sold it to me.

"Here's your whip. Give us back the money."

Angrily the woman handed her some kind of coin. My mother contended that the coin had been worth more. The woman claimed that that was not true. My mother lost her patience and spat out, "Deceiving a child!" The woman cried out that the whip was worth more than the coin I had given her and that she had only meant to please a child who longed to have a whip.

The result was that the whip stayed with the woman storekeeper. That long whip with the red tassel that had almost . . . almost . . . been mine. Now, who knew who would be buying it on the morrow.

My mother reproved me, saying that a boy who found anything ought first to show it to his mother. It was possible that I had given away a ducat for that whip. I, who did not know the difference between a crown and a gulden, was equally ignorant about what a ducat looked like.

I promised that next time I would show her first whatever I might find.

But I never found anything ever again. In no city, anywhere in the world. Kolomey was the only town where I found anything . . . something that glittered and with which I had bought a whip.

I mourned that lost whip for a very long time. It appeared often in my dreams, accusing me of having abandoned it. As for the garden bench, we were at swords drawn. I was angry at it and would not look at it when I passed the town garden on my way to Hebrew school.

At Kolomey, in those long-ago childhood days that I remember so well, I experienced a second great "loss." The loss that grownups call "dying" and "death." It should be clear that I did not know what the words meant. Like every child at that age, I believed that everything was eternal. My Stopchet grandfather and grandmother, my aunts and uncles and the Kolomey cousins. My father and mother, my little brother and sister. Certainly—and of course.

Abruptly my grandfather Abraham stopped coming to Kolomey. I knew that when he came to Kolomey with his horses and wagon, he stopped at the hay market, where one could be dazzled at the sight of so many wagons and horses. But my grandfather stopped coming.

Once, late at night, we children heard a sharp outcry. We frightened children watched as our father and mother dressed hastily. Mother was sobbing loudly. Father was pale. They left the house together, wailing, leaving us children alone. We cried our throats raw until we fell asleep.

But it never even occurred to me to connect that night scene with my grandfather. And so, I waited for him, day after day, and could not understand why he did not come.

My grandfather Abraham was a silent man with large, mournful eyes. His black beard had gray stripes in it. I loved him very much. I loved riding with him from Stopchet to Kolomey and back. I remember those journeys well. I remember my grandfather as in a dream.

I've traveled all over the world. I've roamed its highways and byways. But no place has sunk so deeply into my mind as the road between Stopchet and Kolomey. That couple of miles connecting the east Galician village with the "Jewish town," as Shlomo Bikel* called Kolomey, was transformed into verse.

But that would happen later. Meanwhile, a Jewish boy waited for his grandfather. And if the grandfather did not come, the boy decided to look for him. He sought him at the hay market, where his grandfather used to stop with his wagon and horses along with other wagon-drivers who kept the shafts of their wagons raised up high. He sought him there and did not find him.

There, there, that horse, it seems, is grandfather's, but that horse next to the one with the white spot on its forehead is certainly not grandfather's. And there are two horses that look like my grandfather's. But what's that colt doing here? Grandfather did not have a colt.

I crept about among the wagon-drivers and the horses for so long that the colt grew nervous and kicked out at me with its hind hoofs and I fell. Luckily, it was not a hard blow. I was on my feet at once and continued my search, but this time, I avoided the nervous colt that kicked out at a boy searching for his grandfather.

A man who was harnessing his horses noticed how I was wandering about like someone lost, looking closely at the horses, perhaps . . . perhaps . . . .

The man asked, "Hey, boy. Who are you looking for?"

"My grandfather."

"What's your grandfather's name?"

"Grandfather."

"Where is he from?"

"From Stopchet."

The stranger finished harnessing his horses. He set me on the seat of his wagon. He even let me hold the whip. For a while, he drove about the town with me, then he let me off at city hall, where among other men, I recognized the tall, strong figure of my uncle Yossl.

For some days and weeks, I continued to search for my grandfather and did not understand why there was no sign of him. "He's not here," was a reply I could not understand. How could it be possible that a grandfather was "not here"? But eventually, I did find him. Not at the hay market in Kolomey nor in Stopchet. Many years later I found him in my mind and in my poems.

Several years before the Second World War, my grandfather Abraham was revealed to me as a tragic extension of the Abraham figure in the Five Books of Moses, but this time he was not taking his son Isaac to the place of sacrifice. Instead, it was his grandson, Isaac. The latter sacrifice was not averted by a miracle. The Isaacs of Poland, Lithuania, Russia, and Ruthenia—of the entire European continent—are now heaps of ash in those sites of sacrifice.

The "other" Father Abraham figure of the Bible and the wagon-driver of Stopchet have become one. They have been fused in a single tragic historical fate.

What else do I remember of those childhood years in Kolomey? A lot. Quite a lot.

I want to talk only about a single episode that was later worked into my book, *The Marvelous Adventures of Shmuel-Aba Abervo or The Book of Paradise*.

It's a story about a goat; about a sense of justice in the soul of a child. About an adventure that ended in a fiasco on the Sabbath-calm streets of Kolomey.

I had two uncles in Kolomey. Both of them were upholsterers. The older uncle, Hersh-Mekhl, had a large family. A houseful of some ten children. The second uncle, Uncle Yossl, had no children. Later on he adopted a little girl and raised her as his daughter.

Uncle Hersh-Mekhl, though he worked hard, was as poor as poor can be. Just think of it. A household of so many children. There, a loaf of bread vanished before it was put on the table.

By contrast, things were much better for Uncle Yossl. He rarely worked. Generally he was to be found at the marketplace. He was one of those hail-fellow-well-met people, known to everyone, Jew or Gentile, in Kolomey. A spectacle that gave us children a great deal of pleasure was the sight of him marching with the veterans when they were celebrating Franz-Joseph's birthday.* We were proud of my uncle Yossl. Everyone liked him. He was very generous and liked to do favors for people.

Kolomey's young scamps trembled with fear of his blows. They were more like thunderclaps than blows. The truth is, he rarely struck anyone. But if a Gentile spoke harsh words to a Jew, that Gentile was not to be envied. My uncle would later send oranges to the battered Gentile in the hospital. And when the man was discharged, my uncle Yossl was there, waiting at the hospital's gate. Pressing a coin into the man's hand, he advised him henceforth to be a good citizen. To be civil and friendly and not to behave like a lout.

That's the sort of man he was—my uncle Yossl, the upholsterer of Kolomey.

His wife, my aunt Rukhtshe, was an altogether different person. A barren woman and a coddled beauty, she suffered always from imaginary illnesses. Bizarre caprices that my uncle indulged.

Once, she got it into her head that my uncle should buy her a goat. Goat's milk, it was said, was healthful. And who needed health more than my aunt Rukhtshe? My uncle Yossl bought her a goat.

Aunt Rukhtshe's goat was a phenomenon for all of us children who went to stare at it as at an amazing sight. But to my child's mind, there seemed to be something wrong. Who needed the goat more? The aunt who had no children, or the aunt who had a houseful of children?

So I decided to "kidnap" the goat and take it to the place where it would make a life-or-death difference.

I reasoned that the best time to do the kidnapping would be on a Sabbath, after the midday meal, when my aunt Rukhtshe and my uncle Yossl lay down to rest after they had eaten their heavy, filling Sabbath food.

And it was indeed on a Sabbath that I untied the goat and started to lead her out of her little stall. But the goat resisted, and so, with all my might, I dragged her along. Slowly, slowly, I got her out into the street. The danger lay in being seen by someone at the window.

I dragged the stubborn goat. Any minute now we would be near the window. Another few steps and I would be beyond peril.

Just then, my aunt, looking out of the window, saw me dragging the goat. She cried out so loudly she could be heard ten blocks away, "Yossl . . . the goat . . . Itzik . . . the goat."

Hearing my aunt's cry, I started to run. The goat, which I had hardly been able to drag earlier, now began leaping over me. I ran faster; the goat leaped more wildly. My uncle, in his underwear, came out of the house. My aunt, in her slip, kept yelling at the top of her voice, "Itzik . . . the goat . . . Itzik . . . the goat . . . "

I no longer pulled the goat; the goat pulled me. She made terrified wild leaps as she dragged me along. The street that moments ago had been empty was now thronged with men, women, and children, all of them shrieking in aid of my aunt's "Itzik . . . the goat . . . Itzik . . . the goat . . . "

Finally, someone caught the goat. I was picked up, unconscious from the dusty ground . . . .

My childhood attempt to right a wrong, to achieve justice, was not a success. Bruised and battered, I lay in bed. The goat was once more in the possession of my barren aunt Rukhtshe, who suffered from imaginary illnesses.

Those then were the adventures I had in my very early childhood years in the town of Kolomey. When so many things are unclear, when so much of what is happening in the world cannot be understood, those childhood desires rise trembling before my eyes: a whip with a red tassel, a child losing a grandfather whom he can now hardly remember, and an effort to transport a goat to a place where, in a just world, she belonged. That's what I remember.

And something more of that town of Jews is still with me.

AT GRANDMOTHER TAUBE'S IN STOPCHET

The only grandfather and grandmother that I knew were my father's parents. My grandfather Abraham died when I was yet a child and I can hardly remember him. My memories of my grandmother Taube are much clearer and more meaningful. And I want to tell about her.

She was a small, thin woman, but very agile. Everything she did was done quickly. She cooked, tidied up, baked. She raised geese. The large room in the house was a miniature store where one could buy a liter of milk, a bar of chocolate. Almost anything.

Her two daughters, Brayne and Mayke, helped her out. Aunt Brayne was a pretty girl with golden brown braids that, when she combed them out, reached to her knees. She had mischievous blue eyes. Aunt Mayke was the younger one. Her hair was flax blond. She never unbound her hair frivolously, like her older sister. She was a generally inward person, quiet, thoughtful, restrained. The blue of her eyes was brighter, without a mischievous spark. She moved quietly, worked quietly. Even her smile had something otherworldly in it. I know now that those who smile like that are destined to die young. And yet it was she who was once the target of my grandmother Taube's furious anger.

One evening, Aunt Mayke was standing on the threshold of the house. A young Ukrainian schoolteacher went by. Seeing a pretty young Jewish woman standing in front of the house, he doffed his hat to her. Aunt Mayke acknowledged the gesture with a nod.

Just then, Grandmother Taube looked out of a window and took in the entire scene. She called Aunt Mayke in and began to question her.

"How come you know that Ukrainian Gentile?"

"I don't know him."

"Then why did he take his hat off for you?"

"I don't know."

"Why did you nod your head to him?"

"Since he greeted me, I . . . "

The more Aunt Mayke justified herself, the less my grandmother believed her. She suspected that my aunt knew the Ukrainian teacher. People don't greet each other for no reason. Those who know each other exchange such greetings. How did it happen that the Ukrainian knew her? When did they get to know each other?

Aunt Mayke burst into tears. To my grandmother, that weeping was simply proof that there was something wrong. She shook her finger at my aunt and warned, "Rather than with a Gentile, I'd rather see you dead."

It's possible that it really was nothing more than a chance greeting and that my grandmother was mistaken in her suspicions. But one thing is clear. Jewish mothers trembled over their daughters and wanted, with all their might, to keep them from being alienated. They had reasons enough for their suspicions. They well knew the Ukrainians and their hatred of Jews. In the Hitler era, the Ukrainians of east Galicia revealed what they were made of. How many such quiet, virtuous Aunt Maykes died at the hands of Ukrainians . . . .

It is fortunate that my aunt Mayke died young, even before the First World War. She died young, naturally, and not at the hands of a Ukrainian schoolteacher who doffed his hat to her once, in the days of Franz-Joseph.

It is no wonder that, with two such radiant aunts, I felt, as the saying goes, like a fish in water. They caressed me, and my grandmother Taube let me have anything I wanted. Their little town was always a holiday place for me. I yearned for it all year long and could hardly wait for summer vacation when I might once again travel to Stopchet.

In the wagon, I counted the telegraph poles on the way to Kolomey. How many telegraph poles, do you suppose, were there alongside the railroad tracks from Czernowitz to Kolomey? In those childhood years, I used to know the number well enough, but now I have forgotten it.

When I sat on the wagon I even tried to count the willows along the way from Kolomey to Stopchet, but I never succeeded because I invariably fell asleep and, still fast asleep, was carried into my grandmother's house.

And when I woke, it was a golden dawn and my Aunt Brayne was standing before the mirror combing her golden brown hair, which reached to her knees. My Aunt Mayke, a flaxen blond, drifted silently, as always, through the room; she bent over me and gently touched my lips with hers. "Good morning to you, dear Itzik."

She swayed away from my cot, and as always, went silently about her housework with the secret of her early death locked so deeply within her that no one had any inkling of it. It occurred to no one that she was to be with us only for a while.

Barefoot, and carrying a long twig in her hand, she used to drive my grandmother's geese out of their pen and to the meadows on the outskirts of town. There they stayed for the entire day along with geese that belonged to other Jewish families. In the evening, the geese came home by themselves. Hundreds of them. As they came into the town, they would sort themselves out. Each gander, with his own troop, found his way home and to the woman who owned him. At the gate, a bowl of water had been readied for the geese who, after a day of gaggling in the meadows, slaked their thirst with it. Grandmother Taube used to open the gate to let the geese into their pen, where for a while longer, they continued their gaggling, chatting among themselves until they fell asleep.

I liked looking out of the window to watch my Aunt Mayke driving the geese through the town and out to the meadow. Barefoot, and with the twig in her hand, she looked exactly like a Gentile village girl. She came back alone, in a summery stillness, with the scent of the meadow in her braids and in her clothes.

I did not leave the house until after my Aunt Mayke had driven the geese to the meadow. It wasn't the geese I was afraid of. It was the gander. I could never understand why he hated me so much. Whenever he saw me, he made for me, with his neck outstretched. That enemy always terrified me.

My good grandmother Taube often protected me when that gander stretched his neck out and came at me; and when she was not there, it was my two aunts who protected me.

When I asked my grandmother what it was that the gander had against me—what harm had I ever done him, she replied, "The gander is a stupid fool. He himself doesn't know what he wants. He's just a gander, and a fool."

My aunt Brayne had another explanation. There was a saucy twinkle in her laughing blue eyes: "The gander thinks you want to marry one of his geese and take her away. That upsets him."

And when I asked her how I, a little boy, could marry a goose, she laughed and said it was what the gander thought.

"Then he really is a fool, as Grandma Taube says."

"He's jealous, Itzik dear. He loves his geese. Do you understand?"

My aunt Mayke also protected me from the gander. She simply drove him away, without offering any reasons for why she did so.

I feared the gander throughout all of the time that I was in my grandmother Taube's house in Stopchet.

That gander came to a bad end, as I will tell you a bit later.

In addition to the gander I had other troubles. For instance: having to drink milk. My grandmother ran after me, the glass of milk in her hand, and when she caught me, she compelled me to drink it. Had it been only one glass of milk per day, I might have tolerated it. But there was more than one; more than four glasses every day. In the midst of my most enjoyable games, there she was, Grandmother Taube with a glass of milk in her hand.

But I found a way of dealing with that, too.

There was a well outside my grandmother's house. It had a long pole to which one attached a bucket that was then let down to dip up water. Half the town got its water from that well. The water that spilled from the overflowing bucket mixed with the earth so that there was always plenty of delicious mud around the well, even in the hottest days of summer. Now, there is a rule: wherever there is mud, there has to be a connoisseur of mud; and generally, the best connoisseur of delicious mud is a pig.

And indeed, there was always a huge fat pig lying in the mud. He snorted with pleasure, and it was difficult to drive him away. No matter how often the women shouted "Sooey" at him, the pig pretended that it was not he that they meant. He lay in the greasy mud belching with pleasure.

And it was the pig who frequently rescued me from my grandmother Taube and her glass of milk. When my grandmother chased me, the glass of milk in her hand, and nearly, nearly caught me, I would leap onto the pig lying in the mud. The pig snorted, but that was all. As if he were in his father's vineyard, he continued to lie in the mud. I rode him, like a conqueror. My grandmother could not reach me. Here, I was safe.

And, indeed, my grandmother was stopped in her tracks, looking at me from a distance, afraid to come closer, lest she come into contact with the pig. She brought to bear every diplomatic trick she could think of to lure me away from the pig. She promised me chocolates and bonbons. She jingled her keys to make me think they were money that she promised to give me. But it was all to no avail. I would not dismount from the pig until she had poured the milk out onto the ground.

My two aunts had their work cut out for them getting me cleaned up. But the triumph was mine: I only drank milk when I wanted to, and not when my grandmother thought I should.

That was the only time in my life when a pig came to my aid. No other pig in the world has ever done me another good deed.

That very evening, when my grandmother Taube was eating supper, I sat opposite her, mimicking the way she chewed with the teeth that were left in her mouth. My good natured grandmother laughed. My Aunt Brayne spoke up, "Er iz gor an akter" (He's some actor). "Avade iz er a naketer" (Of course he's naked), then said it again to get the most out of her pun (*an akter . . . a naketer*). "Who ever saw such a thing: a Jewish boy jumping onto a filthy pig and getting himself so muddied. Tomorrow, God willing, his muddy clothes will be clean. Next time he'll know that a pig is both filthy and *treyf*.*

But the greatest adventure I had in those distant childhood years concerned my grandmother's geese and in particular that enemy of mine, my grandmother's gander.

One fine Thursday, my aunt Mayke herded the geese out to the meadow. She came home alone, as always. My grandmother had decided to clean and air out everything thoroughly in the house: clothes and bedclothes. Everything was taken out of drawers, the bedding from the beds. My grandmother and my aunts were frantically busy. I wandered about, now here, now there, feeling superfluous. No one paid me any attention.

Among the things that had been taken out of the drawers was a bottle of brandy that had been my grandfather's. He used to make kiddush with that brandy every Friday evening. When no one was looking, I took the bottle. I thought it was water. I carried it out and poured it into the basin of water that was always left out for the geese when they came back each evening from the meadow.

This time, when the geese had drunk their fill of their water, something happened that no one could explain. The geese began to wobble; to flap their wings; to twist and turn their heads. They fluttered wildly about, now here, now there. The gander's behavior was particularly wild. He clapped his wings together, restless, unable to find a place to settle.

My grandmother stood, wringing her hands.

"The geese have gone mad. I'm going to have insane cracklings."

When the drunken gander saw me, he extended his neck and made for me, his bill at the ready. I was terrified. My aunt Mayke seized his wings. I stood by, trembling and pale.

Gradually, the drunken geese were carried into their pen. The gander continued to play all sorts of tricks, until finally, he, too, quieted down.

My grandmother consulted a conjuress to take off whatever hex was afflicting me. The conjuress dripped candle wax that took on the shape of the gander.

No. That was not the end of the matter. Every Hanukkah my grandmother sent a slaughtered goose to each of her scattered children.

One winter's afternoon, when I came home from school, I found my mother unpacking a package that had just arrived. It was, as always at this time of year, the goose for Hanukkah. But this time, it was not a goose. Instead, it was he himself, my archenemy, the gander.

My good grandmother Taube had sacrificed her gander. An atonement for my childhood fear. There he lay before me—slaughtered. What is noteworthy is that I felt absolutely no sense of revenge. I even refused to eat his cracklings, though I was particularly fond of goose cracklings.

That was the end of the worst enemy I had during my childhood years.

My grandmother Taube, as a refugee from the Russian invasion of Galicia, died in a town in Bohemia that was called Bohemian Brod.

In one of my poems, she escapes from her grave in Bohemian Brod and returns home to her native soil in the small town of Stopchet at the foot of the Carpathian Mountains where are the graves of those dear to her.

A PORTRAIT OF A TAILOR'S WORKSHOP

I've already spoken about my father's fleeing on foot from Stopchet to Kolomey because my grandfather was displeased with him for wanting to be a craftsman—a tailor. After my grandfather died, there was further upheaval in the family.

One after another, my father's brothers left home and went to Kolomey, to Czernowitz, and there they learned to be tailors. Even the youngest of my father's brothers, Uncle Notte, who until my grandfather's death had helped him on his short trips, also became an apprentice to my father.

I can see Notte now, as if it had happened only yesterday, wearing a sweaty shirt and sitting on the coach box, the whip in his hand, a torn straw hat on his head. He urges the horses on, crying, "Giddyap, go, faster." Faster toward home, toward Stopchet. My grandfather sits in the wagon: his face yellow as wax, his eyes wide and sad. I'm sitting beside my grandfather. He caresses me with a weary hand and asks me what I've learned in Hebrew school. Uncle Notte, a robust youth, starts to whistle. I like that, but it doesn't please my grandfather. Angrily, he cries, "What's all this whistling in the midst of things? You'll have time enough to whistle after I'm dead."

Uncle Notte stops whistling. The word "dead" dampens his enthusiasm. He knows that Grandfather is ill and that that's why he sits depressed and silent in the wagon leaving him, a mere urchin, to drive the horses, making the whip whistle.

"Giddyap, horse. Giddyap Chestnut, giddyap Bay."

I envy Uncle Notte because he's sitting on the coach box; because he's holding the reins and the whip. Inwardly, I think that when I am as big as my uncle Notte, I, too, will get to sit on the coach box and drive the horses. I'll even be allowed to whistle because what is forbidden to my uncle Notte is not forbidden to me. My grandfather indulges me in everything. My grandmother, too. All, all of them indulge me. Even at the Feast of Tabernacles, my grandfather took me into the stable and perched me on top of a horse, because that was what I wanted though he gently reproved me "Don't you want to be a *mentsh?** Won't you eat in the *suke?*"* My grandfather didn't know that I wanted to be a mentsh: to eat in the suke as well as to sit on top of a horse.

When my grandfather died, the horses and the wagon were sold and my uncle Notte went off to Czernowitz to become his oldest brother's apprentice.

That brother, my father, was a very severe master. He was especially stern with his brother. If something was not done right—a lapel not properly basted—angry words were immediately heard: "Clumsy oaf!" "Bungler!"

My uncle Notte turned red as a beet. The reproaches before the journeymen embarrassed him. After all, the master was his own brother. My mother always tried to smooth things over with a kind word; with a reproach for my father, "You'll achieve more with kindness. Showing by example is the better way to teach."

But my mother's pedagogic ideas had no effect. An hour or two later my father's voice could again be heard, "Clumsy oaf!" "Bungler!"

I don't know whether my uncle Notte ever learned the craft. He was a boy who had grown up in a small town. He had always helped my grandfather with his horses. He had worked with him on his short trips to the Carpathian forests, to Kolomey. The needle, the thimble, and the sewing machine were foreign to him. What was familiar to him was the horse and the whip, the drive through the forest, the hard labor in the open air. He was a young oak with a soft voice and courteous manners.

In 1914, he was drafted into the Austrian army. He served on the Italian front in a regiment from Kolomey. He was severely wounded in one of the battles and died in a Czech military hospital, a sacrifice for the Austrian fatherland that produced the Hitlers, the Globatshniks, the Eichmanns, the Kaltenbruners, and other such worthies.

I can't help thinking that the name Notte came into our family under an unlucky star. My uncle Notte was killed in the First World War. My brother Notte died of hunger in Samarkand in Soviet Russia. Notte was twenty-four years old; my brother thirty-nine.

My father's other two brothers, my uncle Dovidl and my uncle Alter, learned the trade and became first-class master tailors.

What did a tailor's workshop look like in the first years of the twentieth century? I don't mean its physical appearance but the general mood of such a place. I emphasize the word "mood" because in Yiddish [gemit] it is the word that rhymes with "song" [lid].

In any case, that's the way it was in our home. The master, the master's wife, the journeymen tailors, and one or two apprentices were as one family. My mother cooked and baked khalah, the Sabbath loaf, and on Sunday, bread. An out-of-town journeyman ate with us and slept in our house. Not even the journeymen who had families in Czernowitz ever went to a restaurant. Instead, they took their second breakfast and their midday meal with us. At night, things were altogether different. The apprentices both ate and slept in the workroom, where at night, cots were arranged only to be folded up again by day.

My father had a good reputation as a tailor. Indeed, he loved the work. He paid more attention to the work itself than to the amount of money he might earn. He spent hours on end sketching designs and projects on paper. Even when a client was satisfied, my father himself was not and continued to find faults that the client had not noticed. Obviously, given such pedanticism, our workshop produced only one, or at most two pieces of work per week.

Even so, things would have been all right. One made a living. My father charged a good price for his work, but he also paid his journeymen the highest wages. A weak journeyman did not last long with us. The moment my father became aware that the work was not good then he sent him packing. In addition to such epithets as "Clumsy oaf!" and "Bungler!" my father added the advice that he should immediately apprentice himself to a cobbler or to a patch-tailor.

By contrast, he had the highest respect for those who were skilled. Often it happened that when my father was paying out the wages at the end of the week, it struck him that he, the master tailor, was left with less money than any of his journeymen. But it was worthwhile. The best customers came to him. The cream of the town's society. The "Herr Professor" and the "Herr Jurist." And who knows who else?

There were times, however, when my father abandoned his work. Some sort of unrest, a sense of dissatisfaction, drove him from home. The journeymen stood about without work. Suits remained unfinished. Customers came for their first fitting, for their second fitting, and my father was not at home. Everything began to turn topsy-turvy. My mother wept, but it did no good. When he was seized by the obsession, my father abandoned everything. He hung out at night with his good-buddy friends until he got hold of himself and started anew. For a while, and then the process was repeated over and over again.

Things came to such a pass that we had to sneak away from our house at dawn, when everyone was still sleeping. Quietly, secretly, everything was loaded onto a wagon and without so much as a "by your leave," we left the house on Harmuzaku Street and made our way to some sort of cellar apartment with mildew on the walls.

That was our last home in Czernowitz. There we were overtaken by the First World War and we fled before the czar's army took Czernowitz for the second time.

That move marked a great decline for us. Once we had lived in the Herrngass, the loveliest promenade in town. From the Herrngass to our cellar apartment was truly downhill. The way up was marked by the difference between homes in which one worked by the light of kerosene lamps and those in which one worked by electric light. The way down was the basement apartment with its damp walls and kerosene lamps.

In the basement apartment, my father worked alone, without journeymen, without even an apprentice. My brother and I became newspaper vendors. We went through the streets shouting the news in the *Morgn Blat,* the *Algemeine Zeitung,* "Archduke Franz Ferdinand Shot in Sarajevo." Our mother took the few pennies we earned. We were often hungry. It was to such a pass that my father's bohemianism led us.

My mother often sighed, lamenting our condition. "With such talented hands—and my children have to go about cracking pumpkin seeds to satisfy their hunger."

But let us turn back to the time when things were good. When we lived respectably in the Russishergass, the Herrngass, the Harmuzakugass, when the house was jammed with work; the sewing machines pounded; the needles flew.

The tailors' room was filled with song and laughter. Everyone sang. The best of the singers was a journeyman named Leybele Beker. He was a slender youth some twenty years old. His face looked wasted and pale. He was the first to devote himself to me. He developed in me a feeling for poetry. He taught me to recite Schiller's "Glocke" and Goethe's "Erlkönig," Heine's "Zwei Grenadieren." I used often to visit him at his home as a friend.

"Is Leybele at home?" His mother, the widow, knew that her Leybele was my friend, that he spent time with me and lent me his books, and therefore she treated me always as one of the family. Often, she would express her regrets that my visit was futile because her Leybele had gone away. She did not know where.

That Leybele Becker used to sing Yiddish folksongs as he worked, most of them love songs that were so beautiful and sung with so much feeling that my mother often stood behind the door wiping her eyes with her apron.

It was said that Leybele Becker had a girlfriend whom he loved dearly. She had gone off to America and he longed for her with all his might. And that was why he sang with such sincerity. I suppose the songs were well known, but no one sang them as well as he did. He put his heart and soul and all his yearning into them. His songs were truly winged. And if that maiden's heart on the other side of the ocean was as filled with longing as his was, she would not have stayed one minute longer in that distant America and would have returned at once.

> I loved a tailor-maiden
> Who came from far-off Vi-en;
> She traveled to her parents
> To see them once again.

The tailor maiden never came back from Vi-en, and perhaps it is a good thing that she did not, because if she had, Leybele Becker might have stopped singing, and that would have been a pity; a great pity.

Like my uncle Notte, Leybele Becker was killed in the First World War.

There was a second journeyman tailor named Aba who worked for us for a little while. I don't remember his family name. He had long hair, like a girl's, and a carelessly tied necktie. He was an anarchist who told me that there was no god and that the kaiser ought to be overthrown. I did not agree with him. How could one overthrow such a nice old kaiser? What had he done to deserve that? If one knocked him off his throne, he might be bruised. And how could one say that there was no god? How did Aba know that?

Aba made a gesture with his hand. "You're still too young. When you're older . . . ."

The conversations with the journeyman Aba disturbed me greatly. In my mind's eye I can see the kaiser Franz-Joseph sitting as always on his throne: he is having his usual afternoon nap. Then all at once, here comes Aba with his long hair and his carelessly tied necktie and seizes the sleeping kaiser and throws him down from his throne. The kaiser groans, "Oh, my back."

Aba runs away and I come in. I help the kaiser up from the floor. The kaiser groans. Slowly, I help him to seat himself again on his throne.

The kaiser asks me to pick up the crown that has fallen from his head. Without his crown, he is not a kaiser. There it is where it has rolled, under the cupboard.

I creep under the cupboard, pull out the crown. It's covered with dust and spiderwebs. I dust off the crown and hand it to the kaiser. "Please, Herr Kaiser."

The kaiser puts the crown on. He wants to groan; to say, "Oh, my back." But it strikes him that it isn't fitting for him to groan like a woman in labor.

Suddenly, he asks me, "Who was that person who wanted to throw me off my throne?"

Now, I'm in a quandary. To tell or not to tell. It strikes me that the kaiser wants me to be a snitcher. I had heard in Hebrew school that in the Other World snitchers were hanged by their tongues. Quickly, I reply, "I don't know, Herr Kaiser."

However, the kaiser is stubborn. He doesn't give up. "Did he have long hair and a carelessly tied necktie?"

"I don't know, Herr Kaiser."

The kaiser thinks for a while. "Yes, yes. It was those fellows with long hair and the carelessly tied neckties who slew my sainted queen, Elizabet." The kaiser wipes his eyes with a handkerchief. I'm aware that I don't have a handkerchief so I wipe my eyes on my sleeve. We both love the queen Elizabet. The kaiser because of her beauty; and I because she had loved the poet Heine and had had a monument made for him on the island of Corfu.

"There," says the kaiser, patting me on the head and pinching my cheek." There. Go on home and tell your father that this coming week I'll order three new suits from him."

Those were the sorts of fantasies that I had from the time that the journeyman tailor Aba told me that there was no god and that the kaiser ought to be overthrown. And that he, Aba, was an anarchist. In my fantasies, I undertook to defend the kaiser against unjust treatment. As regards God, I waited, expecting moment by moment for the earth to open up and swallow Aba, the anarchist, the blasphemer. I kept my distance from him, so that when the punishment came, I would avoid it.

Aba's words turned me pious. I prayed every day, never skipping a word. I became even more loyal to the kaiser. With great feeling, I sang the song,

The kaiser is a dear, dear man,
He lives in far Vienna.

Aba the journeyman tailor did not stay with us for very long. He had come to Czernowitz because his brother was serving there in the army. One day, his brother swallowed poison, and it was only with great difficulty that his life was saved. From then on, Aba looked after him. He worked for my father, and whenever he could, he visited his brother, encouraged him, helped him, supported him, doing what he could to make his brother's life in the barracks easier.

♦ ♦ ♦

Max was the third of the journeyman tailors who were engraved in my memory. He was a tall youngster. He was so tall that he had to walk with a stoop. He was a true prankster. He could mimic animals of every sort: a rooster, a cat, a dog, a horse. He mimicked them with such speed and such skill that one would have thought they were all there in the room, neighing behind your back, barking at your feet, meowing on the other side of the window, crowing right in your ears. Though everyone knew him, Max's menagerie was invariably surprising. It was always so unexpected that no one knew where it came from. He himself sat seriously at work, his needle moving at a furious pace, the sewing machine stitching away. The press iron glided along swiftly, swiftly. Then all at once, Max lifted his innocent, simpleton's eyes, "What happened?"

The surprise dissipated. Everyone laughed, Max excepted. From the vicinity of the sewing machine could be heard the oink of a pig driven away from his wallow or the death rattle of a slain rooster.

This Max was a brilliant worker—one of the best-paid. He spent all his earnings on chocolate. All of his pockets were filled with chocolate. All kinds of chocolate. He was always taking a piece of chocolate out of his pocket and popping it into his mouth.

His breakfast was chocolate. His lunch was chocolate, and his supper, once again, was chocolate. No one could understand why he did not tire of it. Sooner or later one could tire of any food. But not Max.

No one could understand why he dressed as he did. Such a first-class wage earner dressing that way. No amount of scolding made any difference. The sleeves of his jacket were too short. His trousers were patched or, often, so torn that one could see entire parts of his body showing through.

The neighbors used to complain about him: "Why isn't he embarrassed before women; before young girls? Feh, and a thousand times feh."

But Max was not embarrassed. Quite the opposite. If the neighbors were still sleeping when he came to work in the morning, he woke them with a long sustained cry to let them know that Max was going to his work, and anyone who did not want to look at his torn trousers should bind his eyes with a horse's tail.

My father thought well of him because he was a master at his work. I liked him because of his cheerful indifference. Besides that, he taught me to distinguish one kind of chocolate from another. I learned the names of the various chocolate manufacturers throughout the entire Austro-Hungarian empire, and why one chocolate cost more than another.

When he came to work for my father, he was known as "The tall Max." But after a few weeks, he was called "The sweet Max."

"The sweet Max" brought a good deal of joy and laughter into my father's workroom. I admired the way he artfully imitated so many animals that the whole room was transformed in a single moment into some kind of a zoo. I admired him for the courage he showed by living in a different way from that dictated by respectable people. For the courage he showed by wearing torn trousers "with his rear sticking out" to spite the "stiff collars and the pressed pants." For his encyclopedic knowledge of the chocolate manufacturers; and for his ability to eat chocolate day in and day out without its doing him any harm.

Another "character" was the journeyman tailor Khaim, who was called "the Gypsy Baron." He did, in fact, look like a Gypsy. Small, sprightly, mercurial. He could not sit still in one place. One moment, he was in a chair, in another moment, on top of a table. One moment on the cupboard, and the next on top of the clay oven. In the summer, quick as a wink, he was out in the courtyard on an old trestle bed that rocked on three sickly legs and that had been put outdoors as something that had outlived its usefulness. Everyone who tried to sit on the trestle bed fell from it. But not the Gypsy Baron. He balanced so skillfully on it that the trestle bed stayed steady on its three lame feet as if they were whole.

No one ever knew where he might be "sitting."

There he was, at the very tip of the only tree in the courtyard. And throughout it all, he never let go of the work he had in his hand. His needle flew, quickly, quickly, and then his voice was heard, "Done."

It took my father several minutes to identify where the call came from, whether from the cupboard or the oven or the tree. But what the Baron handed over was first-rate work. He was the fastest worker that my father ever had. Nor was it ever second-rate, because second-rate, for my father, was taboo. "Clumsy oaf!" "Bungler!" "You're all thumbs!" And such a worker did not last with us for so much as half a day.

My father handed the Gypsy Baron another piece of work, and there he was, sitting at the table, on the oven, on the trestle bed in the courtyard, at the top of the tree, plying his needle at top speed as if a thousand devils were chasing him.

No one knew where the Gypsy Baron came from. He himself was secretive about it. Every three or four months he disappeared for several days. When he returned, he always had a different explanation: he had been at his mother's in Stanisla; with his wife in Keresmezshe; with his bride in Kraków. The names of the places were always different. Finally, it was concluded that he had actually been to Digression Land, where the devil says "Good night." His brown face with its small black mustache was one huge smile. He said, Germanizing his Yiddish, "All right, then, that's how it is. *Wie zagen Sie?* How do you say? Digression Land. Next month, my wife will die. Funeral. *Leichenbagegenish.** You understand?"

The small mustache twisted as if he meant to weep, and no one knew whether he was joking or whether he actually had a wife who would die precisely a month from now. Most probably it was a pretext to disappear again for a few days. Because when he returned from another of his disappearances, he said that his wife was in good health and as strong as a horse; that she was pregnant and that soon he would have to go back for the circumcision ceremony.

I have merely given several sketches of journeymen tailors in my father's workshop long ago. Long ago, in the days of my childhood.

This portrait of a tailor's workshop would not be complete if I did not also say something about at least one of the apprentices.

A master tailor received an apprentice for a period of three years. Until he learned his craft, the apprentice was given food and a place to sleep in his master's house.

There were many apprentices in our house who did not last even for two weeks. It was my fault.

My father judged the apprentice by whether he learned his craft in addition to his other duties: helping the master's wife; serving the journeyman tailors. I judged the apprentice by whether he could tell stories. If he could, then everything went swimmingly. If he couldn't, I plagued him so much that he had to leave.

One of the apprentices who could tell stories was Shmulik, a village lad from Brezev. He was a strong, strapping fellow with a face full of freckles. He told weird stories about witches and warlocks; about princes and princesses who were tricked into caves; about trees that walked to Vienna in order to tell the kaiser that his daughter had married a ghost. The ghost had put all the postmen in the country to sleep, and the trees therefore became letter carriers in order to bring the report to the kaiser.

I swallowed his wild tales avidly and wanted more, and Shmulik told one story after the other until I fell asleep.

But Shmulik could not fall asleep. His primitive village soul was terrified by the stories he told. He lay all night on his trundle bed, unable to sleep a wink. The next day he went about in a daze, like a zombie. Whatever he was told to do he did just the opposite. Several days went by before he came to himself. He literally trembled with fear when he was left with the children on a Saturday night when the master and his wife went off to enjoy themselves, either to the theater or to a tavern.

I could hardly wait for those Saturday nights that made Shmulik tremble.

"Shmulik, tell!"

And Shmulik tried to tell, and to soften his tales a bit. The witch no longer had a single eye in the middle of her forehead. Instead, she had two eyes, like other people. But I remembered well the story from a week ago. I would not allow him to change the tale. The witch had to have one eye in the middle of her forehead. That eye had to glow like a burning coal. Shmulik, squirming, paced back and forth as I recalled to him each of the horrors of his tale. He was trapped by his own stories. And I would not allow him to go free.

Once on a Saturday evening my mother was waiting for my father to come back from the city. She lay down on the sofa. All at once, she sensed that someone was dancing behind her head. She opened her eyes. No one was there. She dozed off again. Again, someone was dancing. She leaped up from the sofa and saw something white disappearing into the next room. She ran into the room and saw Shmulik leaping into his trundle bed.

"What's going on, Shmulik? Why were you dancing behind me?"

And Shmulik told her that one of the journeyman tailors had taken him to a Yiddish theater. There he had seen someone playing Lust, the Evil Inclination. From then on the Evil Inclination came and danced behind Shmulik's head nightly.

"And that's why you danced behind me? Where's the sense in that?"

For Shmulik, sense had nothing to do with the matter. His village soul was filled with superstitious fears and his dancing in his drawers behind my mother was a primitive erotic impulse. He had seen the Evil Inclination in the Yiddish theater and its image would not let him be. Just as his fantasies about ghosts and demons had turned into realities that frightened him and kept him awake at night.

The Jewish tailor's workshop in Czernowitz is now no more than a memory. The master tailor, his wife, the journeyman tailors, and the apprentices are ashes and sorrow. Longing—just a finger touching the ashes—and the images for a moment are once again real.

◆ ◆ ◆ *Fiction*

EXCERPTS FROM *THE BOOK OF PARADISE*

1. My Last Day in Eden

The time that I spent in Paradise was the most beautiful of my life. To this moment, my heart aches and I get tears in my eyes when I remember those happy days.

Often I close my eyes and live again those splendid years, years that will never return—unless the Messiah should come.

In these dreaming moments, I even forget that my wings were shorn before I was sent down to this world. I spread my arms, and I try to fly . . . . Only when I have fallen to the ground and feel a sharp pain in my bottom do I remember that it's all too late—that only the people in Eden have wings.

And for just this reason, I have decided to tell everything that befell me—both before my birth and after it. I shall describe it, not to deceive unbelievers, but to console myself. I know that many people have already described their lives in the various languages of the world. I myself have read a hundred such life histories, and I must confess that, at every point, I sensed in them human vanity—and falsehood, that falsehood which paints itself in rosy colors and paints others in the darkest black. Such life histories are nothing more than a deceiving stupidity that fools especially the authors themselves.

I, on the other hand, mean to tell everything as it was, without diminishing it by so much as a hair. I'm not out to convince anyone that I was particularly virtuous in Paradise. Good Lord, no. I did my share of harm as well as good. But in my story, where I have done harm, I will say so, and where I behaved well, I shall tell accurately just how it was.

I know that many people will ask me, "How come? How is it possible for a person to remember so precisely what happened to him before his birth?" Maybe such questioners will bring evidence that such a thing is impossible. Everyone knows that just before a person is born an angel comes and gives him a snap on the nose that makes him instantly forget all of his past—even the Torah, which he was studying just before his descent into the sinful world.

Those who make this point are right. Actually, that's how it is. That *is* what happens to every person before he arrives in this world. An angel does give everyone's nose a snap, and in fact, he does forget everything. But in my case, a miracle happened—a most remarkable miracle. And I will tell about this miracle at once, so that people will not go around whispering that I, Shmuel-Aba Abervo, am spinning a yarn or turning out lies.

On that day when I was turned over to the care of the angel who was to conduct me down to this world, I happened to be sitting under an Eden tree, enjoying the canaries that had "burst into song," as the Scripture says. By the way, I should tell you that, by comparison with the canaries of Eden, earthly canaries are simply less than nothing. In the first place, the Eden canaries are twenty times bigger, and when they sing—well, it's just not possible to describe their song in any earthly tongue. One needs to hear them with one's own ears to understand the difference.

It was twilight. The Gemora teacher, Reb Maier-Parakh, an angel with heavy, dark gray wings, had gone to the angels' prayer house for his evening devotions, and his students had scattered. Some of them were playing tag while others sat around telling stories about thieves and robbers. I went off to my beloved Eden tree to listen to the singing of the canaries.

I must confess that my greatest weakness, at that time, was the singing of the canaries of Eden. While they were singing, I could forget all the world.

So there I am, lying under the Eden tree; the canaries are singing; large butterflies are fluttering over the grass, playing tag. When I speak of the Eden butterflies, you must not suppose that they are in any way like those summer butterflies you see on Earth. If you think that, you are making a big mistake. The butterfly of Eden is nineteen times as large as those on Earth. Each butterfly is a different color—one is blue, one green, one red, another white, still another black. In short, it is not possible to describe them, since human language lacks the words for all the colors that exist in Eden.

There I am, then, lying under the tree. Suddenly, I hear a well-known voice—like a silver bell.

"Shmuel-Aba. Shmuel-Aba."

I look about and see my friend Pisherl, a mischievous little angel with dark, intelligent eyes. As always, his mouth is smeared with plum jam. He is fluttering over me with his thin, bright wings. Then he settles at my feet.

"What is it, Pisherl? What's going on? Don't keep me in suspense."

Pisherl wipes the sweat from his wings and whispers into my ear, "Shmuel-Aba, it's bad. I've just found out you're to be sent to Earth this very day. It's your fate to become a human being. Do you know what that means? A human being!"

My heart began to beat, "Thump. Thump. Thump."

"Pisherl. What are you saying? Who told you? How do you know?"

Pisherl told me how it chanced that he was flying past the Eden tavern, At the Sign of the Zaddik Noah. There, in the barroom, sat Shimon-Ber, the greatest drunkard of all the angels in Eden.

"He was drinking ninety-six proof and was cursing a blue streak," Pisherl continued. "I gathered that he was in a fury because he was being sent on an errand. He's supposed to take you down to Earth, and then he's supposed to snap your nose with his finger so you'll forget everything: Eden, Torah, everything you've learned—and me, too, your friend Pisherl."

And Pisherl burst into tears. Several drops fell on my right hand. They were large and hot.

My friend's tears moved me to the point of tears. I caressed his dear head and tried to console him. "Don't cry, Pisherl. You know the kind of thing a drunken angel in a bar will say. Well, just let's see him try to take me. I'll tear out that red beard of his. I'll scratch his face up. So help me, I'll bite his red nose right off."

But Pisherl could not be quieted. He wailed at the top of his voice. "You don't know the sort of bandit he is—that Shimon-Ber. That cruel bastard."

I knew that Pisherl was telling the truth—after all, this Shimon-Ber made all the other angels tremble. He was almost never sober. To fall into his clutches was worse than falling into Hell. And yet, he was the very one chosen to take the children down to be born on Earth and to give them that famous snap on the nose.

I quivered like a fish in water. I began to imagine how it would be. This drunkard would lead me by the hand. If I were unwilling to go, he would throw me over his shoulder. Soon, we would be at the frontiers of Eden. I could already hear the drunken angel's voice, "Let's have your nose, fellow. A snap of the finger—and off with you."

In expectation of that snap, everyone shivered; they were even more frightened of it than of being born on Earth. That drunken snap of the finger had undone more than one little angel. Whenever you see a pug-nosed child anywhere in the world, you may be sure it was Shimon-Ber who caused it by snapping his nose too hard.

"Well, Pisherl. What now? What do you think? What's to be done?" I asked my friend.

"There's nothing to be done," Pisherl answered sadly. "It's too bad, but your fate is sealed. You'd never squirm out of Shimon-Ber's hands, even if you had eighteen heads. Maybe it would be best if you—"

"What? What?" I asked, looking intently into his eyes.

"If you went along with him willingly. Don't resist. And don't cry. Shimon-Ber hates being resisted. He hates tears. If you cry, you may get such a snap from him that, God forbid, you'll arrive on Earth without any nose at all. Some face you'll have then—may Shimon-Ber be cursed that way."

From Pisherl's answer, I understood that I would not be able to escape the drunken angel. All the while that Pisherl was talking, I was holding my nose, already sympathizing with my whole heart over the misfortune that, God forbid, would befall it. Deep in my soul, I was praying to the Lord of the Universe to guard and protect it.

As I was making my silent prayer to the Lord of the Universe to protect my nose, Pisherl was sitting pensively on the grass nearby, a finger at his temple. Evidently, he was thinking something.

Suddenly his dark, intelligent eyes began to sparkle. Whenever Pisherl gets an idea, his eyes glisten.

"Shmuel-Aba. D'you know something . . . ?"

"What, Pisherl?"

He looked around to be sure that no one was listening; then he whispered in my ear, "In our cellar at home, there's a bottle of Messiah wine* that my father keeps (as medicine). I'll give it to you to take along on your journey."

"What do you mean—you'll *give* me the bottle for my journey," I said querulously. "Does it belong to you? And what good is it likely to do *me?*"

Pisherl smiled. "It's easy to see that you need to be led by the hand. What's so hard to understand? You'll give the bottle of wine to Shimon-Ber. He'll be so delighted with it that you can make a deal with him so he won't snap your nose too hard."

"What are you talking about, Pisherl?" I cried in a loud voice. "Do you mean to say you'll *steal?* What about 'Thou shalt not steal . . . '?"

Pisherl burst into laughter. "Idiot, thou son of Stupid. Don't you know that 'Thou shalt not steal' is for people, and not for angels? Come on. Show me . . . tell me. Where in the Torah is it written that the Lord of the Universe commanded the angels, 'Thou shalt not steal'? Where, unless it's in the Noplace Book?"

I could see that my friend was cleverer than I, and that he was right. Just the same, I still couldn't understand. Suppose I did give the angel Shimon-Ber the bottle of Messiah wine, and Shimon-Ber then did give me only a light snap on the nose—still, snap it he would, and however lightly he did it, I would have to forget all that had happened to me in Eden—and that would be a great pity.

Evidently, Pisherl understood my thoughts. From his pocket, he took out a bit of clay; he began to work it with his fingers, kneading and twisting, until at last he had shaped a nose that he handed me, saying, "While

Shimon-Ber is drinking the wine, you put on this clay nose. When he snaps at you, he'll hit the clay, miss your nose, and you'll escape him completely. Be sure to remember everything; and, when you are on Earth, see to it that you tell everyone that there is a Pisherl in Eden."

He rose, smoothed out his wings, and in a clear voice said, "Come. Soon Shimon-Ber will be looking for you. It will be better if you approach him yourself. But first, let's fly to my house."

That was my last flight over Eden with my dear friend.

It was not long before we alighted at the house of Pisherl's father, calf-eyed Shlomo-Zalman, the tailor with the lumpy Adam's apple. On the wall of the house there hung a sign of an angel with patched wings—to indicate that Pisherl's father was a patch-tailor who fixed worn-out wings.

Pisherl went into the house and I waited outside. Very soon, he came out again, carrying the Messiah wine under a wing. He handed me the bottle and said, "Here, take it, Shmuel-Aba. And fly at once to the tavern At the Sign of the Zaddik Noah. Better for you to go to Shimon-Ber than that he should come to you."

We kissed each other, hugged each other, kissed each other again, and hugged each other once more, and who knows how long we might have continued had not Pisherl's mother, the angel Hannah-Deborah, called from the window, "Pisherl. The tripe is getting cold. Come and eat."

We kissed each other once again, and we touched wings. Pisherl went into the house to eat his supper, and I flew off in the direction of the tavern At the Sign of the Zaddik Noah.

It was already dark in Eden. In the houses where the angels lived with their families, the lamps were burning. Bearded angels were bent over yellowed holy books. Fat lady angels with triple chins were patching shirts; young mother angels were rocking cradles, lulling the first-born little ones with song.

Sleep my angel, sleep, my darling,
Sleep my angel, sleep, my sweet,
In your mother's cradle, darling,
    Rest your lovely wings.
            Ai, lu, lu.

As I flew by, I looked into first one, then another of the windows. I was very envious of them—the young and the old angels. They would sleep through the night, and in the morning they would wake up still in Eden. And I? Where would I be? It was sheer luck that the wind cooled the tear on my cheek, or else the tear would have burned a hole in my face.

I landed in front of the tavern. I peeped through the window and saw a couple of coarse angels, the kind that do the rough work for the *zaddikim**—plowing their fields, taking in their harvest, and getting a fig for their pains. They were sitting at small tables, drinking spirits, smoking cheap tobacco, and continually spitting at the floor through their teeth.

At a table to one side sat the angel Shimon-Ber. His red beard was disheveled, his eyes screwed up. It looked as if he had already poured a good deal into himself. The moment I saw him, my heart pounded with fear. "So, this is the angel who is to lead me out of Eden," I thought. And no matter how hard I tried, I could not persuade myself to go in.

I stood thus, for some little while, undecided, until at last I got my courage up. "It has to happen sometime," I said to myself and went in.

The moment he saw me, he tried to rise to greet me with a "welcome." But he was too drunk, and his wings got twisted in some way so that he fell backward to his seat. I ran to him and helped to smooth his wings so that, though he might not be able to stand straight, at least he would be able to fly. And, indeed, we were both in flight toward the border that separates the other world from this one.

We took off on Thursday at ten p.m., and we arrived at the border on Friday before the blessing of the Sabbath candles.

You may be sure that our flight was by no means easy. The angel Shimon-Ber, was, as I've said, thoroughly drunk. He kept losing the way, with the result that, after three hours of flying we came upon a familiar chimney—that belonging to the tavern At the Sign of the Zaddik Noah. Shimon-Ber had been drawn to the place where he usually spent his days and nights.

We all but had ourselves a little accident. The night in Eden was dark—not a sign of a star. Shimon-Ber had left his lantern in the tavern, so we were flying blind—without an inkling of where we were.

In the darkness, Shimon-Ber collided with another angel, the angel of dreams, who was, just then, flying down to Earth. In the collision, one of the wings of the angel of dreams was hurt. Shimon-Ber cursed and the angel of dreams wept. He would be unable to fly now, and the people below would have to sleep without dreams. He limped off on one wing to Shlomo-Zalman, the patch-tailor, to get the hurt wing fixed, and we—that is, Shimon-Ber and I—continued on our way to the border.

One other result of the collision was that Shimon-Ber became a trifle more sober. He took out his pipe and stuffed it with coarse tobacco. He lighted a match and, puffing on his pipe, flew on—with me.

Every pull on his pipe created a little glow, so that, from time to time we could see where we were in the world.

We passed the Eden mill. It stood on a hill, its vanes exposed to all the winds. In Eden, many stories are told about this mill. By day, it's a mill like any other—grinding wheat and corn; but at night, it's a place for imps and devils.

I know you don't believe me. How can there be devils in Eden? I wondered that, too, when I first heard of it. I was told about them by my friend Pisherl. I myself never saw any imps or devils, but every angel will tell you what happened to Raphael, the barber-surgeon of Eden. Once, at night, when he was going to see a patient, he passed the Eden mill and heard strange cries. Suddenly, he saw before him a long tongue that an imp had put through a peephole in the mill. The angel Raphael cried out, "Hear, O Israel," and fell down in a swoon. He was found at dawn, lying near the mill, and was roused with great difficulty. From that time on, he suffered from a severe impediment, stuttering.

We, that is, the angel Shimon-Ber and I, flew on. Not a word was spoken between us. What Shimon-Ber might have been thinking, I can't tell. How could I know that? But what I was thinking and feeling, that, as you see, I do remember. And what thoughts!

I thought of my friend Pisherl, sleeping in his little bed. He is uncovered. He has kicked the bedclothes to the ground. Even in sleep, he's mischievous; there's no one like him. He's got his finger in his mouth. Who knows? He may be dreaming of me, his friend, from whom he parted today forever.

I felt like crying. Sobs were already gathering in my throat, but when I remembered that the angel Shimon-Ber hated tears, I restrained myself and let out only the gentlest of sighs.

Toward dawn, the angel Shimon-Ber became entirely sober. The morning wind was sharp and cold and we were both seized with shivers. My teeth were chattering.

"Ai, some cold," grumbled Shimon-Ber, beginning to flap his huge, cottony wings to keep warm. With every flap of his wings, he looked back in the direction of the tavern At the Sign of the Zaddik Noah.

I was not long in understanding that this was the moment to offer him the bottle of Messiah wine my friend Pisherl had given me.

"Reb Shimon-Ber," I called, frightening myself with my daring. "Reb Shimon-Ber. A good little glass of spirits would come in handy now— to warm up with, eh? What do you think, Reb Shimon-Ber?"

At the word "spirits," the angel slapped his gray, cottony wings together with such force that he frightened a couple of blue Eden swallows that were just getting ready to sing "O, Creator of the World."

"Oh! A little glass of spirits," he cried with such a voice that ten Eden hares swooned with fright and a couple of pregnant lionesses miscarried on the spot.

From under my right wing, I took the little bottle of Messiah wine, and showed it to him. He did several loop-the-loops in the air from sheer joy. At first, I thought he had gone out of his mind. And, for a moment, I was frightened. Dealing with a crazy angel is no small matter. To this day, I shudder when I remember the young angel Pearl, who went insane because of an unfortunate love affair. O Lord, what a fuss she kicked up. She all but turned Eden topsy-turvy.

But to conclude. As soon as Shimon-Ber saw the bottle in my hand, he flew up to me, snatched it away, pulled the cork with his teeth, and began to slurp. You ought to know, by the way, that Messiah wine is heavy. Each drop weighs two and a half pounds.

"D'you know what, Shmuel-Aba?" he said. "Let's go down for a bit. We can still manage to get to the border in time." He took out his brass watch and studied the red face of the dial. We came down on a field in Eden.

When Shimon-Ber had finished swilling all there was in the bottle he became very jolly. He pinched my cheek and said gruffly, "You're a fine fellow, Shmuel-Aba."

We resumed our journey and said our morning prayers in flight. At precisely five o'clock in the evening, we arrived at the border. At its farthest edge, Shimon-Ber ordered me to stand on one foot and to recite all the Torah that I had learned. I did as he ordered. When I had finished, he took out a huge pair of shears and began to clip off my wings. While he was clipping, I managed to stick on the clay nose. He was so drunk from the Messiah wine that he noticed nothing.

"Now, let's have your nose, and let's give it a snap."

"Reb Shimon-Ber," I said, pleading, "please. A light snap, Reb Shimon-Ber." In fact, I had found favor in his eyes and so he gave my nose so gentle a snap that I all but did not feel it.

"And now—off with you."

I looked back for the last time. I saw the entire panorama of Eden as it was being dipped in pure gold. I took a final look at my wings lying on the ground.

"Good-by, Reb Shimon-Ber," I said to the angel with the cottony wings, and I descended.

4. My Friend Pisherl

On the second evening, when my parents, the rabbi, the rabbinical judge, and the rich man were already seated around the table, I rolled up my sleeves and resumed my narrative.

I met my friend Pisherl in the Hebrew school run by Maier-Parakh, the Gemora teacher, where we were both pupils. I liked him from the start. That little angel with the dark, intelligent eyes pleased everyone who ever met him, with the understandable exception of the Gemora teacher, Reb Maier-Parakh, whom he tormented severely.

To be truthful, the Gemora teacher had reason for being angry with my friend Pisherl. My friend all but crippled him once with a prank he played on him. It was a Tuesday afternoon and the Gemora teacher was hearing us repeat our lessons. He threatened us with his cat-o'-nine-tails, waving it over our heads, back and forth, until at last he began to snort, and finally, as was his custom, he fell asleep. The cat-o'-nine-tails fell from his hand.

Pisherl's eyes glittered. Turning to us, his fellow pupils, he asked, "Fellows, can you keep a secret?"

We replied that we could, and waited with great interest to see what would happen. We understood that Pisherl was up to something.

Pisherl took a piece of tar from his pocket. On tiptoes, he went up to the Gemora teacher, whose wings drooped wearily. Slowly, Pisherl lifted the teacher's right wing, smeared it with the tar, and pasted it down to the bench. Having finished with the right wing, he smeared the left.

We were choking with laughter, imagining the moment when the Gemora teacher would wake up. We waited and waited, but he slept on. He seemed to have no intention of waking.

Seeing that he would not wake up, my friend Pisherl went up to him and shouted into his ear, "Rabbi, time for evening prayers."

The Gemora teacher woke up and started to fly to the synagogue, wrenching the wings pasted to the bench so hard that he pulled the wingtips quite off. He fell to the ground, yowling with pain. His wife, Golda, an angel with a cataract in her right eye, flew in from the kitchen. She set up a cry, and sent at once for Raphael, the barber-surgeon angel. He, in turn, sent to the Eden pharmacy for an adhesive bandage with which he pasted the Gemora teacher's wingtips back on.

From that time on, the Gemora teacher had it in for my friend Pisherl. He (that is, my friend Pisherl) was beaten whether he was guilty or not. But my friend was one of those pranksters whom no amount of beating could deter from playing tricks. And it was just for this reason that he was dear to me. I was bound to him, body and soul, as in turn he was to me. Whenever anything occurred to me, he was the first to know; and he, for his part, always consulted me.

I had but to ask, "Pisherl, what do you think . . . ?" and Pisherl immediately put his finger to his head, thought for a while, and then came up with the right suggestion: "Shmuel-Aba, suppose you try . . . " I told him everything I thought. I hid nothing from my comrade who was as dear to me as a brother, and perhaps even dearer.

I know that you will say that the trick Pisherl played on the Gemora teacher was not particularly original. Every schoolboy on Earth can brag of similar tricks played on teachers. To this, I reply, first, that this was not the only stunt Pisherl pulled in Eden and, second, that earthly schoolboys are liars, boasting of imaginary accomplishments, while Pisherl actually performed *his* tricks.

One day, Pisherl came to me. He seemed very downcast. He looked at me for a moment with his melancholy eyes and said, "Do you know what? I'll tell you something, Shmuel-Aba. There is no justice in Eden."

I looked at him with astonishment. I had no idea what would make Pisherl say such a thing. He sighed. "You know, Shmuel-Aba, I have an uncle, the angel Khaim-Nogid.* He has his own house on Elijah-the-Prophet Boulevard. A house with a balcony and a brand-new tin roof."

"I know, Pisherl," I replied. "Your uncle is the official liquor dealer of Eden. He's said to be as rich as Korah."*

"And a great pig," Pisherl added. "In the Christian Eden, a pig his size would be enough for a huge feast."

"But why are you telling me about him, Pisherl. I'm curious."

"Listen carefully," Pisherl said. "This uncle of mine, this pig, has a goat that gives twenty quarts of milk every twelve minutes. You and I are going to take the goat from its stall and lead it away."

"Where will we take it, Pisherl? Explain yourself. Don't keep me dangling."

"To my uncle Joel, the bookbinder angel, who lives on Yohanan-the-Cobbler Street.* He has tuberculosis and needs the goat's milk more than my uncle the angel Khaim-Nogid does."

"You're right, Pisherl," I agreed. "There really isn't any justice in Eden. The uncle who is rich and healthy as a bear has a goat that gives milk, though he needs it like ten thousand plagues; and the poor uncle, who is sick with tuberculosis and needs the milk to sustain his very life, has a fig for his pains."

Pisherl put his finger to his forehead and thought for a while. (My friend always put a finger to his forehead when he was thinking.) "Shmuel-Aba, do you know what?"

"What, Pisherl?"

"We must steal the goat from my uncle Khaim-Nogid and give it to my uncle the angel Joel."

"Good, Pisherl," I agreed. "But when? Think it over. It has to be done at just the right time."

Pisherl laughed. "It'll be all right, Shmuel-Aba. My uncle Khaim-

Nogid takes a nap at noon, and my aunt, the angel Yentl, is away then, being measured for a new pair of wings at the tailor's."

"Well," I said impatiently, "well."

"While she's gone, I'll get the goat out of its stable and lead it to my poor uncle. You'll stand watch in the street, in case my aunt should come back."

"Good, Pisherl. I'm ready. When do you suppose we can pull it off?"

"What do you mean, when?" Pisherl gestured with a wing. "Tomorrow noon, right after lunch."

We agreed on a meeting place. Pisherl described it carefully to me. I went around in a daze for the rest of the day. All night long, I was obsessed by a dream of a goat that gave twenty quarts of milk every twelve minutes.

The next day, precisely at the time arranged, my friend and I made off quickly for Elijah-the-Prophet Boulevard, where Pisherl's rich uncle lived.

Elijah-the-Prophet Boulevard was very lovely. That's where the crème de la crème of Eden lived. The loveliest house belonged to the zaddik of Sadgura.* He cut the same wide swath in Eden as he had on Earth. It's worth mentioning that this was the boulevard on which Rahab the whore had opened a salon where the richest of the female angels went to have their nails manicured. In Eden, by the way, she had become very pious and read the pious books so that she knew them almost all by heart. As for the manicuring profession, she had very little enthusiasm for it, but a living is a living. In Eden, everyone had almost forgotten that she had once been a whore.

My friend Pisherl and I stationed ourselves before the angel Khaim-Nogid's house and waited for Yentl to leave. When she did, it would be the sign that Pisherl's uncle was taking his nap.

We waited for about half an hour, then Pisherl's aunt, the rich angel's wife, flew out of her house. We looked after her until she disappeared.

"I hope she croaks," Pisherl cursed. "She goes about squandering a fortune on fashion, at the same time as Aunt Rivtsche can't even permit herself the expense of a patch job for her old wings that are so worn through that anyone seeing her thinks she's a beggar and wants to give her alms."

My friend Pisherl wanted to go directly into the courtyard where the goat's stall was, but just at that moment, an old Jew went by, a stout stick in his hand. He stopped my friend and asked, "Where are you going, little angel?"

My friend Pisherl recognized the old fellow at once. It was the prophet Elijah. In the old days, he used to drop down to Earth from time to time to help a poor man or to perform a miracle so that some unlucky fellow might have a little something for his Sabbath. But recent times had turned him bitter. Poor people on Earth had stopped believing in his help and had decided to help themselves. Scornfully, the prophet Elijah had said, "Let them help themselves, those . . . how do they call themselves there? . . . those . . . shoshialists?"

Ever since he had given up his visits to Earth, he went about aimlessly in Eden, strolling down the boulevard that bore his name. He would not have walked down any other street for a king's ransom.

"Where are you going, little angel?"

I was frightened, thinking the whole plan was now ruined. Imagine! Right in the middle of our plot, the prophet Elijah. He always loved to poke his nose into everything. But my friend Pisherl did not lose his head. He knew the old fellow's weakness—to be talked to about the miracles he had accomplished in the days when he was still pleased to perform them. (He can still do them, but he doesn't want to.)

"Let them help themselves . . . the . . . how do they call themselves . . . the shoshialists?" Having said the word "shoshialists," he spat. Pisherl told him he was right, and went on to tell the old fellow such stories about himself as made the old fellow smile. He took every word that Pisherl said to be the truth. At long last, he took his leave. Pisherl wiped the sweat from his brow.

"Now, Shmuel-Aba," he said, "be careful. Let me know if anyone comes. If they do, God forbid, put your fingers in your mouth and whistle."

"Good," I replied. "But do your best to make it quick, Pisherl."

My friend was gone for some while. Every moment seemed like an eternity. I turned my head to the right and to the left, checking whether, God forbid, anyone was coming. My heart beat crazily.

Pisherl came out leading his uncle's goat on a rope.

"Quickly, Pisherl, quickly. Let's fly to your uncle Joel's. I have a hunch something's going to happen."

"Dope," Pisherl said. "We have to go on foot. A goat hasn't got wings."

We had just taken a few steps when we saw Pisherl's aunt, the rich angel Yentl, flying back in a great hurry. Evidently, she had forgotten something at home. She saw us and immediately raised a hue and cry. My friend and I flew off, making our getaway. The goat dangled in the air, uttering a fearful *meh* over the boulevard.

Pisherl did not let go of the rope. We flew on, panting. Shmaya, the policeman, an angel in a green uniform, who stood at the intersection directing traffic so that the angels, God forbid, would not collide with one another, blew his whistle.

A real chase began. Shmaya, the policeman, still blowing his whistle, was after us. Aunt Yentl, who was a corpulent angel, wheezed like a goose and shouted, "Thieves. Give me back the goat. Woe is me, woe is me. Give me back my goat."

"Pisherl, hold tight to the rope," I cried.

The goat shuddered in midair. Its *meh* was deafening.

"Old Elijah delayed us too long," panted my friend, grasping the rope more firmly.

"He shows up most where he's least expected," I said. We flew on.

Our wings were flapping so wildly that I was hardly able to catch my breath. We were young, and our wings were still unworn. We made a number of zigzags. At one moment we thought we had lost our pursuers, but then we heard their wings flapping behind us again.

The goat was so frightened that her udders opened and the milk began to pour down. Little angels who could not yet fly stood below with open mouths, enjoying every drop that fell!

We arrived at Yohanan-the-Cobbler Street a good bit ahead of our pursuers and alighted. Pisherl knocked at his poverty-stricken uncle's window. His uncle, the angel Joel the bookbinder, came out. He coughed and asked us what was the matter.

"We brought you Uncle Khaim-Nogid's goat. You need it more than he does."

"Who asked you for the favor?" shouted the bookbinder, giving Pisherl two resounding slaps.

At that moment, our pursuers descended. Aunt Yentl was red as a beet. She was shrieking and crying, "The goat. Thieves. Give me back the goat."

Shmaya, the policeman angel in the green uniform, made out a report in which he named us both. Aunt Yentl took the goat by the rope, and promised to fix us properly with Maier-Parakh, the Gemora teacher. She gave the rope a pull and started home with the goat. Saddened and ashamed, my friend and I exchanged looks.

We went home. What Pisherl was thinking, I don't know, but I know that my own heart ached sadly.

For a while, Pisherl kept silent. I did not want to ask him anything. What had happened, had happened. At some point, he lifted his head, and looking at me with his dark, intelligent eyes, he said, "D'you know what, Shmuel Aba?"

"How should I know?" I answered. "Am I a prophet?"

"I've been thinking," Pisherl said, "that as long as the rich uncles don't permit it, and the poor ones don't want it, there'll be no justice in Eden."

6. In King David's Estates

The next night when the rabbi, the rabbinical judge, and the rich man were again at our table waiting for me to go on with my narrative, I watched them for a while. They were pale and had slept insufficiently. The rabbi's beard, or so it seemed to me, was whiter by a hair. Evidently the stories of the Eden ghosts had severely disturbed him.

"Well," my father muttered, "Well. Tell on. You can see they're waiting to hear you, and yet you just sit there like a clod."

When she heard the word "clod," my mother, who was standing at the door, was instantly ready to come to my defense . . . to tell my father what's what; but this time I wouldn't let her. One look from me, and she stayed rooted to the spot. My father, who was already trembling before the storm, calmed down, and I resumed my story.

After all the sights I had seen on that white moonlit night, I was unable to think of sleep. I waited with difficulty until it was dawn in Eden; then I flew quickly to my friend Pisherl's house. I knocked at his window. Pisherl was still asleep. He did not hear my tapping. I knocked harder—so hard that my fingers hurt. At long last, I woke him.

"Pisherl, come. Hurry, quickly."

"What's the matter, Shmuel-Aba?" my friend inquired, rubbing his eyes.

"Come on out. You'll soon know." My whole body was trembling. My friend came out.

Taking him by the hand, I looked into his sleepy eyes and said, "Let's fly to the King David Wood."

We flew. On the way, I told him about all the nightmares that had appeared to me. Pisherl sighed. My story made a deep impression on him. Giving his wings a shake, he said, "I've never yet seen such things as you tell me of, Shmuel-Aba. I've heard a great deal, but I've seen nothing. It seems one sees such things only on sleepless nights. You were lucky to have had a sleepless night. I envy you, Shmuel-Aba."

I couldn't understand him. His words seemed strange. What was there to be envious of? When I said as much to him, he looked at me with a strangely distant look. "Whatever the day hides or blinds with its sunlight, the night reveals. It lifts the veil of things and you get to look into the abyss. It's a pity I slept through such an eventful night."

We flew on. The early sunlight warmed our wings. The Eden wind was young and fresh. He played with our hair prankishly, wondering at his own temerity. When we approached the King David Wood, the wind left us, springing quickly in among the trees to tell the Eden rabbits that guests were coming of whom they need not be afraid. The two "flyers" had not brought bows and arrows along.

My friend and I let ourselves down near the entrance to the wood.

"Right here," I said, pointing, "right here is where the crazy angel Pearl disappeared into the wood. I was afraid to follow her. Come, Pisherl. Maybe we can still find her." We went into the wood and looked for tracks of the crazy one but found none. Birds were twittering in the trees. Dew glistened on the grass in large silver drops.

"Perhaps the drops are tears unfortunate love has wept on the grass," I said to my friend.

"It may be," Pisherl whispered. We stopped before a large, wild, dew-filled Eden rose. With awe and piety, we recited a chapter of the psalms, but the tears remained.

"What happened to Pearl's tracks?" I asked my friend.

"No doubt the Eden streetsweeper swept them away. That's the way things are done in Eden. The day isn't supposed to know that often the nights are filled with nonsense and madness."

"Then it's useless to search. Let's turn back, Pisherl."

Pisherl was lost in thought. His finger was at his forehead. I stood by and waited to see what he would think up.

A bird flew over Pisherl's head and whistled, "Pee. Pee." All the birds knew my friend Pisherl. They were fond of him and often greeted him. In bird language, "Pee. Pee," means "Pisherl."

"We won't go to Hebrew school today," Pisherl said finally.

"But what of the Gemora teacher, Maier-Parakh? He'll beat the day-lights out of us tomorrow."

"To Hell with him," said my friend with a wave of his hand.

"Agreed," I said. "To Hell with him. The monster."

We lingered a bit longer, listening to the birds sing, breathing deeply the smell of the grass.

"Come, Shmuel-Aba."

"Where, Pisherl?"

"We'll fly to King David's estates."

"To King David's estates? Will they let us in?"

"I have a friend there. A shepherd angel named Laibl. I haven't seem him in a month of Sundays."

"Is it far from here, Pisherl?"

"A couple of hours' flight to the east. Our King David is terribly rich. He goes about all day with a golden crown on his head, his hands clasped behind his back, watching the angels at work sowing his fields. He dearly loves to hear his psalms being sung. He thinks his songs are the most beautiful in the world, and the angels who work for him are obliged to sing them as they work."

"Good, Pisherl. We'll fly there and listen to the angels singing King David's psalms."

We spread our wings and started. Our flight lay toward the east. The sun dazzled our eyes. For the first half hour, it was difficult flying into the sun. Then we got used to it. I was already burning with curiosity to see the estates of King David.

My friend pointed down with his finger. "Shmuel-Aba, do you see?"

I looked and saw green fields stretching far out toward the horizon. On the right hand, there were huge verdant forests; on the left, a river that looked like a silver belt the queen of Sheba might have lost. I could not contain myself and cried out, "Oh . . . how lovely."

We dropped down a bit in order to see better. In the fields stood the peasant angels, their long shirts out of their trousers. They were plowing and sowing. Huge drops of sweat dripped from their foreheads. The angels sang:

When dawn lights up the windows,
We're driven out of doors,
Out of our dingy corners,
Out of the shabby house.

Cuckoo, cuckoo, you're a witness
To all that we endure;
Tell our woe to blessed God;
Take Him our silent tear.

Tell Him that we plow the fields,
And take the harvest in,
And tell him that our children starve,
At night, when we come home.

Cuckoo, cuckoo, you're a witness
To all that we endure;
Tell our woe to blessed God;
Take Him our silent tear.

"Why are their songs so sad?" I asked.

"Why? Is that your question?" My friend sighed. "Just look at the lives they lead, and you won't need to ask. May those who envy them be condemned to live as they do." He pointed. I looked down and saw small low huts of clay with straw-thatched roofs. "There, in those huts. That's where the poor angels live. They never get enough to eat; they never dream a dream to its end."

"Why is their fate so dismal, Pisherl?"

"Why? You ask 'why'?" Pisherl gritted his teeth. "Because there is no justice in heaven. In appearance, they are angels just like all the others. They have wings; they sing psalms. Just the same—look at them."

A tear fell from Pisherl's eyes. I caught it in my hand. It was hot.

"I gather, then, that Eden isn't Eden for everyone?" I inquired.

"For the time being, no," my friend answered. And we flew on.

"And this is all happening in King David's estates," I thought. Aloud, I said, "Where's the justice in it?"

Pisherl turned. "Fool. Don't you remember what the patriarch Abraham said on that Sabbath walk? 'Justice shmustice.'"

I remembered the conversation of the patriarchs and I turned red with shame. "Well, what about King David?" I inquired. "What does King David do?"

"If only all the angels could live like him. He carries on in Eden as God would in France. He goes around all day with nothing to do. Or else he plays on his harp, or he dallies with Abishag; and when he gets bored he bothers the pretty daughters of the poor angels."

"He hasn't forgotten his old tricks?"

"No. On the contrary. In Eden he can really do them. After all . . . King David!"

We flew over the silver Eden River. Barefoot women angels were standing at the river's edge washing clothes. One of them, a young angel with red, swollen hands, was singing:

Well for you zaddikim,
Oh, it's well for you.
At the Eden stream,
We wash your clothes for you.

And what you have made dirty,
We can wash it here,
And what you have bespattered,
We will make it fair.

The other angels, old as well as young, who were standing bent over at the water's edge, replied in chorus:

Praise to the Creator
Who rules the world His way,
Who set the whole Creation
In a just array.

Of one, he made a harpist,
Another washes clothes,
While still another labors
Sweating in the fields.

From the clay huts there could be heard the sounds of infants. They lay alone in their cribs, crying their hearts out. Braina, the Eden wet nurse, an angel with huge, full breasts, went from hut to hut nursing the little angels. The lord of the estates had hired her for this purpose so that the darlings wouldn't keep their mothers from their work.

"Where does Braina get the milk to nurse so many of the little angels?" I asked my friend.

"How come you don't understand, dummy?" grumbled Pisherl. "She waters it."

We flew on, turning now to the right toward the gardens. The sun was growing hot. We looked for a shady corner. In the midst of a luxuriant park, there stood a marble palace. The windows of the palace were wide open. Two young female angels, with down clinging to their hair, were airing out the bedclothes.

Pisherl said, "That's the palace of King David. It has more than a hundred rooms. King David, his wives, and his mistresses live there."

Awed, I said, "A lovely palace. It would be worth taking a look at what goes on there."

"God forbid," cried Pisherl. "No sooner across the threshold and you'd be caught by the eunuchs and forced to become a page."

"A page in King David's household! Can that be so bad, Pisherl?"

"Wish it on your worst enemy, Shmuel-Aba. You simply don't know what you're talking about. That's all you need—to stand around all day, holding King David's train or tickling the soles of his feet."

I shuddered to the tips of my wings. I imagined a couple of sweaty feet with huge corns on the toes. It was my job to tickle them. The sweat was suffocating; King David was continually angry, shouting,

"Harder, harder. Tickle harder, Shmuel-Aba. What are you? A page or a clod?" Brrr . . . I shuddered again.

We could hear the sound of a harp. Pisherl pricked up his ears. "Do you hear, Shmuel-Aba?"

"I hear, Pisherl."

"King David is playing his harp. Let's fly, but on wingtips, silently, so he won't hear us."

We flew toward the sound of the music. Under a shady oak, King David sat. He was playing the harp. Near him sat a young girl with black, wavy hair and a raspberry birthmark on her left cheek. My friend and I settled down near the couple. I looked at King David. He was a man of middle height, corpulent, with sharp green eyes. His little beard was reddish, cut somewhat close.

"He's the one who wrote the psalms?" I asked my friend in a whisper.

My friend put his finger to his mouth, "Shhhh . . . ." I understood. Now it was best to be silent and to listen. It must be said that King David played quite well. The girl beside him grew lovelier as he played. When he finished, I saw an eagle circling over his head. There was the sound of a thousand voices from the trees in the garden. "King David of Israel, long life to you."

The king smiled. He seemed pleased. The girl stood up.

"Where are you off to in such a hurry, Shulamith? Why is it you're so pressed for time?" said the king, taking her by the hand.

"I must go, father-in-law. Solomon may be looking for me already in the vineyard. You know, if I'm even a little bit late, he starts looking for me. By now, he's sung the 'Song of Songs' a dozen times."

But King David would not let her go. He pulled her down to him under the shady tree and embraced her. "Dear Shulamith . . . little dove . . . kitten . . . ." Shulamith tore herself from his arms. Her hair tumbled down; her face was aglow.

"Leave me in peace, father-in-law," she breathed excitedly. "It's a sin. You're blaspheming against your psalms."

"If you want me to, kitten," whispered King David, "I'll write even better psalms for you. Another 'Song of Songs,' like Solomon's . . . only more beautiful . . . " We heard the sound of a kiss, then of another, then a third. Shulamith pleaded, tearing herself from his arms. "Let go, I beg you. Let me go, father-in-law! Solomon will find out. There'll be a scandal."

"He'll find out nothing, kitten. Like hell he'll find out, my dove . . . ."

"The birds will tell him, father-in-law. Solomon understands the language of the birds."

"The birds in my estates," the king was panting, "will tell him nothing. The birds in my estates are loyal to me."

Again we heard a kiss, a second, a third. Who knows where it all would have led, had not King David heard Bathsheba calling, "David. Where are you, David?"

Shulamith started to her feet, patted her hair, and, quick as a doe, aroused and inflamed as she was, she was gone. King David rose, took his harp, and started off in the direction of the marble palace. We watched him go until he disappeared among the trees.

From the fields there came the song of the laboring angels. It had the aura of raisins and almonds, of sweat and psalms. I looked at my friend. He looked at me. We understood each other.

"What if Bathsheba knew what just happened here?" I said.

"Bathsheba is used to such goings-on, but if Abishag were to find out . . . don't even ask what would happen."

"Well, what about King Solomon? What if *he* knew? Would he be silent?"

"He'd tear the entire 'Song of Songs' up in his rage. It would be better if he didn't find out. It would be a pity to lose the 'Song of Songs.'"

"No skin off my nose. Let them tear hell out of each other."

We wiped the dust from our wings and took to the air. The sun was already low on the horizon.

9. *A Terrible Tale of the Messiah-Ox*

Pisherl woke up. He was delighted when, on coming into the workroom, he discovered I was there. He ran up and embraced me as if we hadn't seen each other in years.

"Have you been here long, Shmuel-Aba?"

"I've been waiting for more than an hour. Praise God, you've had a good sleep."

We went over to the open window and looked out. There, in the meadow, the Messiah-Ox* was grazing. The three barefoot angels who looked after him were playing cards.

I said to my friend, "The Messiah-Ox gets fatter every year. By the time the Messiah comes, he'll be too fat to move."

Pisherl was silent. We saw the angel Khasya walking across the Eden meadow. She was in her ninth month, and she took a walk every evening to get a bit of fresh air. "Pisherl, why is she wearing a red apron?" I asked my friend. "If the Messiah-Ox sees it, God forbid, there may be an accident."

"You're right. That's right," said Pisherl. And both of us began to signal to her, waving our hands, motioning to the pregnant angel to turn back, in God's name, while there was still time. But the angel Khasya didn't understand our signals. She went peacefully on, getting closer to the place where the Messiah-Ox was grazing. The Messiah-Ox saw the red apron and his eyes lighted up. We thought that at any moment he would fling himself at her.

But we were mistaken. He did not take kindly to the red apron, it is true, but to our great surprise, he kept his peace. Evidently, it occurred to him that he was no ordinary ox. He was, indeed, the Messiah-Ox, for whom it was not fitting to fly into a rage over a piece of red cloth, like a common bull. Nevertheless, it was fated that a calamity should happen.

The angel Khasya was by no means overly bright. One might say that there was more beast in her than in the Messiah-Ox. When she was quite close, only a few paces from the grazing animal, she stopped to watch his pleasant cud-chewing. She stood for a while, admiring his appetite. The three barefoot angels were quarreling over their cards. One argued this way, the other that way, and the third disagreed with the other two. They were so engrossed by their quarrel that they did not notice that the pregnant angel went up to the Messiah-Ox and patted his neck.

"Let her . . . ," thought the Messiah-Ox. "Let her pat as much as her heart desires. If she'd only take off the red apron, all would be well." But, as Pisherl's mother, the angel Hannah-Deborah, says, "A fool brings trouble." The pregnant angel did not appreciate the Messiah-Ox's great forbearance. She patted and patted him. Suddenly she whispered in his ear, "The Messiah is coming."

The Messiah-Ox's entire huge body shuddered. "The Messiah is coming!" That meant that at any minute they would come to slaughter him. His body would be cut into pieces of meat. The meat would be cooked and the zaddikim would devour his flesh appreciatively: "Ah . . . ah . . . a true taste of Eden." It made the ox wild. "The Messiah is coming . . . danger near . . . time to run . . . escape . . . escape from the slaughter knife."

The Messiah-Ox did not know (what is an ox supposed to know?) that this was just the pregnant angel Khasya's idea of a joke; there was still plenty of time left for him to graze on the Eden meadow before the Messiah was due to come. Suddenly, he bent his head, and catching the pregnant angel up on his horns, he began to run wildly.

My friend Pisherl and I set up a shout; we shouted with all of our strength. "The Messiah-Ox is running away; the Messiah-Ox is running away."

The three cowherds jumped up and started to whistle at the ox, and to chase him. The angel Khasya, quivering on his horns, set up such a yowling that young and old ran to see what had happened. They asked each other, "What is it, eh? What happened?"

"The Messiah-Ox hooked a pregnant angel on his horns and ran off."

"Let's chase him."

"Let's catch him. Let's bring him back."

"To hell with the angel. The Messiah-Ox is more important. What will the zaddikim do without the Messiah-Ox if the Messiah should come?"

Now a real chase began. Angels, young and old—anyone with wings—flew after the Messiah-Ox. The enraged animal ran like a thousand devils. No doubt the image of the knife that would slaughter him was before his eyes. He was running away from the great feast of his flesh that the Messiah would make for the zaddikim. The pregnant angel twitched on his horns and waved her arms about, screaming and fainting at intervals, only to rouse herself to scream again.

We chased the Messiah-Ox. Before us flew the three cowherds; behind us, the angels, with or without beards. My friend Pisherl and I were the only children in pursuit. Some of the angels grew tired. They lost themselves in the crowd, panting, wiping the sweat from their wings, and finally they flew home.

"He's strong as iron, that Messiah-Ox."

"Did you ever see such running? Faster than the fastest Eden rabbit."

"The stupid female really scared him; she ought to be put in the courtyard of the synagogue and whipped until she promises never to play such practical jokes again."

That's the sort of thing the angels who returned to their homes were saying. Meanwhile, the Messiah-Ox continued to run away. We pursued him.

That Messiah-Ox did considerable damage in his flight. He ran across gardens, over newly sown fields where he trod down everything. He knocked over a couple of little angels who were playing ring-around-the-rosy. An old angel who was standing at the edge of a village playing a barrel organ was dealt such a blow that he turned several somersaults in the air before he fell in a dead faint from which he was revived only after the greatest difficulties.

"Pisherl! Do you see? He's heading westward, toward the border of the Christian Eden."

"I see, Shmuel-Aba. I see. May you live to tell me better news." It was beginning to get dark. The chase after the Messiah-Ox became more intense. If he was to be caught, it would have to be soon.

That was what we thought. But the Messiah-Ox had other ideas.

The pregnant angel quivering on his horns had no more strength left even to shriek. She was hoarse as a frog; her groans could barely be heard.

The Messiah-Ox's three cowherds were white as chalk. What would happen to them if, God forbid, the Messiah-Ox should cross the border into the Christian Eden? And by all indications, that was already happening. The bells of the Orthodox church were ringing, "Ding-dong. Ding-dong."

The leaps and dashes of the Messiah-Ox were so fierce that he was soon afoam with sweat. The border was very close. Already the Christian border guards, blond angels with blue eyes, could be seen. They wore huge boots and stood leaning on their pikes.

"Pisherl, what's going to happen?"

"A disaster," groaned my friend Pisherl. "A disaster, Shmuel-Aba."

The Messiah-Ox, the pregnant angel on his horns, crossed the border. Some of the Christian border guards tried to stop him, but he plunged on. Our angels, that is, the Jewish angels, drew up at the border. They could pursue the Messiah-Ox no farther. Or, to put it better, the Christian angels would have forbidden the pursuit.

Sad and shamefaced, we descended. We had no idea what to do, but stood looking after the Messiah-Ox as he disappeared in the distant fields.

An angel said, "Maybe they've caught him."

"What if they have," another angel retorted. "What good will it do us?"

"They're just as likely, God forbid, to make non-Kosher beef of him," a third angel observed.

"Our Messiah-Ox, God be praised, is fat enough. They can certainly make a feast of him."

"Our zaddikim are going to be left with their tongues hanging out. They've spent a lifetime sharpening their teeth and now what—no Messiah-Ox."

"Bite your tongue," said the angel Henzl angrily.

"Where do you get that 'no Messiah-Ox'? He's here, all right. And how! All he's done is cross over into the Christian Eden—we have to see about getting him back." The angel Henzl smoothed his wispy beard importantly while he tried to think of some means of freeing the Messiah-Ox.

"What's to be done, Reb Henzl?" asked a short angel with a dense beard. "Advise us, Reb Henzl."

The angel Henzl made no reply. He went up to the Christian border guards and began to talk with them, partly in their language, partly in Yiddish, and partly with expressive gestures. "Our Messiah-Ox," the angel Henzl said, "crossed . . . made escape . . . your paradise."

"What?" asked the angel Vassil, the squadron leader of the Christian border guard.

"Our Messiah-Ox . . . to your paradise," said the angel Henzl once more; then he made signs to indicate someone running. The Christian border guard burst into laughter. He gave his mustaches a twitch and said fiercely, "Beat it, filthy Jew."

The angel Henzl shuddered. We stood around him, our wings lowered, as if we were lost. From the fields of the Christian Eden, we heard the sound of a "hurrah" and then laughter. Evidently some of the Christian angels had succeeded in catching the Messiah-Ox. We stood on our side of the border listening to the Christians' joy. Our hearts beat like crazy watches. The angel Hillel, the street sweeper, sighed deeply. It was a sigh that could have been heard over a seven-mile radius.

The three barefoot cowherds stood about, looking as if they had been whipped. What were they to say when they were finally brought up on the carpet? ("So that's how you watched the Messiah-Ox, bastards." And the zaddikim would spit full in their faces—and they would be right, too. They just *had* to play cards, and while they played, the disaster happened.)

The laughter in the fields of the Christian Eden grew louder. "They're leading the Messiah-Ox toward the Christian stables. They're going to put that pious, Kosher animal near the same trough where they feed their pigs. Woe to them!"

The angel Henzl said, as if to no one in particular, "From bad to worse. They may even slaughter the Messiah-Ox with a non-Kosher knife. What will the holy zaddikim say? How will the Great Feast look without the Messiah-Ox? Angels! Help. What's to be done? Suggest something."

"Suggest something! Easier said than done."

The night was pitch black. Our angels stood at the border, their wings drooping, not knowing what to do with themselves.

One of the barefoot cowherds said, "Do you know what? Let's light a fire meanwhile. We can warm up, and at the same time, we can consider how to break the news to Eden."

The idea of the fire pleased everyone. As I said, it was already late at night and we were shivering. The three cowherds gathered kindling and built a fire around which we sat.

Each of us put a finger to his forehead, thinking, trying to come up with a suggestion.

"What do you say, Pisherl?"

"What should I say, Shmuel-Aba? It's good and disgusting."

"Now *they* have the Messiah-Ox, and we have a fig for our pains, Pisherl."

"Then we'll have to do without the Messiah-Ox, Shmuel-Aba. When the Messiah comes, we can eat the Leviathan. The flesh of the Leviathan is tastier than that of the Messiah-Ox."

The angel Henzl, who was listening to our conversation, flared up. Beside himself with rage, he delivered a speech that was continually interrupted by his swallowing the wrong way; but he went on.

"So, the punks are ready to leave the Messiah-Ox in the Christian Eden! Who says we'll leave the Messiah-Ox to 'them'? Have we herded him these thousands of years only to let them make a feast of him? Haven't they pigs enough over there? Do we have to leave them the Messiah-Ox as well? Let there be chaos; let there be darkness, do you hear? Let there be darkness, but let the Messiah-Ox be returned to us."

My friend Pisherl and I were frightened. We began to stammer, to apologize. "Don't be angry, Reb Henzl. We meant no harm, God forbid. We only wanted . . . we only said . . . you understand, Reb Henzl."

But the angel Henzl is difficult to calm once he gets worked up. He loomed above the fire and talked and talked, droning on like a mill. None of us understood a word.

Suddenly, with a flap of his wings, he extinguished the fire that had been flickering in the field and cried at the top of his voice, "Angels, up! Why are you crouched like crones before a fire? Let's rouse all of Eden. Let's make an uproar. Let us confront our disaster. Woe unto me, that I have lived to see this day."

We got up, spread our wings, and flew. The angel Henzl went before us; his wings flapping fearfully, he shouted, "Like hell we'll let them have the Messiah-Ox. The Messiah-Ox is ours. We'll bring him back to our Eden by fair means—or foul."

10. *The Turmoil over the Flight of the Messiah-Ox*

The news that the Messiah-Ox had escaped set all Eden in a dither. One bird told another; one wind told another. In the morning, as we were coming back home, we found crowds of zaddikim already in the streets. They were disturbed, gesticulating, unable to believe that it had really happened.

"Escaped . . . really . . . the Messiah-Ox?" the rabbi of Apt* asked the rabbi of Lublin.* "It can't be. Such a thing was never heard of."

The white head of the rabbi of Lublin trembled. One could see he was vexed. "The very birds are calling the news on the housetops and you go on with your, 'It's not possible.'"

The rabbi of Apt was tenacious. "Maybe it's only a dream, and all of this anxiety is for nothing."

The rabbi of Lublin shook his head. "A dream . . . a dream . . . . If only it *were* a dream."

"No doubt they'll bring him back," said the rabbi of Apt, trying to console himself. "What do the saints in the Christian Eden need the Messiah-Ox for? They prefer pig meat, and they have pigs in plenty."

The rabbi of Lublin accepted a pinch of snuff from the rabbi of Apt. He sniffed deeply, then sneezed aloud.

"You sneezed on the truth," said the rabbi of Apt, though he did not believe it himself.

I poked my friend Pisherl. "Where are the Messiah-Ox's three cowherds?" I asked. "They were with us just a while ago. Where did they disappear?"

"Why do you ask me? Can't you see for yourself that the cowherds are scared? The zaddikim are furious with them for losing the Messiah-Ox. No doubt the cowherds are hiding somewhere in an attic."

We saw a cluster of people. In the middle stood the rabbi of Sadgura. His beard was disheveled; his eyes glittered. He was literally giving off sparks. "Where are they, the scoundrels? Where are the cowherds? They ought to be punished as they deserve. The little bastards ought to have their wings broken. They ought to be driven out of Eden; they, and their wives, and their children, and their children's children." The zaddikim nodded their heads, agreeing with his bitter words.

We saw the rabbi of Horodenka,* running breathlessly. His gabardine was unpinned and he had lost a slipper on the way. Now, he ran up to the crowd, panting, "What a calamity! What a grief! What will I do with the gold fork and knife I bought especially for the Great Feast? What a calamity!" The rabbi of Horodenka was a small man with a long beard. One could say without exaggeration that his beard reached to his knees. Pisherl could contain himself no longer and burst out laughing.

"Don't laugh, Pisherl," I said. "It's a sin."

"How can I help laughing? Just look at the little rabbi. One slipper on, the other off. God be praised, what an appetite he has." Our luck was that the zaddikim were so engrossed in their discussion that none of them heard Pisherl's sly remarks.

"What's to be done? What's to be done?" the rabbi of Sadgura said, wringing his hands. "What sort of Great Feast can it possibly be without the Messiah-Ox?"

"We ought to cry woe . . . cry woe in the streets," the rabbi of Horodenka said heatedly. "Only think, such a thing has never happened before."

"This must be Satan's meddling," said the rabbi of Sadgura. "Where did the beast get the sense to think of running away?"

"Right. Right," the rabbi of Horodenka cried. "It's the work of Satan. Satan, may his name be cursed, has sneaked into Eden."

"We ought to inspect the *mezuzahs*,"* the rabbi of Zalishtchik suggested from the midst of the crowd. "Maybe a mezuzah has been defiled and that's the source of the whole calamity."

"Come," whispered Pisherl in my ear. "Let's leave these Galicians. Let them quarrel to their heart's content about spoiled mezuzahs. Let us fly on."

"Where, Pisherl?"

"I thought we might fly over and hear what the holy patriarchs have to say about the escape of the Messiah-Ox."

We left the crowd of Galician rabbis and flew in the direction of the Three Patriarchs' Allée, where the patriarchs lived in their villas. On the way there, we passed a number of zaddikim standing around in smaller or larger clusters. As we flew, we heard occasional words, "Messiah-Ox . . . escaped . . . cowherds . . . card-playing . . . to the Christian paradise . . . they must be punished . . . have their wings broken . . . what will the Messiah say?"

"The Messiah-Ox pulled off a real stunt, Pisherl. The zaddikim are at their wits' end. The Maggid of Kozienice* has even forgotten to wear his fringed garment . . . ."

"And the grandfather of Shpola,* Shmuel-Aba, has torn whole handfuls out of his beard; and how he beat his fists against his head, crying, 'My God, Jews. My God. What will we do if, God forbid, the Messiah should choose to come today?'"

"Tell me, Pisherl, where do these zaddikim get their remarkable appetites?"

"You ask funny questions. Don't you know that the zaddikim don't work? They never so much as put their hands in cold water. They go about all day long with nothing to do but to breathe the air; and it's said that the air is a great inducer of appetite."

We started down the Elijah-the-Prophet Boulevard. The morning sun covered the roofs with gold. The boulevard was empty. The richer angels were still asleep, and those zaddikim who lived on the boulevard had gone to consult with the others about the calamity.

Shmaya, the policeman in the green uniform, stood at the corner, yawning, his wings drooping. He had his truncheon in his hand as usual, but this time he didn't know what to do with it. My friend Pisherl and I had a moment of pity for him. He stood so alone, so lost with nobody before whom to be important. We flew over his head, made several loop-the-loops hand in hand, and sang a little song that Pisherl had invented after the policeman had turned in his report about us and the goat:

Shmaya, Shmaya, po-lice-man
With his stick stuck in his hand,
Stands upon the boulevard;
Like a dummy, like a fool
Wears a uniform of green.
Entirely green, his uniform . . .
Thinks he's great, thinks he's swell.
Come and see, O come and see,
You and him and her and me,
Come snicker at the likes of him.

Shmaya the policeman turned red as a beet. When he spotted us, he waved his stick and, foaming at the mouth, started after us, his wings outspread. But we were lucky. Just at that moment, Elijah the Prophet, who was taking his first stroll of the day on his boulevard, made his appearance. "Shmaya, where are you flying, hah? Why are you so excited, Shmaya?"

Shmaya folded his wings again. It appeared that he was ashamed to tell Elijah that we had sung a satirical song at him. He saluted the old prophet with a smile. "Good morning, Reb Elijah. Have you heard, Reb Elijah, the Messiah-Ox has run off. All the zaddikim in Eden are terribly upset about it, and you, Reb Elijah, are strolling about as if nothing had happened."

"I know. I know the Messiah-Ox has escaped and that the zaddikim are all agog. Let them, let them boil away. They have something to stew about. They are fortunate in having sound teeth, God be praised, while I," and here the old prophet showed his gums, "as it turns out, have nothing with which to chew my portion of the Messiah-Ox."

We left the old prophet talking to the cop and flew on in the direction of the Three Patriarchs' Allée. "Do you know what I think, Shmuel-Aba?"

"How should I know what you think, Pisherl?"

"I think there must be considerable confusion among the patriarchs. I'm curious to see the patriarch Isaac. He's a great gourmand, our patriarch Isaac. He'd give you almost anything you can think of for a piece of good meat."

"How do you know that, Pisherl?"

Pisherl showed his astonishment. "Shmuel-Aba, have you forgotten what we learned in school? It's written clearly in the Bible that the patriarch Isaac loved Esau better because he regularly brought his father a portion of the meat from his hunting expeditions." Pisherl thought for a while. "And second, Shmuel-Aba, . . . second, I myself saw how, one evening, when Isaac came to the meadow where the Messiah-Ox was grazing . . . how he brought with him a piece of chalk . . . ."

"What was the chalk for, Pisherl?"

"He made a mark on the Messiah-Ox's right side, to designate which piece was to be his at the coming of the Messiah."

"But the patriarch Isaac is blind. How could he have known where to make the mark?"

"Leave it to him, Shmuel-Aba," replied Pisherl. "Blind as he is, he tapped about with his finger and found the fat spot. Then he made his mark."

We turned into the Baal-Shem Alley. It was a poverty-stricken alley; nevertheless, it was sunny. Here, the very poorest of the angels lived. They were so poor that there was only a single pair of wings to a household. When one member of the family took the wings to leave the house, the rest had to stay at home until he returned.

But in this alley, great wonder stories are told. Hungry as they are, they believe in miracles. Their stories are indeed remarkably lovely. But hunger does its work too, goading and goading, frequently interfering with their sleep.

Lovely little angels were playing in the alley. They were holding each other by the hand, turning in a circle and singing:

> Hi and ho and hmph,
> Rivtsche is a nymph,
> She is a *grande dame*
> And Berkeh is her man.
> They fly about, these strollers,
> In wings of many colors.
> All know them, both together—
> In her hat, a feather;
> He wears a silken top hat.
> They have no children—that's flat
> But wine and honey in a can
> They've plenty, may they both be damned.

I pointed to the children playing in the Baal-Shem Alley. "Pisherl, the children are so poor and dirty, let's drop down and play with them a bit."

"God forbid," said Pisherl. "Have you forgotten, Shmuel-Aba? We're flying to the holy patriarchs to hear what they'll say about the Messiah-Ox."

"Only for a moment, Pisherl," I pleaded. "Let's just play a moment, then we'll fly on."

"No. Not this time. We've got to go. We'll play with them some other time," he said sternly. I had no choice but to give in. The alley curved and we had to fly carefully, slowly, to avoid scraping our wings.

No sooner had we left the Baal-Shem Alley and turned right than we recognized a familiar street. It was the Street of the Lovers of Israel. Here there lived Reb Moishe Leib of Sasov,* Reb Velvl of Zbarazh,* and Reb Levi Yitskhok of Berdichev. These zaddikim own small properties here. Behind every house, there's a cherry orchard. It's clear that they are not the richest of the zaddikim; there are a great many who are much richer; still, things are not too bad for them. They have no anxieties about making a living. They spend their days praying that God will have pity on the children of Israel and make room for them in Eden.

We looked down and saw a man of middle height, wearing a simple gabardine and, though it was really a warm day, his fur hat. He stood in the middle of the street, his head raised to the clouds, his arms lifted to the heavens. He was whispering.

"It's the rabbi of Berdichev," my friend Pisherl said in my ear, "Reb Levi Yitskhok of Berdichev. No doubt, he's talking things over with the Almighty. In the hour of calamity, he always stands in the middle of the street with his Sabbath clothes on and weeps and pleads with God."

"Let's find out what Reb Levi Yitskhok is saying to God, Pisherl."

"All right, Shmuel-Aba," my friend agreed. "We'll drop down and listen to one of his prayers in Yiddish. But remember, we won't stay too long."

"Only one prayer, Pisherl. I want to hear one prayer and no more. We settled down quietly a few paces from the rabbi of Berdichev and listened. The rabbi of Berdichev stood, as I've said, with his arms outstretched to the heavens. He was pleading, and his pleas would have moved a stone:

A good morning to you, O Lord of the Universe.
I, Levi Yitskhok of Berdichev,
Have come to you with a plea.
Where is justice, O Lord of the Universe,
And why do you plague your zaddikim, O Lord of the Universe?
Is it true that they followed in your ways?
You'll have to agree that they did . . . oh, yes.
Is it true that they obeyed your laws?

Once again, oh, yes.
Did you not promise them Eden?
Once again, Yes.
And the Messiah-Ox and the Leviathan?
And the red Messiah wine?
Once more, the answer is yes.

So where is the Messiah-Ox,
Father in Heaven?
Escaped to the Christians,
Father in Heaven.
Then bring him back to us again,
Father in Heaven,
Don't make a mockery of the Great Feast,
Father in Heaven.

I don't plead on my account,
Father beloved,
But for your zaddikim,
Father most faithful.

The rabbi of Berdichev waved back and forth, like a reed bent by the wind. There were tears in his voice, real tears.

"The rabbi of Berdichev must be a good man, Pisherl."

"A very good man, Shmuel-Aba. But let's keep going."

We flew on. Soon we were in the Three Patriarchs' Allée. By day, it was deserted; the benches that stood on both sides of the street were vacant. Only in the evening did the Allée begin to show life; then the betrothed couples appeared, whispering and kissing each other, vowing their love by the stars and the moon.

In the Three Patriarchs' Allée, it is always shadier than anywhere else. The birches along the roadside guard the Allée faithfully; not every sunbeam is privileged to get through.

At a distance, we discerned three Jews in fur hats who were walking along, waving their hands about. Judging by the movement of their shadows, we concluded that they were quarreling. As they drew nearer, we recognized the holy patriarchs walking rapidly.

The patriarch Isaac was in the middle. As always, he wore dark glasses. His speech was nervous, more nearly a shout than talk. "And I tell you, without the Messiah-Ox, Eden is not Eden. Whoever heard of a Jewish Eden without a Messiah-Ox? What sort of feast will the Great Feast be without so much as a morsel of meat? No feast at all, do you hear? No feast at all."

The patriarch Jacob, who was walking on the left, agreed with his father. He, too, thought that without the Messiah-Ox, the Great Feast would be an empty form. "Esau is lucky," Jacob said bitterly. "We, the zaddikim of the Jewish Eden, put the Messiah-Ox out to pasture, and he, Esau, will get the joy of it. Father, that son of yours was always your favorite. Now you're being repaid. He'll eat up your portion of the Messiah-Ox as well."

"Don't even mention his name," the patriarch Isaac cried in a loud voice. "I don't want to hear his filthy name."

The patriarch Abraham pulled Jacob by the sleeve. "Jacob, why are you tormenting your father? If he's made a mistake, do you have to keep reminding him of it? He thought that Esau would straighten up and become a somebody, and so he cared for him. Had he known that he would turn into a Gentile, he would have destroyed him root and branch."

The patriarch Jacob would not yield the point. He said that even if Esau had been—no matter what—Isaac would still have preferred him, just as long as Esau continued to bring him occasional tidbits to eat. His father (so Jacob argued) had always preferred his stomach to the Torah, and now he had . . . .

The patriarch Isaac turned red with rage. A vein in his forehead swelled. He wanted to lunge at Jacob; to give it to him properly; to beat hell out of him.

But the patriarch Abraham interposed, scolding, "Here I've called a council together in the Great Synagogue and you're squabbling, ready to come to blows. Pfooh!"

Abraham's scolding helped calm Isaac down. He walked on silently, his head bowed.

"Did you hear, Shmuel-Aba? The patriarchs have called a council in the Great Synagogue. Let's go and listen, but be quick, Shmuel-Aba. If we get there in time we can hide so they won't drive us away."

"Good Pisherl. Let's go."

We flew off. Below us, the patriarchs looked like three dots. "Quickly, quickly," Pisherl urged, and we flew to the Great Synagogue.

At the synagogue, there were already a number of the zaddikim. Naphthali, the caretaker of the synagogue, a man with a hump and a goat's beard, had flown from one villa to another, informing the zaddikim that the patriarchs Abraham, Isaac, and Jacob were calling together a council. The zaddikim had needed no urging to attend. Each one took a walking stick in hand and went at once.

My friend Pisherl and I went into the synagogue. No one noticed us, since they were all engrossed in themselves and in the escape of the Messiah-Ox. Hiding behind a bench that stood on the south side, we watched and listened.

The synagogue filled up. There was no longer even standing room, and yet more and more late zaddikim pressed in. They pushed and shoved, elbowing each other, treading on each other's corns, until finally they got in. The air was so thick that we—my friend Pisherl and I—could hardly breathe. "What good is all this going to do us?" I asked Pisherl.

"Shhh-Shmuel-Aba." Pisherl put his hand over my mouth. "They'll hear us and throw us out."

Abraham, the oldest of the patriarchs, appeared on the podium. With the thumb of his right hand stuck in his waistband, he waved his left hand over the heads of the audience. "A great disaster has befallen us, friends," he began. "The Messiah-Ox has escaped; and not merely escaped as occasionally happens with an ox, but he's run off to the Christian Eden. Now, where did the Messiah-Ox get the intelligence to escape?-that's a question that cannot be answered at this time, my friends.

"At this time, we need to consider . . . to investigate . . . to find an idea that will help us bring him back, back to his place in the Jewish Eden." The audience set up a commotion. A man with a grizzled beard began thrusting about with his elbows, pushing closer and closer to the podium.

"I have a parable," he cried. "Friends, I have a parable just suited to this occasion—a precious parable, with a golden moral. Once upon a time, there was a king who had three—"

"No need for parables, Preacher of Dubno,"* cried voices in the audience. "We need advice, not parables." But the Dubno preacher was stubborn. He shouted everyone down and pushed his way, with all his force, toward the podium.

"You will regret it, gentlemen. It's a precious parable. The moral is a golden moral. Once there was a king—" The preacher of Dubno might have succeeded in telling his parable if a drum roll had not been heard at the door.

A Zaddik cried out, "King Solomon has driven up. He's just getting out of his carriage." For a moment the synagogue grew still, then the buzzing began again.

"King Solomon . . . the wisest man . . . he has the brains of a prime minister . . . fool . . . a king is greater . . . the king is a lord, and a minister is no more than a servant." Quarrels broke out. There were cries of "oaf," "fool," and other such nicknames. Suddenly, the voice of the synagogue caretaker was heard at the back. "Make way for King Solomon."

King Solomon thrust his way toward the podium at once. He was sweating like a beaver and wiping his forehead with a silk handkerchief.

The synagogue grew hushed. Solomon's tall, broad-shouldered figure, his fox-red beard, his sharp, intelligent eyes commanded respect. He spoke softly, unhurriedly. "As soon as I heard the full story, I wasted no time, but sent a letter off to the Christian saints . . . if you know what I mean . . . I wrote to them about this and that and how much would they want for the return of the Messiah-Ox . . . if you know what I mean. We are ready to do business, I wrote . . . though we can do without the Messiah-Ox . . . he's not so very necessary to us and—"

At this point, the patriarch Isaac could contain himself no longer. He leaped from his seat and cried, "What do you mean we don't need him? We *need* him. Without the Messiah-Ox . . . where does he get off writing 'them' that we can do without the Messiah-Ox?"

King Solomon smiled wisely and reassured the outraged Isaac. "It's only a manner of speaking, if you know what I mean, Reb Isaac. One mustn't let them know that the Messiah-Ox is the apple of our eye. If they knew, they would ask for his weight in gold . . . if you know what I mean." Putting his finger to his forehead, he added slyly, "That's diplomacy, Reb Isaac. Diplomacy. One needs to understand it . . . if you know what I mean."

All the zaddikim nodded, agreeing that King Solomon was right, that he was indeed a wise man—if you turned Eden upside-down, you wouldn't find his match.

"So . . . I . . . if you know what I mean," continued Solomon, "so I wrote a letter inquiring how much they wanted. I sent the letter off with one of my postal pigeons. I estimate that we'll have a reply on the morning of the day after tomorrow."

A commotion began down below. "Where does he get off writing without our knowledge? We might at least have been informed of the contents of the letter. After all, we have a small stake in the matter . . . ."

King Solomon always hated back talk. Drawing himself up to his full height, his beard flaming, his eyes ablaze, he roared, "Attention!" with the voice of a lion.

The zaddikim stopped in their tracks, like soldiers before their commanding officer. There was not so much as the flicker of an eyelid. They stood this way for some fifteen minutes until King Solomon said, "Enough. Now you can go home. And when I get a reply from the Christian Eden, I'll let you know." He stepped down from the podium and pushed his way through the crowd. Outside, his gilded coach was waiting.

No sooner was Solomon gone than a dispute broke out. It was argued that King Solomon ought to have consulted with the zaddikim. Wise though he might be, he was, after all, only one man, and they were numerous. And though the zaddikim might not be as wise as he, still, their numbers counted for something.

"He's always behaved like this. He's always done just what he wanted, and paid about as much attention to us as to the cat . . . ."

"Pfooh! Pfooh! Jews, you're talking against a king . . . against a king," cried a small Zaddik with a sparse beard.

Away was made for the holy patriarchs. They left the synagogue and went home. "Then we may expect an answer on the morning of the day after tomorrow," said the patriarch Isaac.

The patriarch Abraham comforted him, "Don't worry. The reply will be favorable."

"May your wish pass from your mouth to God's ear, Father. And amen," sighed the patriarch Isaac. The patriarchs continued on their way.

11. *Our Mission*

Several days went by, but there was no reply. The zaddikim became extremely nervous. At night, they said prayers; by day, they peered their eyes out, watching for the postal pigeon that was to bring the reply; but there was no pigeon nor any reply to be seen.

"They're making dreadful fun of us," said the patriarch Isaac. "Woe unto my old age that I should have lived to see this . . . ."

"Your Esau," Jacob taunted him, "your favorite son. He knows that his father is dying for a piece of Messiah-Ox—and there is none."

"Still talking back to your father." The patriarch Abraham turned his dark eyes on him. "Where is 'Honor thy father . . . ,' Jacob?"

Jacob's wife, Rachel, ran into the house. She was breathless. From under her wig there peeped strands of her own hair. She was still slender and lovely. No sooner did Jacob see her than he became a different man. His eyes lighted up; he ran to her, caressed her head, and said, "Why are you running so, darling? May your loveliness be blessed."

Rachel looked up at him affectionately and said, "I met Esther on the street. She still carries herself as if she were a queen. A silk dress in the middle of the week, a gold ring on every finger, a strand of pearls around her neck. May such things be said about every Jewish daughter. I pretended I didn't see her and wanted to pass her by. I'm not fond of the beauty. But she stopped me and said, 'I want to tell you . . . a fast is what's needed. If you want the Messiah-Ox back, the best remedy will be a fast.'"

The patriarch Abraham said, "That's right. She's right. A fast must be declared in Eden."

In short, a fast was declared. Everyone fasted. The zaddikim became so weak that they could hardly keep on their feet, but there was still no sign of the postal pigeon.

A strange thing happened in the course of those fast days. The angel Shimon-Ber, as was his custom, got drunk and beat his wife to within an inch of her life. He dragged her by the hair through Eden, raving in his drunken voice, "What do you need the Messiah-Ox for, zaddikim? You need an animal? Here! I've got one for you. I'll let you have her for a bottle of ninety-six."

They tried to calm him down; to explain to him that the angel he was dragging by the hair was not an animal but his own wife who was in her seventh month. He would have none of it, but kept up his continual shouting. "A half pint of vodka and the creature is yours, zaddikim."

The Eden police were called. Several angels in green uniforms came flying and at last, with great difficulty, were able to bind Shimon-Ber. They took him off to sober up in the Eden jail. His wife was revived only after the greatest difficulties. She was taken home more dead than alive.

"He has to choose just such dreadful days as these in which to get drunk," the zaddikim grumbled. "That Shimon-Ber ought to have been a Christian and not a Jewish angel."

Finally, on the twelfth day, there was news that the postal pigeon had returned, bringing a letter from the Christian Eden. King Solomon had the letter. Though no one as yet knew its contents, there was great joy. People kissed each other in the streets, tears in their eyes.

On that very day, King Solomon called together a council. He read the reply to everyone:

To the most worthy and well-born saints of the Jewish Eden: Our reply to your letter is thus and thus. Your Messiah-Ox crossed our borders without passport or visa. According to the laws of our Eden he must be punished for the damage he created with six months at hard labor and half a pound of hay as a daily food allowance.

As for the pregnant angel whom he brought with him on his horns, we stand ready to return her to you. But the infant, born in our territory, will be baptized and will remain with us.

We are prepared to send the Messiah-Ox to you just as soon as he has served his sentence and worked off the damages assessed against him.

When King Solomon had read the letter, there was weeping and wailing in the Jewish Eden. Zaddikim ran about like poisoned mice, unable to find a resting place. They wrung their hands and wailed in anguish, "Who ever heard of such a thing? Six months in jail! Half a pound of hay per day. To work out damages . . . . They'll send the Messiah-Ox back to us nothing but skin and bones."

The wives of the zaddikim squealed, "Such a thing hasn't been heard of since the world began. To take a Jewish infant angel and baptize him. Woe to us who have lived to see such a thing."

Only one person did not lose his head. That was King Solomon. He wrote a second letter making various proposals, in the course of which he flattered the Christian saints. The wise king knew that flattery was a fine remedy against opposition.

The answer to the second letter came three days later. King Solomon read it before the chief of the zaddikim.

> To the most honorable King Solomon, the wisest of the wise. This is to inform you that we have received your letter. We have agreed to accept a diamond from your crown as payment for the damages caused by the Messiah-Ox. But the Ox will still have to serve his sentence for crossing the border without passport or visa. The law is the law; but to show that we want to meet you halfway, we have imposed only a three months' sentence. As for the infant born on our soil, we have already baptized him and named him Peter. The newly delivered mother is at your disposition. You may have her back whenever you like.

"Three months on jail food, and that's the end of the Messiah-Ox," wailed the patriarch Isaac.

"A Jewish infant, baptized," cried Mother Sarah, wringing her hands. She was joined in her sorrow by Rebecca, Leah, and Rachel.

"What a calamity; how shameful. And all on account of the stupidity of the cowherds," the zaddikim cried.

King Solomon wrote a third letter, agreeing that the Messiah-Ox deserved to be punished, but he argued that three months was too long. Furthermore, three months on prison food would kill the animal; he proposed therefore, that they, the Christian saints, should permit two Jewish cowherds to look after the Messiah-Ox for the time of his incarceration. "We stand ready," King Solomon wrote, "to send several wagons of hay so that he will have enough to eat." As for the baptized infant angel—he would let that matter drop. "Regarding the Messiah-Ox, I await a prompt reply."

The postal pigeon took the letter and delivered it to the Christian Eden. An answer came at the end of three days. Again, King Solomon read the letter to the zaddikim. Once again, the Christian saints made no difficulties. They agreed to let the Jewish Eden send over two angels who would look after the Messiah-Ox until he had done his time, but they warned that cowherds were not to be sent. If the Messiah-Ox were to see a Jewish cowherd, he would run wild again. The best idea would be for the zaddikim to send two little angels whom the Messiah-Ox would trust. As for the Ox's punishment, the Christian saints would cut his sentence to six weeks. That much time, he would have to serve. Regarding the diamond, they said that King Solomon could send it along with the little angels who would be sent to look after the Messiah-Ox.

This letter pleased everyone. "The saints of the Christian Eden can be talked to. One can see that from this letter."

"Well. Whom shall we send?" the patriarch Abraham inquired, stroking his dignified beard. The zaddikim considered the matter, suggesting first one and then another. Finally, someone mentioned Pisherl as "a bright little angel who knows what's what."

"And the second one?" someone inquired.

"The second one? I think the second one might be . . . ."

"Well, who? Let's hear who? There's someone who keeps on saying 'the second one . . . the second one . . .' and there's no name to be heard," murmured others.

"I think the second should be Pisherl's friend, Shmuel-Aba. They're very fond of each other . . . like two brothers. And as for Shmuel-Aba, he's as bright as they come."

In short, it was decided that I and my friend Pisherl should fly to the Christian Eden to look after the Messiah-Ox. We were told to go to Zaidl, the Eden photographer, to get passport photos made.

We went off happily. Zaidl, the Eden photographer, was delighted to see us and pinched each of us on the cheek. "How good that you've come. I'll read you the Purim play I've just written."

Zaidl, the Eden photographer, was a longhaired angel who wore glasses. He had one weakness—he wrote a new Purim play every week and would read it to anyone he could catch.

We explained that we had come to be photographed and that we had no time now to listen because we were flying on a mission to the Christian Eden. When, with God's help, we got back again, he could read to us as much as he liked.

The angel Zaidl turned glum. He very much wanted to read his play, but there was nothing to do except put it off until we returned. "By then," he promised us, "I'll have six new Purim plays. Remember to come, lads. You'll enjoy yourselves."

He photographed us and had the pictures ready on the spot. We went to the police department, where our passports were made out. With them in hand, we went to say good-bye to Pisherl's parents.

Pisherl's mother wiped her eyes with her apron. "Be careful, Pisherl. Don't catch cold on the way, God forbid."

And Pisherl's father, Shlomo-Zalman, the patch-tailor, told us sternly, "Don't let the Christian angels talk you into anything. Don't eat any pork, do you hear?" He gave us a heedful of similar *don'ts* and ended finally on a hiccup, "And don't forget you are Jewish angels, and that it's an honor to be an angel in the Jewish Eden."

We promised him everything he wished. Pisherl's mother gave us several buckwheat cookies to take along, and we said good-bye.

"Fly in good health and come back well," they cried after us.

"Now, Shmuel-Aba, we have to fly to King Solomon's to get the diamond. From there, we'll go straight on to the border." We rose up higher and higher into the air. It was something of a long trip to King Solomon's estates, but we were so excited by the journey that we didn't even notice the passage of time.

"Shmuel-Aba, do you see there, the building with the golden roof? That's King Solomon's palace."

We dropped down. The angels who guarded the palace had been told of our coming and they let us in at once.

We approached a silver stream. Shulamith sat at its edge, her bare feet in the water. She was catching fish in a golden net. "If she only knew that we saw her at King David's palace. What do you suppose she'd do?"

"We're on an important mission, Shmuel-Aba. And you have to think up stupidities."

We crossed the wooden bridge. Behind us, we could hear Shulamith singing.

> With you together,
> My beloved,
> I would go
> As deep as Hell.

> How grim, my dear,
> To be in Hell,
> Where prayers are useless
> And tears as well.

> Tears are no solace,
> No solace is prayer,
> But a song of true love
> May comfort us there.

We turned off to one side and Shulamith's song became fainter and fainter. Already, it was almost out of earshot. My friend and I were very fond of songs, and at any other time we would have lingered for an hour or two to listen, but now, when we were getting ready to fly off on such a long journey, we had no time.

We found King Solomon standing in the courtyard. He was wearing a silk robe and slippers. His crown glittered on his head. He was engaged in conversation with a cocky little rooster. As is well known, King Solomon understood the language of the beasts, the birds, and the fowl. We saw for ourselves how he put questions to the rooster and how the rooster replied, but we were not able to understand the answers.

We were becoming impatient. Who knew how long they might stand talking this way; and we had such a long journey before us.

Pisherl poked me, "Well, Shmuel-Aba."

"What Pisherl?"

"Let's approach him."

We approached and bowed before the king. The king interrupted his conversation with the rooster.

"Your majesty, we've come for the diamond. We're flying to the Christian Eden to look after the Messiah-Ox." King Solomon took his crown off and removed the diamond from it. He played with it for a moment or two. The diamond sparkled, dazzling our eyes.

"Take it, lads. And see that you don't lose it. It's an expensive gem-worth twenty-five thousand korona."

We took the diamond, promising the king that we would guard it like the eyes in our heads. He waved his hand, indicating that we could fly off.

"We're off, Shmuel-Aba."

We spread our wings and flew in the direction of the border. We arrived there in the evening between twilight and evening prayers. Bells were ringing in all the churches. The twilight, the festive singing, and the sound of the bells appeared strange and foreign to us. We pressed closer, fearful lest we lose one another.

An angel in a blue uniform with two crosses on his wings examined our passports. Two other angels in gray uniforms searched us to see whether, God forbid, we might not be smuggling any Talmuds in. The Talmud is regarded as a most terrible thing in the Christian Eden.

The border formalities lasted more than an hour but they found nothing on us and our passports were in order.

The angel in the blue uniform led us to a huge iron gate. He knocked three times and demanded entry. A voice that we recognized at once as belonging to an old man was heard on the other side of the gate. "Who knocks there?" it inquired.

"Saint Peter, it's me, the angel Theodore, the border guard. I've brought you a couple of little kikes from the Jewish Eden." We could hear a key being inserted in a lock. The lock groaned and the huge, heavy door swung open.

A little old man with a long white beard and twinkly eyes stood before us. He was baldheaded. In his right hand, he held the Eden key. He looked us over for a bit. The cross on his chest was of pure gold. The angel in the blue uniform saluted. Saint Peter made the sign of the cross over him and told him to go. The border had been left unguarded long enough.

The old gatekeeper told us to follow him. We entered and Saint Peter shut the gate again, saying, "No doubt you're hungry from your long trip. Rest here for a while. Tomorrow morning, a messenger will come to take you to the prison stables where the Messiah-Ox is."

Not far from the gate, there was a house where Saint Peter lived. It was an extremely dark night and a votive candle was already burning in his window. "You don't need to be afraid, lads. Nothing bad will happen to you. Come with me." He went before us and we followed. I don't know about Pisherl, but my heart was beating loudly.

We entered the house. It was roomy, and there were icons hanging from every wall. There was a table in the middle of the room and the old fellow told us to sit down.

We seated ourselves at the table. He gave each of us a hunk of black bread and some cheese, smiling at us meanwhile. "You won't eat any pork, eh? If you only knew the taste of a bit of pork. But then, you're stubborn. You don't want any. A splendid food, a bit of pork. Even your teacher at Hebrew school tells you to *khazer** well."

We didn't reply, but ate our bread and cheese. After our journey, we were really terribly hungry. The old fellow inquired about the zaddikim. He particularly wanted to know whether our patriarchs were well or having troubles of any kind.

Pisherl said that everything was in good order. Except for the problem with the Messiah-Ox, all was well.

"Tomorrow, you'll be taken to the Messiah-Ox," Saint Peter said. "But see that you don't go wandering off from your quarters. And don't go flying around our paradise. Among us, Jewish angels are not liked. See that you behave yourselves. Be discreet, and you won't get your wings broken."

We promised not to irritate anyone. If only we were not picked on, all would be well.

"The best thing," the old fellow advised us, "would be to mind your own business. If our saints should be on their way to prayer, don't let them catch a glimpse of you. If you see a procession, get out of sight so no one will see hide nor hair of you."

"Some mess," I thought. "We'll have to hide to keep from being seen. What's the point of the whole thing if we're not to see anything, no matter what?"

Pisherl and I exchanged glances. We understood each other. Evidently he, too, had regrets for the entire affair. Old Peter's eyes began to close. He led us to a separate little room where there were no icons. "You'll spend the night here, fellows. And if you should have to do an 'angelic' thing, you can do it through the window."

The old man went back to his room. Pisherl and I remained by ourselves looking at each other with mournful eyes. I went to the window and looked out. The sky was clouded over; there was the smell of rain. We were not very light of heart. We thought of home and prayed to God that the weeks would pass quickly. There was a streak of lightning outside that illuminated our room for a moment. Then there was a second flash. Thunder grumbled and grumbled until, with a crash, it fell to the ground. We blessed ourselves aloud. In the other room, we could hear Saint Peter snoring.

"Shmuel-Aba?"

"What is it, Pisherl?"

"Let's go to sleep. One gets through the night more quickly asleep."

We undressed and went to bed but could not sleep. The lightning and thunder wouldn't permit it. In the Jewish Eden, we had often experienced such nights, but here, in a strange country, far away from all we knew, the stormy night was more fearful.

"Pisherl?"

"What, Shmuel-Aba?"

"Let's tell stories. If we tell stories, the time will pass more quickly."

We huddled closer and Pisherl began to tell the story of a beggar and a prince; but the thunder would not let him finish. Finally, he had to break off his story in the middle. We tried covering ourselves with the bedclothes, but that was no help. We jumped out of bed.

Pisherl opened the window and went outside where he stood in his nightshirt, lightning flashing around him. Anyone who has not seen my friend Pisherl illuminated by lightning doesn't know what loveliness is. "Shmuel-Aba," Pisherl said, "jump down through the window, Shmuel-Aba."

For a while, I hesitated, then I jumped. Just at that moment, the rain poured down and we got wet as fish. Our wings grew so heavy we could hardly lift them.

We went back into the room, water pouring from our heads and wings. The floor turned wet. We crawled back into bed and huddled close against each other, trying to get warm. Outside, the rain continued to pour down.

"Pisherl, do you hear?"

"What, Shmuel-Aba?"

"What the rain says." It was going "tap . . . tap . . . drop . . . bzsh . . . tap . . . a-drop . . . bzsh . . . ."

Our arms wound around each other, we fell asleep. In my dream, King Solomon was conversing with the rooster. I understood every word they said to each other. "How are you, rooster? And how are your thousand wives?" the king asked.

"Thank you so much, king, for your kind question. My wives are laying eggs and cackling, and, the Lord be praised, they are well. And how are your thousand wives, king?"

"Without meaning to be sinful, still . . . do you know something, rooster, among my thousand wives there isn't one who is entirely right." King Solomon grew thoughtful.

"If that's the case, O king, I'm luckier than you. My wives are doing fine. Not one of them is barren. If you want my advice, king, take a few more wives. A good one is bound to show up."

"Rooster, maybe you're right. So long as there's life, one ought to keep looking. A good one may turn up." Suddenly, a strange thing happened. As I watched, King Solomon turned into a rooster. His comb was fiery red. He flapped his wings and flew up to the top of a fence. "Cock-a-doodle-do."

At this cry, I woke up. "A curious dream," I thought. Outside, it was already dawn. The Eden roosters were crowing. My friend was still asleep. Evidently, he was very tired. He had his right hand over his heart and he was smiling. Asleep as he was, he was very lovely. Unable to restrain myself, I kissed him on the forehead.

I crept quietly out of bed. It seemed a pity to wake him. I went to the window and looked out. After last night's rain, the earth was fresh. The grass smelled . . . it was a delight to the soul. The birds in the trees were singing.

"Lovely is thy creation, O Lord of the Universe," I whispered. "But I can't understand why you needed three Edens. Wouldn't it have been

better to have one for everyone? No passports; no visas; no quarrels."
My heretical thought frightened me. "Some nerve," I scolded myself.
"You are going to teach wisdom to the Lord of the World, Shmuel-Aba?
He has more wisdom in the least fingernail of his smallest finger than
you'll ever have in your entire body."

The sun rose in the east. It was huge, brilliant. One golden ray fell on
Pisherl's nose and tickled it so long that he finally woke up.

"Good morning, Pisherl."

Pisherl rubbed his eyes. He seemed for an instant to have forgotten
where he was. Then he jumped out of bed. We washed ourselves and
said our morning prayers. Our spirits were considerably improved.

We went into Saint Peter's room. The old man wasn't there. He had
gone to church to say his prayers. There was a pitcher of milk on the
table. We drank the milk and ate some black bread. In the distance, we
could hear the ringing of bells.

Peter came home. Seeing us, he smiled good-humoredly and gave
each of us a pinch on the cheek. "Well, boys. Have you prayed this
morning?" he inquired.

"Of course we have. Do you suppose we'd have eaten without saying
our morning prayers? How would that have looked?"

"All right, all right," the old man smiled. The angel who is to take you
to the Messiah-Ox is expected at any minute. Remember, behave your-
selves and all will be well."

We looked at him and swore to behave ourselves. He nodded his
head, satisfied. Once at the table, he crossed himself and began to eat.
As we watched him, we felt ourselves growing more comfortable with
him. The clock on the wall struck seven.

12. Anyella

Saint Peter wiped his lips, stroked his beard, and asked us to give him
the diamond out of King Solomon's crown. Pisherl handed it over. Pe-
ter examined it from all sides, smacking his lips all the while. "A rare
diamond. A diamond of a diamond. A diamond like this is worth—I
don't myself know how much!"

The old fellow opened a drawer from which he took a sheet of paper and wrote out a receipt—a declaration that he had received the diamond. Pisherl put the receipt away. Peter cleared the table. The clock on the wall struck nine.

We heard a knock on the door, and before the old saint could say, "Come in," the door was opened and there entered a tall, broad-shouldered angel with piercing gray eyes. He bowed before the old apostle, flapped his wings three times, and said, "I've come for the little kikes. My name is Dmitri; I'm going to take them to the Messiah-Ox." He cast a baleful look at us. His piercing eyes and his tightly twirled mustaches made it clear that he was an enemy of the Jews—a real anti-Semite.

Old Peter whispered something into his ear. We stood to one side, trembling. The angel Dmitri gave his mustaches a twirl and with a venomous smile, he said, "Let's go, Jewboys."

We had no choice but to go with him. The old saint accompanied us to the door.

We took off. The angel Dmitri flew before us, waving his strong, huge wings and singing,

Jew, Jew,
Foolish Jew,
No more Sabbath
Coat for you.

We despised his song, but we could say nothing. We had to listen and be silent. I could see the tears in Pisherl's eyes. The angel Dmitri kept looking back. Our wings were young and weaker than his, but he was angry because we "flew like dying chickens."

He kept tormenting us, making fun of the way we spoke: "Mommy . . . Daddy . . . Mommy . . . Daddy . . . ." God only knows what we endured in the course of our flight with this monster. We cursed the days of our lives and wished our wings had been broken before ever we had started on our journey.

At evening, we alighted near a wood. At our right was the prison stable with its barred windows. An angel with a sword marched back and forth before it, guarding the prisoner. The angel Dmitri led us up to the angel on guard and said something to him in a language we didn't understand. He kept pointing to us all the while. The angel on watch said,

"Good," and Dmitri bade him farewell. He spread his wings and flew away. We could hear his song for a long while, "Jew, Jew, foolish Jew . . . ."

The guard opened a heavy iron gate with a huge key. We went into the prison stable and saw our Messiah-Ox where he lay bound in chains. He was thin as a rail. If we had not known it was he, we would under no circumstances have recognized him.

Pisherl went up to him and caressed him. The Messiah-Ox looked up at him with huge, sorrowful eyes. "Now what did you accomplish by running away," Pisherl said. "A silly female angel makes a joke, and you go running off."

The Messiah-Ox seemed to understand my friend's scolding. He had a look of regret in his eyes. Pisherl consoled him, continuing his caresses. "Only a few more weeks, Messiah-Ox, and we'll go back to the Jewish Eden. You know, we've been sent especially to look after you; and later, we'll take you back home. And next time you'll know better. There'll be such joy when you get back, just you wait and see."

I, too, went up to him and caressed him; I told him how the Eden meadows longed for him. Since his escape, the grass on the meadow had been strangely sad. The crickets no longer sang, and the butterflies fluttered around like orphans, unable to find a resting place.

"But when you come back," Pisherl said, "everything will be all right again. The Eden meadow will blossom, the crickets will sing, and the butterflies will know that the Eden meadow is their home again."

The guard gestured to us. We understood that he wanted us to leave. Time was up for today. We said good-bye to the Messiah-Ox, promising to come tomorrow, and left the prison stable. The guard locked the gate again, and we stood outside, not knowing what to do, where to go, or where we would spend the night.

"Shmuel-Aba?"

"What, Pisherl?"

"How will it all end, Shmuel-Aba?"

"May I know as much about evil as I do the answer to *that*."

The sky grew dark. The stars sparkled over the wood; they were the same stars as at home, and yet, they seemed very strange.

When it was quite dark, we saw an old fellow with a long white beard approaching. He carried a sack on his shoulders. I stared at him and would have sworn it was the prophet Elijah.

Evidently, Pisherl thought so, too. He poked me and whispered, "See, Shmuel-Aba. The prophet Elijah."

"Pisherl, since when does the prophet Elijah wear a cross on his breast?"

The old fellow came up to us. The guard waved his sword and shouted, "Halt." We came to a stop, like soldiers. The old fellow patted our heads, smiling gently and good-humoredly. "So you are the little Jewish angels . . . good . . . I'm Saint Nicholas. I'll show you where you'll be staying for a while. In the meantime, here's a little present. Go on, take it; take it."

He untied his sack and gave Pisherl a leaden soldier, and me a rooster made of tin. The old fellow spoke Hebrew, which pleased us tremendously. He tied his sack again and threw it over his shoulders. "Come on, fellows." He went before us and we followed, feeling very comfortable with him. As we entered the wood, the old angel lighted his lantern.

We went on slowly. By the light of the lantern, we could see the squirrels jumping from tree to tree. We could hear the night birds calling each other. A doe ran across our path. In the distance, we could hear the splashing of water.

The old saint looked back at us frequently and smiled. He said, "You're tired, fellows. Soon, soon, and we'll be at the forest ranger's. That's where you'll stay until the Messiah-Ox has served his sentence."

He was right. We were indeed tired. We had been flying all day with that monster, the angel Dmitri; but we went on, just managing to keep on our feet. The sound of water was getting closer and closer. At the very edge of a river, there stood a small wooden house. The old saint stopped, put his lantern down and knocked, "Open, Ivan. It's me, Saint Nicholas."

The door opened. Ivan the forest ranger came out. He was an angel of middle height with short strong wings.

Saint Nicholas said, "These two little Jewish angels will stay with you, Ivan. See that you take care of them. They won't eat our food, so give them uncooked milk from an earthen vessel and black bread." The old angel bade us farewell and went away. He was soon lost among the forest trees.

We went into the house. On the walls there hung holy pictures. The river could be seen from the window. The forest ranger angel Ivan looked us over from head to toe. He was amazed, and hardly knew what to say. Finally, he made a movement with his hand and said, "Never mind."

The door of the second room opened and a girl angel with blond braids and blue eyes came in. The forest ranger said something to her in a language we did not understand, but we gathered that she was called Anyella.

She went back into the other room. After a short interval, she was back, carrying fresh milk and black bread. We settled ourselves greedily to eat, slurping the milk, munching the fresh rye bread with the greatest joy. The forest ranger angel took his gun down from the wall. He went up to Anyella, kissed her on the forehead, and went off to spend the night guarding the forest. We were left alone with the little girl angel, the forest ranger's daughter. She kept herself busy around the house, tidying up and singing like a canary all the while.

I liked her a lot, that Anyella. Her slightest movement was a delight; but Pisherl was in a transport of joy. He called me aside and whispered, "How beautiful, Shmuel-Aba. I've never seen anything like it. Let her just say the word and I'll stay here, in the Christian Eden. I could look at her from morning till night."

At these words from my friend, I became terribly disturbed. I said to myself, "Those are the very words spoken by the infatuated couples in the Three Patriarchs' Allée." My heart ached. I was afraid that my friend was already lost. "But you're a Jewish angel, Pisherl, and she is a Christian. The two words don't rhyme, Pisherl."

My friend was instantly saddened. I had reminded him of something that hurt.

Outside there were the sounds of the forest and the water. In the house, Anyella went from place to place. Pisherl could not take his eyes from her. I pulled him by the right wing, "Come on, Pisherl. Let's go outside for a bit."

He followed me, in a trance. We sat down at the river's edge. The moon appeared from behind a cloud. Pisherl sighed.

"The real symptoms," I thought. "No sooner does the moon show itself than he sighs. Any minute now and he'll begin to write poetry. That little blond angel has bewitched him."

Pisherl was silent. I listened to the sound of the water. Suddenly, there was a burning sensation on my left wing. It was my friend Pisherl's tear. "God be with you, Pisherl. Why are you crying?"

Without answering my question, he put an arm around me and began to sing:

Dear heart, since I have seen you
Keeping your father's house,
I've sworn a vow to love you
Truly, I confess.

There's no place I can find, dear,
To rest, since you appeared.
Through the streets I wander—
I know I shall go mad.

This was another of Siomkeh's songs. Pisherl did not yet have one of his own; he might still be saved. "Let's get away, away from here, while there is still time; while your love is still only a spark. Once it turns into fire, it'll be too late, Pisherl."

"What, Shmuel-Aba?"

"Let's fly away from here. Quickly. This moment."

"What about the Messiah-Ox, Shmuel-Aba?"

What could I say to that? We had been sent here to look after the Messiah-Ox, and to bring it back home. I thought for a while, and then I said, "Anyella isn't very pretty. Your sister Ettl is much prettier, and other Jewish angels are prettier still."

My friend sighed. "You're speaking nonsense, Shmuel-Aba. Anyella is beautiful. It isn't right to malign an angel, even if she is a foreigner."

"He's caught in the trap," I thought. "He's speaking high-sounding words. May God help him; I don't know if I can."

We heard Anyella, who was standing at the open window, calling, "Hey, boys."

Pisherl trembled. We got up and went into the house.

Anyella made signs to us to show us where to sleep; she led us into a separate room, and then went off to her own chamber. We went to bed. Pisherl talked continually in his sleep, keeping me awake. In the morning, when we got up, Anyella gave us milk and black bread.

The forest ranger angel was already home, sleeping and snoring. Anyella drove the goats out of the stable. My friend Pisherl and I flew off to the prison stable where the Messiah-Ox lay. We wanted to see to it that he was fed on time and not tormented.

After our arrival, the Messiah-Ox's portion of hay was increased. He began to improve, to put on a little weight. With every gram added to his weight, I felt a proportionate joy.

Pisherl, meanwhile, went about troubled. In the course of the days during which the Messiah-Ox gained weight, Pisherl lost it. He was continually disappearing from sight; continually wandering about in the woods, eating without appetite, and sleeping restlessly.

When we returned home to the forest at night, Anyella was waiting for us. She had taken to being quite friendly with us and taught us Christian Eden songs. In return, we taught her Jewish songs. Life was good around that pretty little angel. Pisherl could not tear his eyes from her. When it was his good fortune to sit near her, he turned crimson.

Once, on a Sunday, she invited us to go into the woods with her to gather strawberries. Her father, Ivan the forest ranger, was asleep. Anyella, as always, was very lovely, and it was impossible to refuse her. We went into the forest with her. Unable to fly because of the dense branches, we went on foot. Anyella laughed and sang and played tricks. From time to time, she bent to gather strawberries and dropped them into the pitcher she had brought with her. Occasionally, she broke off an entire cluster and held it to our mouths. Pisherl pulled the berries from the cluster with his lips. They flamed redder than the berries.

He went on with downcast eyes, silent, uttering not a word. I pulled him aside and asked if he wanted to be left alone with Anyella. His eyes lighted up. "You're a real friend, Shmuel-Aba. I'll never forget what you're doing for me. Sneak away so she won't know when you've disappeared."

I did as he asked. While Pisherl and Anyella were bent to the ground, engrossed in gathering strawberries, I disappeared. They did not come back until evening. Anyella was tired. My friend Pisherl was happy.

That night, when I woke from my sleep, I saw my friend standing at the window, holding something in his hand. "Pisherl, why aren't you asleep?"

"I can't sleep, Shmuel-Aba."

I jumped out of bed and went up to him. "What have you got in your hand?"

"Nothing. It's a secret, Shmuel-Aba." He closed his hand more firmly. I was annoyed and said, "Well . . . my best friend has a secret and won't tell me what it is. What's happened to our friendship?"

Pisherl, sensing my anger, came up to me and kissed me. "Shmuel-Aba, if I told you the secret, it would no longer be so beautiful."

"Never mind, Pisherl. I won't tell you any more secrets, either." I could see Pisherl struggling with himself, unable to make up his mind whether to tell or not. I stood by and waited. Pisherl opened his hand and I saw a lock of golden hair. "Did she give you that, Pisherl?"

"She did." I could tell that revealing his secret was very painful to him and I regretted what I had done. I promised myself that I would demand no more secrets from him. But now a devil had mixed into our friendship.

I crawled back in bed. I lay for a while with my eyes wide open. My heart ached curiously. From that night on, whenever I saw my friend with Anyella, I disappeared, acting as if I hadn't seen them. I wandered around alone in the woods or flew idly over the river. The days sped by; who can catch them?

Meanwhile, the Messiah-Ox put on more weight, though in truth not as much as before. There would still be plenty to do in the Jewish Eden before he would be wholly restored.

Pisherl left the care of the Messiah-Ox entirely to me, though it would be wrong to say that he sat with nothing to do. He went about in the forest carving the name "Anyella" on every tree. He wrote "Anyella" with a stick in the sand at the river's edge; and he whispered the name "Anyella" in his sleep. It may be that he wrote poetry, too, but I didn't ask him and he didn't show me any.

Every Saturday, Saint Nicholas came with his sack on his shoulders. He rarely found Pisherl at home, so he had to confine his preaching and his presents to me. "Wouldn't it be better for you, Shmuel-Aba, if you were to stay here and be converted, eh? Our Eden is nicer than yours. You'll be as happy as can be here."

I would not be persuaded but replied, argument by argument: in the first place, how could I be so sure that his Eden was so nice? Had I seen it, after all? They hadn't let me stir in it so much as from here to there. "And in the second place, Reb Nicholas, aren't you forgetting the essential Jew? No small matter, that—the essential Jew!"

The old fellow smiled. "You're stubborn, Shmuel-Aba. And stubbornness is unpleasant." He went away unsuccessful. He came again, and again left with nothing.

To tell the truth, I was really worried by Pisherl. Now that he was gripped by his infatuation, Saint Nicholas might succeed in converting him. I prayed God that the ensuing weeks would pass swiftly and that we would be home soon. Indeed, the weeks flew by, and the day neared when the Messiah-Ox was to be freed.

Later, my friend told me that he had continually prayed for the weeks to lengthen, but my prayer was preferred by God and the weeks had flown. "So you have good proof, Pisherl," I said, "that the Blessed One did not want you to become a convert and marry Anyella."

On the day that the Messiah-Ox was freed, Pisherl was a very sad angel. He was pale, and Anyella went about with tearstained eyes.

Saint Nicholas came very early in the morning with the news that the Messiah-Ox was ready to be turned over to us. We dressed and went outside. Anyella stood at her window, her eyes melancholy and huge.

"Good-bye, Anyella."

"Fly well, Pisherl."

Two cuckoos called to each other in the wood, and the grasses sparkled tears. In Pisherl's eyes, drops of dew glistened. On our way, Saint Nicholas tapped with his stick; the wind lifted the edges of his garment. The sack on his shoulders rolled back and forth. Pisherl was nearby, continually casting glances behind him. Finally, one could no longer see the forest ranger's hut; it was hidden by the trees. Softly, I stroked Pisherl's wing and said, "Pisherl, forget her."

We came to the prison stable. The guard stood before it, his sword in his hand. A few paces farther on stood that monster, the angel Dmitri, holding a paper. We went into the stable with the guard. Dmitri removed the chains from the Messiah-Ox and threw them aside. Saint Nicholas took the sheet of paper from him and read aloud.

"In the presence of Saint Nicholas, of Gregor Stasiuk, the guard, and of the gendarme angel Dmitri, we, the angels Pisherl and Shmuel-Aba, take possession of the Messiah-Ox in order to return him again to the Jewish Eden.

"We undertake to leave the Christian Eden quickly. We will not look about or dawdle anywhere on the way to the border. We understand that the gendarme angel Dmitri will accompany us the entire way, and that we are under his orders."

We signed this paper and made our preparations to go. The Messiah-Ox could hardly keep on his feet, he had gotten so unused to walking. But that monster, the angel Dmitri, would not wait. He was a torment to our souls. "Giddyap, kikes!"

We drove the Messiah-Ox from his stall. Pisherl led him by one horn, and I by the other. Behind us flew the angel Dmitri. He twisted his mustaches and issued commands. "To the right, Jew-boys. Jew-boys, to the left."

It was a hot day. The Eden road was dusty (because of the Messiah-Ox, we went on foot) and our throats were dry. But the brute, Dmitri, tormented us; he would not let us rest for a moment, would not let us drink so much as a drop of water. If the first journey with that anti-Semite was unbearable, the return trip was a veritable death. "And you were ready to stay with such monsters," I said to my friend.

The angel Dmitri imitated us, "Bread, bread . . . mommy, daddy . . . a black year." He kept cutting at the Messiah-Ox with his rubber truncheon.

We walked all that day. When night fell, we were still leading the Messiah-Ox by the horns. Barefoot and hungry, we went on, cursing our days and our years. The boundary was nowhere in sight.

"If only the monster shows up one day in the Jewish Eden, I'll teach him a trick or two," I thought. "Meanwhile, one must put up with it. And be damned before we'll let him know how much he's hurting us."

The angel Dmitri gave a sharp, vicious laugh, "Never mind, kikes. Never mind."

But these torments were as nothing. Toward midnight, Dmitri called out, "Halt." We came to a stop, trembling. With a twist of his mustaches, he commanded us to dance the Mayofes Dance.*

At first, we refused, but when he began to wave his rubber truncheon over our heads, we had no choice but to dance.

To this very day, when I remember that moonlit night, in the middle of the road, I'm overcome with revulsion. We danced, we turned, we flung ourselves about, and flapped our wings. We sweated pitchersful while he, the brute, flew over us, waving his rubber truncheon, wheezing with laughter.

When the dance was finished, and we could hardly stand on our feet, the monster took a piece of pork and ordered us to eat it. We resisted with all our strength, trying to make him understand that Jewish angels were forbidden to eat pork. But it was like talking to a wall; the monster insisted, and we had to taste it.

Grimacing, overcome by revulsion, we ate. Our grimaces seemed to please him. He shook with laughter.

We took up our journey once more, ashamed, degraded. I said to my friend, "Pisherl. Remember, no one in Eden must know that we ate pork. They'd wipe us from the face of the earth. Remember—not a word."

We walked on for the entire night and all of the next day. We did not arrive at the border until evening. We were so tired we could hardly stand.

The angel Dmitri signed over a paper to Saint Peter and took his leave of us. "Good-bye, kikes."

Old Peter put his spectacles on and began to read the document. While he read, we rested and caught our breath. The Messiah-Ox stood stock still.

"A real Haman, that angel Dmitri," cried the rabbinical judge. "And such a fellow is allowed in Eden. God spare us from the like."

"Blessed is the name of God," breathed the rabbi. "So long as the Messiah-Ox was back at last in our Eden. I can just imagine the joy of the zaddikim when he was brought back."

"You can't begin to imagine what went on. There was an entire parade. But I'll talk about that tomorrow, God willing. Now, I'm tired."

My father sat as if stupefied. He could not take his eyes off me. My mother ran up and kissed me, cursing the angel Dmitri meanwhile with powerful curses. "He should have dropped dead, that monster Dmitri. What agony he caused you! May he be flung from one end of Eden to the other until *I* cry, 'Stop.'"

She took me in her arms and put me in the cradle. I could just barely hear the rich man, Reb Mikhel Hurvitz, saying *sonderbar* several times.

I could still feel my mother's kiss on my cheek, and, as in a dream, I heard the visitors saying their good-byes to my father. I fell asleep.

THE TALES OF HERSHEL SUMMERWIND

Tale. Hershel Summerwind told me these stories at Gentile Pantula's tea shop where Jewish porters, water carriers, and such hard laborers used to go to drink tea between five and six in the afternoon.

All the tales Hershel told were strange in the extreme, and all of them were true because they all happened only to him.

If, to the present day, you can still see a sky full of stars you ought to know whom you have to thank for it. No one else but Hershel Summerwind.

It all happened when he, Hershel, was still a little boy in Hebrew school. Altogether some eleven years old.

He was a world-class prankster; and punished by his rabbi with as many blows as he could absorb. Every new whip was tried out on him first.

But the rabbi's blows were as nothing compared with his stepmother's pinches.

Hershel's mother died giving birth to him. And he was born an orphan.

And the stepmother whom his father, after a while, brought home from abroad did not like him—Hershel, that is. And there is reason to think that it was not for nothing. Hershel drove her crazy. If she sent him on an errand, he would be gone the entire day, coming home only in time for dinner.

When his father came home all worn out, tired from the marketplace, the stepmother used to pour her embittered heart out to him. "Hershel this," and "Hershel that."

His father, generally a kind man, never struck him. The truth is, that Hershel's tricks gave him plenty to worry about, and when the stepmother had finished making her list of accusations he would smile sadly, "He'll turn into a proper man, Zlate. Don't worry. You'll see. He'll turn into a proper man . . . only . . . he'll be a poor man."

When the stepmother saw that the father dismissed the whole matter with a word or two, she took matters into her own hands. She knew how to pinch. So she pinched Hershel. Each of her pinches made him see stars, as they say. And Hershel responded to her pinches with new pranks and new tricks.

That's how he was. A genuine world-class prankster.

In their home, there was a rooster who had the run of the house. That rooster did whatever he liked. No one ever bothered him or questioned him. The stepmother, who treated Hershel like a dog, was an absolute cooing dove to the rooster.

The stepmother, who believed in ghosts and transmigrated souls, and demons, had persuaded herself that the soul of her dead first husband, Hersh-Mendel, had transmigrated into the rooster. . . . She recognized him by his "sidelong glance and by the trembling of his head." He was exactly like Hersh-Mendel.

When nobody was at home, she actually called the rooster Hersh-Mendel, and wiped her eyes with a corner of her apron.

"You're doing penance, Hersh-Mendel. You've been turned into a rooster. Woe is me. Who told you to go off chasing the girls, Hersh-Mendel? Now you've transmigrated into a rooster. Woe is me."

A moment later: "Just your luck, Hersh-Mendel, that you've fallen into my hands and that I recognized you. Anyone else would have had you killed long ago; and would have eaten you, long ago and would have forgotten about you, long ago."

And the rooster clearly felt that the stepmother was his friend. Whether he also knew that she had once been his wife, Hershel Summerwind did not know. And what he did not know, he did not want to narrate.

No matter how many hens and roosters had already been killed, Hersh-Mendel, the rooster, was still among the living, guarded and protected by the stepmother who from time to time fed him drumsticks from other poultry.

The stepmother remembered that her first husband, Hersh-Mendel, had dearly loved a chicken drumstick.

It should be evident that Hershel Summerwind hated Hersh-Mendel, because he hated the stepmother.

Whenever he could, he plagued the rooster any way that he could. No need to talk about Hershel plucking the rooster's feathers out one by one.

If the rooster took a little snooze, Hershel woke him up. If he came upon the rooster in the courtyard he chased him until the exhausted rooster flew up to the fence, where he crowed hoarsely for the stepmother's help.

The stepmother, hearing the rooster Hersh-Mendl's desperate cry, came running more dead than alive and saved him from Hershel's clutches.

For the stepmother, each of the rooster's hoarse crowings was one more proof that she had to do with the transmigrated soul of her dead husband, may he rest in peace. He used to crow like that in the synagogue when he was given the honor of reading a lesson from the Torah.

It happened one day that the prankster, Hershel, had been chasing the rooster. The rooster, with disordered wings, ran about as if possessed by an evil spirit, all of which gave Hershel supreme pleasure. As he chased the bird, he sang the song that he had composed a week earlier when he had seen the rooster pecking at a chicken thigh:

Hersh-Mendl, chicken eater,
May you not grow bigger.

The rooster, as was his wont in such a moment of danger, flew up to the fence, but Hershel would not leave him alone. The rooster crowed, calling the stepmother to his aid, but she was not at home. She had just gone to buy something in the grocery store. On her way there she ran into Gitl, the soothsayer, and was carrying on a conversation with her about ghosts, devils, transmigrated souls and other topics of interest to women.

When she got home, she found an excited, happy Hershel chasing the rooster and the rooster crowing at his last gasp.

That Hershel was well and truly given his desserts need hardly be said. The stepmother well and truly twisted his ears. Hershel could hardly tear himself from her clutches. As he ran off he stuck out his tongue and then promptly sang out for everyone on the street to hear:

Hersh-Mendl, chicken eater,
May you not grow bigger.

The stepmother held the rescued rooster in her arms. Pressing him to her heart, she whispered, "You're doing penance, Hersh-Mendl. Woe is me."

She called out to the fleeing Hershel, "Just you wait. When you come home for supper, you'll get yours."

It stands to reason that Hershel did not come home for supper. He prowled the streets hungrily, seeing in his mind's eye how Hersh-Mendel was pecking at a chicken's thigh while the stepmother beside him encouraged him with "Eat, eat, Hersh-Mendel. May it do you good."

Hershel had regrets. What good had it done him? Now, hunger gnawed at him, but he was afraid to go home.

At night, when everyone was asleep, Hershel came home. Silently, walking on tip-toe, he crawled up to the attic where, still hungry, he lay down to sleep.

He had a strange dream. He was himself a saucy young rooster. The stepmother, a fat, respectable hen, was taking him for the first time to Hebrew school.

The teacher—good God—was the rooster, Hersh-Mendel. As Hersh-Mendel habitually did, he held his head to one side as he asked Hershel, "What does *komets alef* * spell?"

The he pecked Hershel on the head.

"And, boy, *kometz gimel?*"*

And again, he pecked Hershel's head.

Hershel, frightened, started up from his sleep and looked about him on every side.

Yes, he was in the attic, and it had all been a dream.

He held his breath and listened intently.

But who is pecking so loudly?

He crawled slowly to the attic window and stuck his head out.

For a moment, Hershel was stunned. The sky was spread out before him. Hersh-Mendel, the rooster, was perched on the black chimney pecking up the stars with his sharp bill.

The foolish rooster thought they were seeds.

Hershel sensed the danger. "To allow Hersh-Mendel to keep pecking at the stars would create havoc for the entire summer night. Not only for this night but for all starry nights in general. Because, as is well known, each night bequeaths the stars as an inheritance for the night to come.

Slowly, Hershel crawled out through the attic window. Slowly, slowly, so that Hersh-Mendel should not hear, he crawled on his stomach, toward the chimney.

And Hersh-Mendel was so busy eating that he heard nothing at all.

Suddenly, Hershel seized him by the wings. Hersh-Mendel, the rooster, was so frightened that he vomited up all the stars he had pecked.

Hershel waved the frightened rooster around over his head and sang a new song that just then occurred to him.

The essence for Hersh-Mendel, pecking stars,
Is the meal the foolish fowl devours.

The stars in the sky looked mischievously down at him. Hershel understood their meaning. "Hershel, we will never forget your good deed."

For the first few minutes, the rooster was so overwhelmed by the way the meal of stars he had been quietly enjoying had been unexpectedly interrupted that he had no idea what had happened to him.

It was only when Hershel began to wave him above his head and dance around the chimney with him like an Indian that he finally uttered a timorous crow.

All the roosters of the town crowed in reply, as is the custom of roosters. There followed such a babel of crowing that the town's householders, thinking it was dawn, started out of their sleep and washed their hands in preparation for their morning prayers.

Hershel's stepmother heard the desperate cries of her transmigrated Hersh—she sensed his danger. Wearing only her nightdress and carrying a poker in her hand, she made her way to the attic where, with difficulty, she squeezed herself through the attic window.

You can imagine the punishment Hershel received. The stepmother did not spare him at all.

To this day, Hershel Summerwind remembers the black and blue marks left by those blows. But it was all worthwhile.

"I saved the stars."

From that night on, there was something not quite right with Hersh-Mendel, the rooster. A couple of weeks later, he laid his head down for the last time in a corner of the courtyard.

And where his soul has transmigrated now, nobody knows. As for Hershel, the blows he received brought him to his senses. The proof: he is still alive and telling true tales of what happened to him.

As, for example, this story of the birds:

This happened about a year ago. He was then a well-built lad of about eighteen or nineteen. His younger sister, Eidel, was already married, but the stepmother, as was her habit, was still grumbling, "Proper folk would think that a boy his age would be a father by now, but this one just hangs about, doing nothing. Chases after girls. You'll have the same fate as overtook my Hersh-Mendel. Mark my words."

Well, a stepmother's grumbling! She had never been his friend, and since the death of the rooster Hersh-Mendel—she had been even less friendly than before.

Incidentally, every year—on the anniversary of the day that the rooster Hersh-Mendel died—she gave candles to be lighted in the synagogue and she paid Ezra the synagogue caretaker to say the prayer for the dead in his name.

To make a long story short, Eidel, Hershel's younger sister, had been fortunate enough to make a good marriage, and before the year was out, she gave birth to a boy. Two days before the circumcision feast, Hershel's father took him aside and said, "My son, harness the horses and drive over to Daraban to Zalman the tavern keeper and tell him, my son, to give you the barrel of wine he set aside for me twenty years ago. This is what you should say, 'God willing, the day after tomorrow will be the happiest day of my life: my first grandson.'

"Take the whip, Hershel. Harness the horse. Go, and come back in good time with the barrel of wine, lest the circumcision feast be spoiled."

Hershel's father and Zalman the tavern keeper were close friends—sworn blood brothers, body and soul. Some twenty years ago, when they had met after a long separation, Zalman the tavern keeper had, with his friend looking on, put down a barrel of wine in his cellar. Clapping his friend on the shoulder, he had said that his friend could send for this barrel of wine whenever the day came that, in his judgment, was the happiest day of his life.

That wine had been in Zalman the tavern keeper's cellar for some twenty years before it was required.

This was the first time in his life that Hershel had ever seen such a radiant look on his father's face. But such radiance is a sign of true happiness.

Hershel harnessed the horse and wagon, took the whip with its red tassel in his hand: "Giddyap, Chestnut, on to Daraban."

It was some distance to Daraban, uphill and downhill, past field and forest, with poplars and birds and golden sunlight along the way.

The horse, well-rested and well-fed, ran along at a good pace, without waiting for Hershel to use his whip.

Hershel was in a supremely good mood. He cracked his whip in the air simply for the fun of it. A rhyme was curling on his lips for a song he was just then inventing.

Not a horse, but a train
Runs, and flies to Daraban.
The horse says, "Hershel, Hershel, stop!
What makes you think you need your whip?"

Hershel did indeed think that his whip was unnecessary. And that's why he thought up the song. Or perhaps it was only because a song made the road pleasanter.

It was evening when he arrived in Daraban. Zalman the tavern keeper welcomed him as if he were a long-lost jewel. It was no small thing—his best friend's only son!

He clapped Hershel on the shoulder, "How is your father? Gotten older, eh?"

And when Hershel had delivered his father's message, Zalman the tavern keeper clapped him on the shoulder again, "Ah, Hershel. I like you. I take it that congratulations are in order. It stands to reason that the wine has grown stronger over the years. Unlike your father, who gets weaker with age." And with a sigh, Zalman the tavern keeper concluded, "Ah, if only people could be like barrels of wine."

Hershel unharnessed the horse, and though he had brought a sack of oats with him from home, Zalman the tavern keeper would not let him untie it. "You'll have your sack of oats for the return trip. Today, if you get my meaning, your horse is my horse's guest. They'll eat from the same trough. My horse is fond of guests. He takes after his owner. You understand me, Hershel?"

When Hershel was done with the horse, Zalman the tavern keeper invited him into the large parlor, poured out two glasses of wine, one for himself and the second one for his guest. "L'khayim, Hershel. And may your father be proud of you!"

Hershel was hungry and tired after his long journey. Zalman the tavern keeper sensed this and said, "Are you hungry, Hershel? My wife is supposed to be back at any moment. She's gone to a funeral."

Hershel knew that Zalman the tavern keeper's wife, Zisl-may all-Jews-be-blessed with-the-like, never failed to attend a Jewish funeral in the town.

Always, on her way back from a funeral, she invariably said, "He had some funeral. May all Jews be blessed with the like!" And that was why she was known in the town as Zisl-may-all-Jews-be-blessed-with-the-like!

When Zisl-may-all-Jews-be-blessed-with-the-like came home and when Zalman the tavern keeper told her what a welcome guest they had, she set to work at once to prepare supper and put off describing the funeral until later.

"He had some funeral. May all Jews be blessed with the like."

The food Hershel was given did not set well with him. The funeral odors that came from the tavern keeper's wife and from her words spoiled his appetite.

Worn out, he flung himself down on his bed. In his dream, he saw the funeral. Four men were carrying the bier. His father, with bowed head, said to the stepmother, who walked silently beside him, "That's the end of Hershel."

And the stepmother said sharply, "That was some brat. It would have been better had he never been born."

Then, suddenly, as if rising out of the ground, there was Zisl, the tavern keeper's wife, tall and lean, her cheeks more sunken than usual. Pointing a finger at the casket, she called loudly, so that everyone might hear, "That was some funeral our Hershel had, may all Jews be blessed with the like."

The tavern keeper's wife disappeared. The funeral disappeared. Who knows what happened? Suddenly, it was a circumcision feast. His—Hershel's circumcision feast. Everyone was celebrating. Wine was being drunk, honeycake eaten. Hershel saw Itche the circumciser approaching him. He had his circumcising knife between his teeth. Hershel wanted to cry out that he had already been circumcised, but he could not utter a sound. He wanted to run away, but his feet felt as heavy as lead.

Hershel started up from his sleep and spat three times to ward off evil omens. Outside, townspeople were already buying and selling. Peasants were already sitting in Zalman the tavern keeper's tavern. They smoked their coarse tobacco and drank wine.

One, two, three. Hershel was up and dressed. He washed, then raced through his prayers, after which he harnessed the horse. Zalman the tavern keeper helped him load the barrel of wine onto the wagon.

"Giddyap, Chestnut!"

Before he left, Zisl-may-all-Jews-be-blessed-with-the-like appeared with a package in her hand. It was food she was giving him to eat on the way. Just think. It was a long day's journey. One has to have a bite of something. With God's help, it would be evening before he reached home.

Hershel took the package but avoided looking into the eyes of the tavern keeper's wife. He did not like her, that funeral-goer who had wobbled into his dream last night quite ready to follow him to his grave.

It was not until he had left Daraban behind that the shadow of last night's dream left him.

Now here was the windmill, and it was here that he turned onto the broad highway that led, uphill and downhill through field and forest to his town.

On the way back, the whip was, once again, unnecessary. Too bad. Having brought it on the way here, it had to be brought back.

It was a hot summer's day. The road, dusty. Hershel removed his jacket.

"Ah, that feels good!"

But the farther he went, the more he felt the sun burning him. His throat felt dry. He had trouble breathing.

Suddenly, it struck Hershel that he was being a perfect fool; there was a barrel of wine lying in the wagon—and he was dying of thirst. True, the barrel of wine was for the circumcision feast, but what harm would it be if he took a little sip to quench his thirst? Who would notice, and who would take it amiss?

Without thinking too long about it, Hershel removed the bung from the barrel, bent down, and took a deep swallow.

The wine, as has been said, was old and strong. The deep swallow Hershel had taken made his head whirl. His eyes began to close and presently, he was asleep. It was pure luck that the horse knew the way home.

He does not remember how long he slept thus. But when he woke, it was to a strange sight. All around the wagon there were more than a hundred birds lying on the ground. And all of them were dead drunk.

It was only then that Hershel realized that he had forgotten to put the bung back into the bunghole. While he slept, the birds had flown down. Each of the birds had taken a sip of the wine and had fallen drunk to the ground.

Hershel sprang down from the wagon. He was afraid that when the birds woke and were sober again that they would fly away. It would be a pity. So many beautiful birds at a time. What a lovely celebration it would be if they could all sing together tomorrow at the circumcision feast.

He found a long thread in his pocket. One by one, he tied the feet of the birds who were fast asleep. When he had tied the feet of all the birds with his long thread, he wound it around his own waist and made a stout knot. Now they could not fly away. Even when they turned sober.

Satisfied with his work, Hershel Summerwind took another sip of wine from the barrel and fell asleep once again.

And when he woke up from his doze, he felt that his feet were dangling in the air and that his head was touching the clouds.

While he had been fast asleep, the birds had wakened. Shaking the sleep off their wings, they had flown upward, carrying Hershel Summerwind with them toward the clouds sailing through the sky.

Fear made Hershel's heart flutter. He heard the neighing of the horse on the road beneath him. It was calling to him, reminding him that he had abandoned the barrel of wine; that the circumcision feast was tomorrow; that his father's festivity would be spoiled.

"Upon my word! What a story," Hershel reproved himself. "Who needed the birds, eh? Now see what you have. They're carrying you off as the devil did the teacher, and who knows where they'll take you?"

Having blamed himself, there was, just the same, no help in sight. What was done was done.

Hershel shouted down to the horse that stood in the middle of the highway and did not know what to do, "Chestnut, take the barrel of wine home. You know the way. May you be well, Chestnut; give my regards to my father. Give Eidel a mazel-tov from me. And a fig for my stepmother."

The horse pricked up its ears the better to hear what Hershel was shouting down to him from under the clouds. Evidently the horse understood, because he yanked on the wagon and started off down the road, alone, without his master, and without the whip.

The birds that were carrying Hershel higher and ever higher burst into song. Their song was delicious. A veritable Song of Songs before the sun, before the wind, before the clouds.

For a while, Hershel listened to their singing, and then he, too, began to sing. He had a fine voice—a music-making throat. The birds were awed. They spoke among themselves, "A strange bird, that one, flying with us, but he knows how to sing."

"Indeed, a strange bird," a second bird said. "And his song is quite different from ours. It smells of ripe red cherries."

"Red cherries?" a young bird called out. "I love ripe cherries."

"That's some smart bird," mocked a middle-aged bird. "Where's the blockhead who doesn't love to peck at cherries?"

"Do you know what, fellows?" said an older bird, "Let's fly to Zaynvl Sadovnik's cherry orchard. The cherries should be ripe now."

"To the cherry orchard! To the cherry orchard!" the birds all cried in chorus and started off at full speed to Tsiganesht, where Zaynvl's cherry orchard was to be found.

"The birds reduced Zaynvl's cherry orchard to an absolute ruin," Hershel recounted. The scarecrows who stood there with brooms in their hands were no help at all.

And indeed, it was thanks to the flight of the birds to Zaynvl's cherry orchard that Hershel was rescued. The flight was frightening. His brain was in a whirl, his eyes grew dim, his ears buzzed. But no sooner had the birds descended to the first of the cherry trees than Hershel tore the thread asunder—one, two—and leaping down from the tree, he jumped over the fence and headed for home.

It was no more than four miles from Tsiganesht to his home. A breathless Hershel ran and ran. More dead than alive, he collapsed in his father's house just after the second evening prayers.

The horse, bearing the barrel of wine, had just then stopped before the door, so that no one had any inkling of what had happened to Hershel.

In the morning, Hershel told his story of the birds and of the great miracle that he had experienced; and to make sure that everyone knew that he was telling the truth, he sang the song that the birds had sung while they were flying through the air.

From this story, we can see what a great and good God we have. If He could rescue and help such a scoundrel as Hershel Summerwind, He will certainly rescue all the honorable and God-fearing Jews who follow God's commandments and who walk in His ways.

Amen, selah.

THE STORY OF THE NOBLEMAN'S MUSTACHES

Story. This story took place in a small Jewish town in Poland. It was inscribed in an old record book. The record book was burned. I am the last one who remembers the story, word for word. And now I'm telling it to you. Listen!

In a small Jewish town there lived a man named Mottl Parnas. He was, by trade, a barber. That is, he made his living by cutting Gentile hair and shaving Gentile skulls.

When there was a fair, peasants from the surrounding region came into the town bearing all sorts of good things. Some of them dropped into Yoyne Zinger's tavern, some of them into Mottl Parnas's to have their hair cut or their skulls shaved.

The copper coins that Mottl Parnas earned on a fair day were welcome guests. With them, he was able to stop the mouths of his wife and children.

But fair days came only a few times a year. So, for Mottl Parnas, things were not so good. And, in general, where income is lacking, domestic peace is lacking, too.

And, indeed, Mottl Parnas lacked domestic peace. His wife, Red Feygele, plagued him continually, honoring him often with blows, and Mottl, though he was a good two heads taller than she was, endured it all silently. Because he was naturally silent: one of those "leave-me-alone-why-are-you-bothering-me" men, with moist, frightened eyes.

And so our Mottl endured his hell in silence as if he were indeed guilty; and with his own hands, all by himself, he seized Prosperity by the cap and threw it out of the house.

The only revenge he ever had was when his wife was in childbed. For him, her shrieks and cries, which reached into the seventh heaven, were sweeter and more delicious than the rebbe's song.

No pauper ever appeared before the rebbe to secure his help in bearing children. Perhaps because Mottl didn't have the money either for the fare or for the rebbe's honorarium. So the Almighty spared him that sort of trouble.

And Red Feygele was frequently in childbed. And the unlucky fellow frequently had the sweet taste of revenge.

And time passed. Perhaps it even hurried or perhaps, as the writers of the storybooks put it, time flew by.

And Mottl Parnas grew older along with his wife, Feygele, and his household increased—every year a new hatchling, a new expense.

Then, however, a story transpired:

There was a nobleman, a lord who ruled over the town and the surrounding region—an exceedingly wicked man. A son-of-a-bitch with Polish mustaches. He whipped his peasants bloody for the smallest infractions. And he hated the Jews with an unfocused but relentless hatred.

This nobleman was a widower. It was whispered that he had poisoned his wife, that sickly, pious noblewoman, because he could not stand the incense with which she had filled all the rooms and the icons that she had installed in every corner, and the frequent fasts that she undertook, and her scrawniness—which was a consequence of those very fasts.

To his friends, he once said, "I need a wife in bed. Who can stand a lifetime sleeping with a prayer?"

But the "prayer of skin and bone"—his wife, that is—persisted in her ways. She lighted candles in the Catholic church; she fasted her fasts and grew scrawnier day by day. A shadow with a gold cross between her withered breasts, she shuffled about the palace muttering prayers and was utterly indifferent to the nobleman's lust.

The nobleman's Evil Inclination, a randy fellow—had a scheme of his own. He led his master—the nobleman, that is—through twisted paths and byways to a bubbling, gurgling, overflowing well in the midst of the forest. And it was there, beside that well that the nobleman found his beautiful Magda Walczynska , a high-born lady from a neighboring estate who happened to be strolling there all alone.

She was beautiful and as lust-inspiring as Mary Magdalene before she became a penitent. And when the lord saw her, he was beside himself. And when he compared her to his parchment-faced "prayer" it was borne in on him what a fool he was. And for the first and only time in his life, he called himself an old jackass—out loud.

After that meeting, a second followed, then a third—in the forest, beside the well, always in secret, so that the "prayer" would not know.

And indeed, the "prayer" did not know. She moved like a nun from one of her icons to another. By the light of the candles that burned day and night before the holy pictures, she herself looked like an icon in motion.

Meanwhile, in the forest, the birds were singing. The trees rustled, and the mischievous wind performed a variety of tricks, frightening the hares and the foxes.

The nobleman is passing by!

He was indeed passing by, but without his dogs or his gun, as was usually his wont. He waited anxiously for the beautiful Mary Magdalene, who, as she usually did, kept him waiting for a good little while before she revealed herself, emerging from among the trees, laughing her delicious laugh.

And it was there, in the forest beside the well that was their usual trysting place, that the plan was born that was to send the "prayer" mounting to heaven where she might pray to all the holy ones to send down blessings to the high-born young woman and the lustful old man with the Polish mustaches.

That is what the peasants in the tavern whispered to one another so that no one might hear and spread the tale because their fear of that lord was so great.

And here is the proof. One night, after the nobleman's wife had kneeled before each of the icons and had piously said her prayers, she lay down to a sleep from which she never rose again.

It may be that he poisoned her or that he simply choked her to death. One guess is as good as another. No one knew for certain. What was known is that the "prayer" had been a stumbling block for the nobleman with the mustaches and for the well-born young woman who, it should be said, was a widow.

The funeral for the "prayer" was quite lively. Three priests babbled prayers for her soul. Peasant women carried holy pictures, and the nobleman walked with his head bowed, like a true mourner.

But soon after her death, the nobleman ordered all of the castle windows to be opened. He drove the incense out of the rooms and sent it after his pious wife in paradise, where it might give pleasure to all the holy folk with whom, no doubt, she was by now intimately acquainted.

Three weeks after his wife's death, indeed, no more than three, the nobleman was to preside over a banquet in honor of the young widow. There, at that banquet, he meant to declare before all the guests, the nobility of the surrounding region, that she was to be his bride. And that the wedding would take place soon, at a time fitting before God and man.

The banquet was planned for a Sunday evening. The lord's servants, on that Sunday, could hardly catch their breath, there was so much to do to prepare the royal meal.

At ten o'clock on that Sunday morning, the landowner ordered that the barber, Mottl Parnas, with all his implements, should be brought to him. Mottl Parnas had a reputation as a barber. He had learned the skill in a big city. In the town, he was said to have "golden hands," and with those "golden hands," as we have seen, he managed on rare occasions to earn a few copper three-ruble coins.

Why the nobleman, as was his usual custom, did not have himself barbered by his valet on that Sunday and instead chose to send for Mottl Parnas remains a question.

Perhaps because he was in a strangely good mood on that day and had treated his servants well, he wanted to give the poor Jewish barber, Mottl Parnas, a chance also to earn a little something, to be pleased on this fortunate day, on which the temptation from the forest would become his fiancée before God and man.

Or perhaps it was simply one of the nobleman's caprices. Whichever it was, when the messenger entered Mottl Parnas's home, Mottl's wife, Red Feygele, was just then honoring him with a dense stream of curses. One of those streams that came Mottl's way every Sunday. Because, you need to know, that Feygele did not curse on the Sabbath. On the Sabbath, she was pious and God-fearing, and read her woman's Bible like every other proper Jewish woman in the town.

And indeed it was for that reason that the Sunday curses and wounding words were especially sharp and stinging, and poor Mottl, had he been able to, would have lighted out for the farthest reaches of the world.

The landowner's messenger arrived just then as a veritable redeemer. Mottl quickly assembled his tools and, with a "Good-bye, Feygele," he strode so quickly off on his long legs that the messenger keeping up with him could hardly catch his breath. But when Mottl neared the hill on which the castle stood, he felt his heart constrict. Any moment now he would be standing before the severe lord with the ferocious mustaches. Had he been able to, Mottl at that moment would have run back at once to hell, that is, to his wife, Red Feygele.

But it was already too late. The terrified eyes of the barber Mottl Parnas grew even more terrified.

The nobleman, as has been said, was, on that Sunday, filled with loving kindness to all and everyone. All that morning he had gone about the vast chambers of his palace, listening to the songs of the canaries in their cages, giving Andzej, the old gardener, a convivial clap on the shoulder, asking his equerry Anton when he meant to marry the stout Maryasha. And thus contented with himself and with everything else, he stroked his long nobleman's mustaches.

Mottl's heartbeat was wild, like the tick of a watch that has gone insane. And now he was standing before the nobleman, whose forehead today shone; there was not a trace of cloud on it anywhere. "Good day," he replied to Mottl's stammered greeting, but his Polish mustaches, long and dangling, looked as threatening as always.

Mottl Parnas said a silent prayer in his heart. "Lord of the Creation, dear Father in Heaven, let the work of my hands succeed; let the nobleman be pleased with it. O, dearest God, make a miracle so that everything goes smoothly, and I live to see my wife and my children."

That was the prayer poor Mottl uttered in his heart. And God heard his prayer, and everything went smoothly. The landowner was a fastidious fellow, like all noblemen. He looked into the mirror and said, "Good work, Mottl!"

For poor Mottl, it was as if a stone had been lifted from his heart. The nobleman was satisfied with his work. The cut of the lord's hair was an absolute wonder. Mottl's "golden hands" had put the proficient valet's work to shame.

Just the same, a disaster was fated to happen.

The nobleman, who was standing before the mirror, said to the barber, "It seems to me, Mottl, that my left mustache is just a little bit longer than the one on the right."

And the longer the lord thought about it, the more certain he became that the left mustache was indeed a bit longer than the one on the right. He said, "The left mustache has to be trimmed just a little to make it even with the one on the right."

Mottl Parnas, who had already begun to pack his implements, shuddered. To touch the nobleman's mustaches, those fierce Polish mustaches, was surely a test. He was struck dumb with fear, and what he had wanted to say, he did not say. That is, that the left mustache was the same length as the right one; and that the nobleman was imagining things and that . . . .

As in a daze, he took up his scissors. For a moment, his heart forgot to pray to Him who lives eternally. In his mind's eye, he suddenly saw his small red-haired wife, Feygele, who uttered a cry, "Don't, Mottl."

Mottl's hand trembled. A piece of noble mustache lay on the floor. Mottl broke out in a cold sweat.

The nobleman leaped from his chair, his brow clouded, his eyes spurting fire. His right mustache hung nobly down as always, but the left one. Jesus, Mary! Jesus, Mary! And today of all days, the day of the banquet. Today of all days, when he had invited all the nobility of the neighboring estates. Today of all days, when he had intended to announce to them all that "the blond temptation from the forest" was to be his bride.

The nobleman looked at the piece of mustache that was rolling about on the floor, he looked at Mottl, the barber, who stood, his mouth open, and his knees trembling.

Abruptly, the lord shouted, "Jan! Stepan!"

Two stout servants came in. They stood by the door and waited for the nobleman's orders.

"Take this kike and give him a hundred and fifty lashes, without pity."

The two servants, Jan and Stepan, seized the bewildered Mottl Parnas—one of them took his head, the other his feet, and they carried him out to the courtyard. There, in the courtyard, they pulled down the poor barber's underpants, and then the two devils, Jan and Stepan, began to count lashes.

For the first twenty lashes, Mottl the barber screamed unearthly cries. By the time they reached thirty he was unconscious.

The landowner, with one short mustache and the other long one, stood at his window and sent down orders. "Pour cold water on him and start again."

Mottl Parnas the barber was carried home at his last gasp. In his delirium, he carried on conversations with his grandfathers in the other world.

"Good day, grandfathers. What do you think? Will they let me into

Paradise? If not, we'll have to bribe someone. After the whipping I got from the lord, I haven't strength enough to go to hell."

Later he was taken to the hospital for the poor, and there, at about ten o'clock that night, he died.

He was a weak man, that Mottl Parnas. He hadn't the strength to survive the hundred and fifty lashes.

When they brought the sad news to Red Feygele that her husband had passed on, and when she looked at her orphans who had been left without a father and without a provider, she was momentarily stunned. But after another moment, a curse burst from her heart: "For the sake of a bit of mustache, they murdered a father of children. Dear Father in Heaven, may that lord's mustaches grow and grow and never stop growing."

There are curses that are dispersed by the wind. There are curses that are dispersed by water. And then there are curses that are fulfilled.

And Feygele's curse was fulfilled.

Just then, the nobleman was sitting at the head of his table. The blond forest "temptation" sat near him. The gentry from the neighboring estates sat around the table. The candelabra shimmered. Wine in the beakers glittered. There was the scent of roses and eau de cologne. There was not the slightest trace left of the former odors of incense and wax candles.

The lord had cut off the second half of his mustache and joined it to the other half that Mottl the barber had spoiled. The truth is that it was not a smooth fit. But he had no other choice. The banquet was already prepared. There was no way to put it off.

The gentry from the neighboring estates did indeed wonder about the nobleman's mustaches that had now in some strange way gotten smaller. (The Polish nobility are connoisseurs of mustaches. Their whole sense of honor is naturally located in their mustaches.) But they kept silent, as if nothing had happened. They asked no questions about anything. Inwardly, each of them thought, "Strange," and continued to eat and to drink all the good things the servants continually put on the table.

But the lord sensed what was pressing on their minds, and when they were all well under the influence of drink, he stood up and told them the story of his mustache misfortune, and that the kike Mottl Parnas was the one to blame, and how he, the nobleman, had punished him.

"The misfortune was fated, ladies and gentlemen, but by the time of the wedding, the mustaches will have grown again. Lord Jesus is a merciful master. Meanwhile, my bride, forgive me."

The nobleman bent down to the blond "temptation" and kissed her. But as he raised his head, the other nobles sat with their mouths open, as if turned to stone.

The blond "temptation" uttered a shriek and fainted.

The landowner was completely confused.

"What's happened, lords, ladies?"

But no one could speak a word. Everyone pointed at him.

He ran to a mirror and was dazed by what he saw. The mustaches that, just a little while ago, had been shamefully sheared had grown and, with each passing moment, were growing longer.

The lord fled from the room. The other nobles slowly came to their senses. And it was only now that anyone thought to tend to the bride-to-be.

When she was conscious again, the lord was standing beside her, and his mustaches had been restored to the length they had been when the banquet began. The nobleman's valet, who had also been frightened at first, had evened them so that they were proper again.

"An illusion!" said the stout Edvard Potocki, and burst into loud laughter.

And the gentry, too, burst out laughing.

The blond temptation, the nobleman's fiancée, opened her eyes. Two huge, blue, terrified eyes.

"What happened, darling?" she whispered.

"Nothing. An illusion, countess," repeated the stout Potocki and laughed again."

"An illusion, darling," murmured the lord, like someone dazed as he bent down to his fiancée and kissed her once more. When he raised his head, those around him stood as if turned to stone. The blond temptation screamed, "Jesus, Maria!" and fainted away again.

The nobleman's mustaches were strangely long, and with every passing moment they grew longer and longer.

"It has the touch of the devil in it," stammered the stout Count Potocki as, trembling, he left the room.

Once more, the nobleman ran out of the hall and came back a while later. With his valet's help, he had again brought the mustaches under control. But he did not find his guests. They had fled, as if driven by angry spirits.

His fiancée, the blond countess, lay on the floor in a faint.

He bent down to her and caressed her hair; his hands were gentle and sad. He whispered: "Wake up, darling, my blond bride of the forest. Evil spirits are playing their dark game with my mustaches. Let us pray to Lord Jesus, our Master, that he may take pity on my mustaches and redeem them from the mocking tricks that the wicked demons are playing on them.

A little later, the scene was very moving. The nobleman on his knees before a picture of his Redeemer. The lady, with her hands folded in prayer, kneeling beside him. The "forest temptation" with a prayer on her lips for the nobleman's mustaches.

And when they rose to their feet, and the lady turned to look at the landowner, her beloved, she started back, crying, "Devil! . . . You . . . Yourself . . . are the devil!!"

She went away. Left the nobleman alone. He stood again before the mirror, looking at his fearful long mustaches that, moment by moment, grew longer and longer.

After that night, the landowner no longer showed himself on the streets of the town. He no longer went hunting as he used to do. He avoided his friends, the gentry of the neighboring estates.

Often, very often, he thought of his fiancée, the blond lady of the forest. With tears in his eyes, he would sigh, "It was not to be, my golden darling."

His valet followed him closely with a scissors in his hand and, whenever it was necessary, trimmed his master's mustaches.

At night, when everyone around him was asleep, he would move like a shadow, a lantern in his hand, to the grave of his pious wife to beg her forgiveness.

The nobleman supposed that it was because of her that he was suffering; that she was the reason for the great punishment that had over-taken him.

Later, when he learned that the Jewish barber, Mottl Parnas, had died of his whipping, it began to dawn on him that there was a link between the death of the barber and the growth of his mustaches.

One night, he stood before Mottl's grave. There he sat, his clenched fists pressed against his breast, and begged the poor Jewish barber to pardon him.

The nobleman even traveled to the rebbe, to whom he gave a gener-ous donation, and asked the rebbe for his blessing.

But the rebbe's blessing did not do him any good. Red Feygele's curse was much stronger.

One fine morning, when the valet, bearing his scissors as usual, ap-proached his master to trim the mustaches that had grown fearfully long overnight, the lord drove him away. "It's not necessary. Go away."

For the first time since the death of the pious lady, his wife, the landowner lighted the candles before the icons with his own hands. And he prayed long and hard before each and every icon, expressing re-morse for his sins.

It was that way all day long—himself, alone before the holy images.

In the evening, when things in the room began to grow dim, and only the great mirror glittered in its golden frame, the nobleman stood before it and regarded his lifeless features and the long mustaches that already reached to his knees. He laughed a sharp, sly laugh. "It will do!"

Toward midnight, he hung himself with his mustaches. Outside, there was a raging wind and rain.

In his final moment, his feverish eyes beheld a large bottom, striped with the marks of the whip; and around it a cluster of children weeping, "Father! Father dear."

And a small, red-haired woman who pointed her finger at the land-owner hanged with his own mustaches, "A fine atonement for his sins!"

From this tale, one should draw the following moral: that one has to avoid being cursed. It's true that this time, the nobleman well and truly deserved his curse. May the Lord preserve us from such noblemen, now and forever. *Amen, selah.*

The rabbi of Chelm, his high forehead furrowed, sat bent over a book. He stroked his snow-white beard and sighed frequently. Each of the rabbi's sighs nearly extinguished the tallow lamp burning on the table.

And there was plenty to sigh about. Just think of it: he carried the burden of an entire town of artless children on his shoulders. Naive children with beards and side curls who couldn't find a solution to the simplest of problems. Anything but. So they came to him, the rabbi of Chelm, to have him untangle whatever the tangle was in which an inhabitant of Chelm might be snarled.

"Lucky for Chelm," thought the clever rabbi of Chelm, "that they have me for their rabbi. Some reputation the town would have if I were not here. Chelm would look like Abdera, the Jewish-Greek town of long ago. Or, on the other hand, like the German town of Schildo. Towns filled with fools, with neither Torah nor wisdom."

And the rabbi of Chelm felt that he was where he belonged. He bore with love the misdeeds of this community of Jews, which scoffers elsewhere referred to as "Chelm Fools," when in truth what they were was a naive people who could be led around by the nose by anyone who so much as looked like a God-fearing person.

"Take, for example," thought the rabbi to himself, "the story of what happened last winter . . . ." The first snow had fallen; a white, tidy snow. Like true children, the Chelmites were delighted with it. They stood looking out of the windows of their houses overwhelmed with wonder at the white brilliance. And gazing at the snow, they began to think that it would be a great pity to tread on that whiteness. What they feared was that the synagogue *shames** who had to wake people for their midnight prayers would play havoc with the pure white snow.

And, as always in a time of trouble, they had come to him, the rabbi of Chelm, for advice on how, at midnight, to keep the shames from treading on the snow. He, the rabbi, had considered and considered (who else if not he?) until he arrived at a solution.

"When it comes time for midnight prayers, let several Chelmites seat the shames on a table and carry him from house to house, and this, necessarily, will keep him from treading on the snow."

But the snow story was as nothing compared with the other achievements of the rabbi of Chelm. His wisdom was spoken of by Jews throughout the entire world. What if scoffers made fun of him— where was the harm? Wisdom scoffed at was still wisdom. And a wise man on whom a fool's cap has been set is still a wise man.

The Warsaw scoffers sneering at him and his congregation troubled him about as much as last year's snow. That's what defined them as scoffers. On the other hand, the sermon given a week ago in Chelm's great synagogue by the preacher of Chelm did trouble him.

In his sermon, Reb Hershl, the preacher of Chelm, had compared the rabbi's wisdom to King Solomon's, and in the course of his sermon he recounted how he, the rabbi of Chelm, had ruled on a question involving the new synagogue that the workmen of Chelm had built.

It had been a difficult question. Whether to paint the synagogue or not? If it were painted, then it might, God forbid, look like a church; on the other hand, if it were not painted, then how would anyone know it was a holy place and not an ordinary building? The rabbi of Chelm, after meditating for three days and three nights, had come upon a solution: first, the synagogue would be painted, and then it would be whitewashed.

The whole town had buzzed with excitement over this brilliant solution. But the rabbi would not hear of comparing it to the wisdom of Solomon! This, not because the rabbi of Chelm was such a modest man, but after all—think: "King Solomon!"

The rabbi of Chelm got up from his chair and began pacing the room. His shadow made strange somersaults on the walls. He paused, looked around on all sides. Strange. It was night once more. Which night was it after the six days of Creation? Who had the gumption to count? The tallow lamp on the table danced. A shimmering star danced at the window.

The rabbi's body trembled. "Oh my! Oh my! There are no bounds to wisdom," he thought. "Everyone in Chelm knows that I am no fool. Indeed, they regard me as a wise man. And certainly King Solomon was a wise man. But how can either of our wisdom be compared to that of the Creator of the world?"

There was a star trembling in the window. How could one tell whether joy made it tremble or fear. Or was its tremor meant to spite him, the rabbi of Chelm?

The rabbi spat three times: ptui, ptui, ptui. His thoughts, heaven preserve us, bordered on the verge of speculation. Satan, may his name be obliterated, probably knew that Chelm was a town and that the rabbi of Chelm was a holy man, and it was worthwhile for Satan to divert the rabbi from the path of righteousness. Who knew how many nets Satan had already spread around him?

To disorganize the evil thought, the rabbi paced the room even more quickly. Whomever else Satan, may his name be obliterated, might ensnare in his net, it would not be him, the rabbi of Chelm. "Beware!"

Abruptly, the rabbi said aloud, "Where do you suppose they can be? It's four weeks since they went off and they haven't been heard of or seen."

"It's not a trivial matter," he grumbled. "I've sent two people out on such an important mission. They left without so much as a good-bye. Then they disappeared as if water had closed over them."

The two messengers he had sent were not ordinary youths; they were respectable householders of Chelm. Red Ziml the ink maker and Black Yossl the dairyman.

Their mission also was unusual.

One fine day, the rabbi of Chelm had begun to think about Justice. That the world needed it. That the world could not survive without it. And, since Chelm was a city in the world, Chelm, too, needed a little bit of Justice. No sooner had the thought occurred to him then he called an assembly together at which it was decided to send two messengers out into the world to buy some Justice for the Chelm community.

Striding back and forth in his house, the rabbi of Chelm heard the night watchman's horn. It was not the usual workweek sound. Instead it sounded a note of either fear or good news.

And indeed, almost at one the door opened and Red Ziml rushed in breathless. His face glowed. He could hardly stammer, "Rabbi. We've brought back an entire barrel of Justice."

If the rabbi of Chelm had not been shy, he would have seized Red Ziml and kissed him. But the rabbi controlled himself and, his voice trembling, said, "Tell me, Ziml, tell me how, and from whom you were able to get such an extraordinary bargain—an entire barrel of Justice."

And Red Ziml told how he and the other messenger, Black Yossl, wandered the four corners of the earth until, in the vicinity of Warsaw, they came upon a tavern in a village. It was the tavern keeper who had the barrel full of Justice. But though you might beat him black and blue, he would not under any circumstance sell it. With great difficulty, they finally persuaded him to let them have it for a purse full of money. But the tavern keeper warned them not to open the barrel en route because, God forbid, the Justice in it might drain away.

"Where? Where is the barrel?" asked the rabbi, hardly able to breathe.

"The barrel is in the middle of the marketplace. Black Yossl is guarding it. You understand, Rabbi, a thief, God forbid, could . . . "

"I understand. I understand," cried the rabbi joyfully. "Now, Ziml, you go and call together the associate rabbi, the ritual slaughterer, the head of the community, and all the other householders, and we'll go to greet the barrel of Justice."

Red Ziml went off. The rabbi of Chelm put on his Sabbath coat and his beaver hat and went happily to the marketplace where the barrel full of Justice stood.

The marketplace was crowded with people. All of Chelm was there. Men, women, and children. Even the Sabbath-goy, Stashek, was there in a cluster of folk. A huge summer moon was a silent witness to the amazing ceremony that was to come.

The crowd made way for the rabbi. The old gray beard slowly approached the barrel. All the people held their breath. The rabbi bent down. Before he opened the barrel to allow Justice to spread all over Chelm, the rabbi, out of sheer curiosity, wanted to sniff it. He wanted to know how Justice smelled.

"People! Ugh!"

"What? Ugh?"

"Justice stinks."

Each and every Chelmite grabbed his nose. Indeed, they could all tell that something was very much amiss.

It was the rabbi who was the first to understand. Turning to the two

Chelmites who stood closest to him, he commanded, "Take the barrel of Justice, out to the field. Dig a hole and bury it there in such a manner that no one will ever know where it has disappeared."

The two Chelmites seized the barrel, and quick as a wink, they were gone.

The rabbi of Chelm called out for everyone to hear, "People, go home. Wash your hands. Say the *asher-yotser* prayer* and remember that Justice is—ugh."

The crowd dispersed, everyone repeating to himself the phrase, "Justice is—ugh."

To this day if you say the word "Justice" to a Chelmite, he will spit and, with a wave of his hand, he'll say, looking directly at you, "Justice is—ugh."

The rabbi remained alone in the marketplace. In the light of the full moon he stood sad and pale, whispering something with his withered lips. Perhaps only the wind knows what it was he whispered, and perhaps not even he. Because after all, when has the wind ever had the time or the patience to hear what a disappointed old man whispers all alone in the middle of a marketplace late at night?

He stood thus for a little while, leaning on his gray stick. Then, slowly, he made his way home.

From every household could be heard the sound of water being poured and the murmuring of the asher-yotser prayer.

Slowly, slowly the old rabbi passed by small straw and shingle-roofed houses of the town of Chelm. So that was what remained of his dream of human Justice. Just that, and nothing more.

He slipped into his house like a shadow. He washed his hands and murmured the prayer.

He lighted a wax candle, took a book out of the bookcase, and looked into it, trying to forget for a moment the goading feeling that comes with a great disappointment.

"A lifetime spent dreaming of Justice. How's one to know that Justice has such a foul stench. How's one to know?"

The old rabbi swayed over his book. With the weary rhythm of a mourner he swayed back and forth. Back and forth.

His shadow moved on the wall—a sort of black rabbi. With the rhythm of a mourner. Back and forth. Back and forth.

But the revelation that the Chelmer rabbi had, namely that "Justice stinks," made an enormous impression in Chelm. It was talked about and wondered at in every household.

The philosopher of Chelm, Nussn-with-the-Spectacles, who was known in Chelm as Nussn the Wise,* actually wanted to write the story down in order to make known the deep maxim at which the rabbi of Chelm had arrived. But the rabbi sternly forbade him to do it.

Just the same, the story became known, just as all the other stories about Chelm have become known. In Jewish households everywhere in the world the wonders of Chelm were told along with the story of the wisest of the Chelmites, the gray old rabbi of Chelm.

They told each other the stories and laughed heartily. The legend grew. The epic in which folly kissed common sense on the forehead.

And one must confess that every one of the Chelmites fulfilled his function perfectly. Not one of them remained backward. The head of the community and the bathhouse attendant, the rich man and the beggar. All of those amazing children of folly, all of those remarkable creatures that Jewish folk-fantasy has conjured up and has masterfully fixed in the legends of Chelm.

But the best of the Chelm figures is still the rabbi of Chelm, may his holy memory be blessed, the fine old man with the high forehead and the snow-white beard. The faithful guardian, protector, and adviser of his exquisite community.

For the sake of the truth one has to add that the rabbi of Chelm was not crushed by his disappointment regarding human justice. It simply made him profoundly sad for a while. But his iron faith in the Justice of the Creator of all the worlds finally purified his feelings.

On one rainy autumn night as he sat bent over a volume, he felt a strange inner lightness. The flame of his wax candle trembled, and lo, the shadow on the wall—the black rabbi—had a different motion than usual.

"A dance! Let us dance a dance in honor of his beloved Name—" the white rabbi said to the black one.

The white rabbi got up from his chair, lifted his coattails, and began to pace, turning around himself.

The black rabbi on the wall, his shadow-image, did the same, lifted his coattails and turned around himself.

At first slowly, then more quickly, more quickly, the snow-white beard waving; the coal-black beard waving: white-black, white-black. One rabbi and two figures. One joy, one praise for the dear Name that has created heaven and earth.

The white rabbi felt a weariness, but he would not yield to it. The black rabbi on the wall felt a weariness but would not yield to it.

The candle on the table began to gutter, gutter, and the rabbi of Chelm fell to the floor.

And in that tiny moment the black rabbi, his shadow-image, also fell.

And there was a hushed silence.

FIRST LETTER TO X. Y.

Dear,

Certainly you were not expecting such a miniature literary weekly as this one. Raised on journals with an endless number of pages and little content, we now trumpet reform. With measured, essential words we will take the measure of modern Jewish literature, modern Jewish thea er, and modern Jewish art and their relationship to the world. There and back, beside the cradle of our project, there stands the shadow of Don Quixote, the father of all illusions. May his accumulated merits stand by us. *Amen, selah.*

Our program: First of all, to pop the lice loudly that have crammed and burrowed their way into the pleasure-pores of Jewish literature. Our specially manicured fingernails are ready. We advertise a mobilization of all troubadours and strugglers east and west, north and south—Come to us. From time to time, literature, too, puts up barricades. Help us to sweep away the false and destructive conjuncture that is crippling the present literary scene, entangling the threads, making the way more difficult for those who are on their way and for those who ought to be on their way.

We want to restore the crown of Jewish melody to persecuted

beauty's head. A marrow-less idler has gnashed his rotten teeth, announcing "an end to melody," and million-voiced epigones have seized upon the slogan and have carried it further; and the effect of that resonance has wrought veritable destruction.

For us, melody is the be-all and end-all. It flutters over the cradle and over the child; it trembles above love and is feverish in the bride's veil; it accompanies marchers and weeps over the solitary; it is jubilant over bread and wine and is tempestuous over hunger and thirst. It embraces grief and joy with black and colorful hands. It closes the dream-exhausted eyes of the dying. Ripe prose is nothing more than a colossal detour to melody. For example, Hamsun.*

In every wanderer who sleeps on the highway blanketed with night and wind, in every child that hangs its smile on the blue mask of evening, in every mother who fearfully takes the pulse of the night, in every louse-infected man who pops like lice the silver stars; in every wind that pursues shadows like fleas; in every village, in every town, in every desert, in every touch, shudder, movement, storm, there dozes the true gold of poetry. And you, Jewish poet whose name is already well known, or who is not yet well known, it is upon you that we place this burden. We do not point the way. That's your business. All roads lead to Rome and all roads lead to the kingdom of beauty. The existence of a literature depends not on dates or paragraphs or on positions that can be elbowed aside but on true and authentic words.

To show the way—Never before has there been an intersection of so many symbols. Our generation wavers between Yes and No. Hamlet's tousled head floats through our sleepless nights. Blood has pictured the agony of our generation and scattered crucifixes over all the roads of the world. Christ's head sobs symbolically in our dreams. Our wounds require consolation. The hand of the holy Saint Francis of Assisi presses upon our heart. Our blood is stormy with revolt. The burden of Prometheus flashes before our eyes. Our nerves yearn toward joy and ecstasy. The golden form of the holy Baal Shem Tov is drawn distinctly upon the horizons.

Chaos, chaos is still our mother. The blasphemous gang with its *Maestoso Patetico*,* its hysterical confusion of images, is gone. The second chapter is open. Our lines of sight, our symbols have become clearer. Depending on who carries Hamlet's head on a platter as Salome carried the head of Saint John; depending on who carries the gleaming mantle of Christ in his hands, or who pursues the Violeta Halos of Hasidism in Yiddish literature. The circle is marked. The finale is intuited. It may be that we are fated, after the destruction of the idols, to ignite new idols and to dance the first idol-worshiping renewal dance.

1929

THE BALLAD: THE VISION OF BLOOD

Night. Figures, masks on the windows. Man, woman, child. A vermin-infested man dozing on the stone ground beside the gate—A madman who looks into a well and asks, "Who am I?" The evening with its perpetually suffering Jesus gesture on the cross. . . . The Giaconda who, out of despair, has hung herself on the first lamp pole and in whose hair is entangled the white half-moon; white and sad as a child's smile.

That is the vision of restless blood; the spurt that erases silent feeling; the hushed lyrical vibrations of the soul. That is the fearful glimpse at the edge of night. Death, madness. That is the wild mystery that dozes in our ecstatic blood—the ballad.

I walk through the dusk, gray and gray. Imprecision stirs at the edge of the horizon. Silhouettes darkly emerge. Trees, houses, lanterns. Old hunch-backed beggars. The blood begins to seethe, swallowing silhouetted panoramas. There is noise, intoxication. And through the union of silhouette and the sound of blood the balladic transformation emerges. The silhouetted beggars, with their heavy dragging tread, carry balladic question marks. And they incise the question marks on the night's stars. Stumbling figures inquire. Lost shapes search. The night is silent, makes no excuse. Does not restore the lost. Now the great bacchanalia begins. The withered hands of the beggars ignite sinful red moons. In the background of the night, and in a wild ecstasy, the wanton deed is born. The befuddled aimless laughter of human despair. The great mystical vision of our blood—ballad.

At night. The child stands before a mirror. The mirror is pure, clear, transparent. What does a child see in the mirror? What is it searching for in the mirror? Nothing. It just gazes into it, musing. Suddenly the mirror darkens. A gray cat leaps by and disappears. A mangy figure stretches out at full length over the mirror. The eyes cold, strange. Its clothes black and strange. The child's face turns white as chalk. It screams a primordial, hysterical scream. That is the bizarre cry of our blood and fear—ballad.

Evening. A shopkeeper stands on the threshold of the little shop. Pale, clever, insightful, realistic. Shopkeeper, who is clever? "I," he replies. "Shopkeeper, who is foolish?" "You," he replies. "Your dream, your yearning, your irrationality." Shopkeeper, what is the world, and what is mind? He pulls a silver dollar out of his pocket. "This. For ten of these you can buy a woman. For twenty of them you can buy mankind. For thirty pieces of silver you can buy and sell Jesus. And for forty, you can buy a first-class God. Phantoms, phantoms. Foolishness. So what! Eh?"

Night falls over the shopman's head. His face turns paler, ghostlier. His hands thinner, ghostlier. Night flings him up to a cloud. The moon, like an abraded white dollar-coin, catches him up and carries him through space, turns, wheels about quickly like a top. The shopkeeper waves his arms about, makes hysterical gestures. The ghostly play of non-sense, dear sirs. Grotesque cynicism on night's flag. Ballad.

A streetwalker wanders through an autumn night. A sad, fine rain in her hair, in her clothes. Surrounded by silence and death. Abandoned shadows huddle in the corners of tall gates. Blue streetlights mirror themselves on the wet sidewalks. The streetwalker's blood pulses rhythmically in time with the dripping of the rain, with the sound of her own silent wandering steps. Autumn evening idyll. Autumn evening elegy. Then suddenly, unwillingly, without warning, the word "Come" escapes from her lips.

An unspecific call to someone unspecified. A shadow has heard it. He gets up from the sidewalk and puts out his hand—"Come." The woman turns pale. "I didn't mean you. It was not you I called."

"But I heard you. You called for no one. I am no one. Your blood, against your will, called out. I am the shadow of your blood; the echo of your blood. Come!"

The autumn idyll by the movement of unspecific blood has been transformed into a tragic ecstasy, into a fantastic union of man with shadow—it has been transformed into ballad.

A disheveled, insane head leans smiling out of the window of the madhouse. His smile is meaningless and moves randomly out through the night. A blue poisoned moon. Beggar children carrying sacks wander about on the road. Hungry souls, they snatch with hungry hands at the blue poisoned moon, mirroring their beggarly faces in the insane smile, and are purified and poisoned. It is the tragic union of child with madness on night's banner—ballad.

Night. The father rides with his child. The child is ill. Its blood feverish with visions of death. There is so much exalted sound in the vision of death. There is so much mystical fear in the magnificent "Erlkönig."

The child is—ballad. Exalted, intoxicated with night and death. The figure of the father is superfluous. A chill, realistic antithesis that begs to be cast out of the entire atmosphere of the ballad.

The ballad—that is the black fantastic crown of poetry, demonic and dark, that floats through our thought and spirit carrying in its dark light endless revelations—fearful bacchanalias. In the gleam of that black crown, Balshazar blasphemed God and died. In the gleam of that wild black crown, the black raven ripped apart the noble blue soul of Edgar Allan Poe.

1929

SHOLEM ALEICHEM, THE ONE AND ONLY

1

In the year 1916, in the very middle of the month of May, he died in the city of New York, the seething cauldron of the United States.

One could tell he was a famous writer because of the funeral he had. It was said that it was one of the biggest funerals ever to have taken place in New York.

Masses of people, their heads bowed, marched by. And a moment before the coffin was shut forever, the collective mourner with thousands of eyes was fixated on the wax-yellow countenance of the dead master as if it wanted to seal into memory that face which, any minute now, was to be given over into the domain of worms and clay.

I remember: a spring day that was fragrant with May flowers: with lilac and cherry blossoms.

At the very center of the synagogue courtyard in Jassy, the capital city of Moldavia, the capital city of Yiddish theater, a pale fifteen-year-old boy before the window of a Yiddish bookstore. Tears well from the boy's eyes.

In the window hangs a newspaper, *The Real Yiddish Future*. On the front page, bordered in black and in the kinds of large Hebrew letters used for New Moon blessings, the headline, "Sholem Aleichem, Dead. Yiddish Laughter Dead." That fifteen-year-old boy then was very far from dreaming that one day he would himself belong to that Yiddish literature and that Sholem Aleichem's existence in it would fill him always with fear and pride.

Pride because this wonderful, singular writer was ours. With fear and despair because how, after Sholem Aleichem, could anyone write at all.

With a beating heart, the boy ran home to tell the tailor, his father, the melancholy news.

For as long as he could remember, his father had been a great Sholem Aleichem admirer. More than that—an exalted apologist for Sholem Aleichem. He himself, in his primitive fashion, had agonized his way through the track that leads from Shomer* to Sholem Aleichem. And it was that simple Sholem Aleichem apologist (of the countless anonymous ones) who, nevertheless, revealed to the sensitive boy the wonder of Sholem Aleichem.

And it was that simple reader who also found the right critical formula to which Yiddish criticism, and the writer of these lines, has only lately arrived over a sea of critical detours.

"Sholem Aleichem, the one and only."

In recognizing the uniqueness of such a manifestation as Sholem Aleichem lies the clear path to understanding him.

Had Yiddish criticism of those days arrived at that uniqueness and its artistic worth it would as a matter of course have been spared a great many of the false conclusions that contributed so greatly to the misunderstanding surrounding Sholem Aleichem. Every such unique figure carries within itself the criteria that help us to understand it.

All external criteria that are applied relative to such manifestations shed unconditionally, and fatally, a false light.

The spiritually enlightened Frenchman Voltaire, thanks to the aesthetic criteria that were external to the phenomenon of Shakespeare, misjudged the magnificence of his uniqueness.

It is a short distance from misjudging to blaspheming. In truth, just a pace away. Indeed, Voltaire blasphemed rather than recognized Shakespeare. And it is not to be wondered at—indeed, it is almost self-evident, that our homegrown enlightened ones were Sholem Aleichem's blasphemers.

With the external method of approach that they applied, they helped—no, they themselves were—the standard-bearers of the false interpretation of Sholem Aleichem's genius.

Regardless of whether such an enlightened one was called Eliezer Shteinman, A. Vayter, Zvi Hirshkan, or something else. For example, a typical enlightenment reflex was Peretz Markish's phrase (at the very time of the critical reappraisal) when, in calling attention to Sholem Aleichem's influences on A. M. Fuchs's stories, he let his tongue run away with him, saying, "Of course, A. M. Fuchs is descended from Sholem Aleichem, but without the glasses or the pointed Van Dyke beard."

And thus it is that a simple everyday Jew could, with his phrase, "There is only one Sholem Aleichem," overthrow all those intellectual enlightened ones with their methods of approach and their interpretations.

"Sholem Aleichem, the one and only."

2

Sholem Aleichem , the one and only.

Of course there is only one Sholem Aleichem, because in him was manifest the transmigrating soul of that eternal laughter that comes to a people only once in an eon. For the Spaniards, that laughter was revealed in the form of Cervantes; for the French, in the shape of Rabelais; for the English, in the form of Dickens.

Sholem Aleichem, the one and only, because figures such as Sholem Aleichem are not merely brilliant rhythmic flashes such as any greater or lesser literature might possess. They are the refinement of generations of gestures, grief, wisdom, and stubbornness.

One and only Sholem Aleichem, because his was the intimate artistic expression of the Jews, which, though it was rooted in the depths of a unique folklore, had nevertheless the marvelous power to rise toward universality.

One and only Sholem Aleichem because what is unique in the history of a literature is his successful synthesis of destiny with a primarily dramatic humor that is balanced between tears and laughter. Two such strange elements that, in Shakespeare, ran parallel to each other and that, only in a few works, paused, magnificently and weirdly, to look into each other's eyes.

Sh. Niger,* who, in his time, sought to establish Sholem Aleichem's literary pedigree, managed to disinter the acute notion that in Sholem Aleichem, Mendele, and Shomer were at odds. Only in his later years did he arrive at the universality of Tevye the dairyman.

At last and about time.

The tracing and the discovery of the relationship between the uniqueness and universality of a work must be the chief attribute of every critic. Only with such a mode of measurement can one arrive at an estimation of the positive or negative worth of any given work.

And Sholem Aleichem was the most original figure that we Jews gave to world literature.

3

I know that in a hastily written article it is by no means possible to elaborate the full uniqueness of Sholem Aleichem. There is only one alternative: the way of suggestiveness. To outline a critical schemata or, to put it better, to offer several theses that can only be justified in a longer monograph.

First of all, the universal moments: the continual reiteration of proletarian themes. As for example:

Of Job, in *Tevye the Dairyman*

Of Don Quixote in *Menakhem Mendl*
Of Mephistopheles in *The Haunted Tailor*
Of Odysseus in *Motl, the Cantor's Son*
Of Chelm in the Kasrilevke tales.
And so on, and so on.

4

The demonic-maniacal in Sholem Aleichem's heroes:

The illusory dybbuk who flings Menakhem-Mendl from one grotesque dramatic situation into another.

The cursing-monomania of Sheyne-Sheyndl that casts its grotesque light over her poverty-stricken and tormented life.

The citation-mania of Tevye the dairyman.

The parable mania of Reb Yusifl of Kasrilevke.

Et cetera, et cetera.

5

Only Shakespeare could probe thus the maniacal in the human condition. For this "Genius of Tragedy" the maniacal human condition was the point of departure from which he deduced heroic-dramatic consequences.

Sholem Aleichem, like no one else in Yiddish literature, had a feel for the elements of ur-tragedy. He was, as the Germans might say, "a playwright in disguise." The form of the theatrical monologue that dominates his work is a classic example. But he did not arrive at the final tragic summing up achieved by the brutal Briton or the "British barbarian," as Voltaire called Shakespeare.

Sholem Aleichem softened the dramatic elements with his lyric-humoristic smile; his deeply humane lyricism. In fact, he was world literature's last great humanist.

6

Though it may sound paradoxical, he was the first Greek in Yiddish literature. "Greek" in the sense of his free and open attraction to the sensuality of language. He liberated Yiddish artistic expression so that it could soar away from Mendele's asceticism and Peretz's rationalistic caution and allusions (see, for instance, Peretz's famous three dots).

He was the first great bacchanalian innovator in Yiddish literature. As usual, the Enlightenment critic did not understand such openness and misinterpreted it. Eliezer Shteinman wrote contemptuously of Sholem Aleichem's clownishness. And Zvi Hirshkan called Sholem Aleichem "the last announcer."

The Enlightenment critic always derogated him, pointing out his folkloric peculiarities.

7

In the light of his work, his pseudonym Sholem Aleichem (Peace unto You) loses its accidental character. It acquires meaning and becomes, in a particular fashion, a key to the mystery of his art that has been revealed under the name Sholem Aleichem.

There is in that name a familiar intimacy that separates a stranger from his wanderings and seats him at the family table as an equal member. The light of the suspended lamp draws him into the nearest circle of light and the hum of the singing samovar and the intimate family melody: "And now, kinsman, I will tell you a story, a sadly happy tale that might have happened to me, to you or to anyone else."

There is, however implicit in that name a pagan ritual, a grotesquely spectral leap with which Jews are wont to greet the nascent moon when it appears over the rooftops and alleys of Jewish villages and towns. It is that "Sholem Aleichem" greeting with which trembling human shadows greet the bizarre and spectral cosmic light of the eternally renewing silver moon. In Sholem Aleichem's work two elements, the bizarre and the spectral, are vividly present: the intimately idyllic and the bizarrely grotesque. That romantic expedition into the spectral-bizarre is, incidentally, characteristic of all the great humorists of world literature.

For Cervantes it found a classical solution in that he identified the fantastic-bizarre moment with the illusoriness of Don Quixote. In his quest for a point of equilibrium between the bizarre and the grotesque he made use of the figure of Sancho Panza. In Dickens, the bizarre-fantastic works itself out in the form of intermezzos (see the ghost stories that he interpolates here and there in his novel *The Pickwick Papers*); or it runs parallel to, and independently of, the story in *The Christmas Carol*. In the work of the German humorist Wilhelm Rabbe, we find the Dickensian method of bizarre-fantastic intermezzos interpolated wherever the realistic manner of the narrative permits it (see his novel *The Sparrow Street Chronicle*). In Chekhov and Gogol, the bizarre-fantastic elements, once again, run alongside the realistic style of the stories and novels. (Compare Chekhov's "The Black Monk" with Gogol's tales "The Nose," "The Overcoat," and others.) In Sholem Aleichem, too, there is the same turn toward the bizarre-fantastic as is to be found in the great humorists already cited. The bizarre-grotesque manifests itself in a whole series of stories that run parallel to his lyric-humoristic manner. Here, I will mention only two of those stories: "Eternal Life" and "A Tale Without a Tail" or, as it was later to be called, "The Haunted Tailor."

In "Eternal Life," a son-in-law who has been supported by his in-laws travels out into the world for the first time—to another town. On the way, in the dark of night, he comes to a snow-covered tavern. The tavern keeper, whose wife has just died, burdens the young man with the duty of acquiring the sort of merit that is rewarded in the "world to come" by asking him to take his wife's corpse to a Jewish cemetery in a nearby village. The journey, over snow-covered, dark roads with the corpse on the sled—made more perilous by his being plagued with frequent wrong turns—is a typical ghost story, exhaling a bizarre romanticism of fear and trembling, which is softened at the story's end when the young man is interrogated and his mistake explained.

"The Haunted Tailor" is more integrated and more accomplished, because the composition has the pervasive mingling of the real with the fantastic.

The tailor, Shimon-Elye Shema-Koleynu, goes to Kozodoyevke (Goatsville) to buy a nanny goat but comes home each time leading a billy goat, which of course does not give milk. The trick is played on him by the Mephistophelian tavern keeper Dodye, whose tavern is precisely at the midpoint on the road to Kozodoyevke. The innkeeper's demonic intrigue takes on a weird and appalling form at the story's end. The billy goat turns into a fantastically grotesque phantom that leaps over rooftops and walls, terrifying people in their houses and turning loose into the village nights a tale that may never be spun to its end.

Seizing that bizarrely fantastic billy by the horns, I make of it a required and characteristic ornament for Sholem Aleichem's monument, which has not yet been set up.

1933

FOLKLORE AND LITERATURE

Modern antisemitism, precisely because it achieved such a brutal form in the classic land of the Jewish Enlightenment Movement, has liquidated—and, one would think, forever—the notion of assimilation as a solution to the Jewish problem. The bewildered Jewish intellectuals seek and grope for a way back, back to a lost Jewish uniqueness—that very uniqueness that had once been liquidated by Enlightenment tropes: "backward," "Asiatic."

Recognizing and finding the way back to one's own people—that is the new slogan and the outstanding tendency of the Jewish intellectuals. Whether they are among those who until now were completely assimilated or whether they are among those who lived within the confines of the community and who over the last decades placed greater emphasis on Europe and with a broad hand opened every gate and doorway to every external influence that, at a particular moment, endangered the inward uniqueness of the folk culture of the Jews.

The first and at the same time the most important step toward the awareness of a folk culture is to recognize the soul of the folk, and the most vivid expression of that soul is its folklore.

When the Polish colonel Adam Koc read his first "Ozon"* declaration on the Warsaw radio, the Jewish-Polish intelligentsia shuddered. The declaration was the first presage of the course of Hitlerism in Poland. Jewish-Polish assimilation groaned deeply. The noble magnificent shades of Mickiewicz and Slowacki blanched. The illusion of a shared Polish culture lowered its wings.

At that moment, how did the ordinary Jew respond—the Jew wearing his small round hat? With a bitter smile, he turned to his fellow Jew and asked, "What did the Kotsker preach about today?"

How much contempt and irony is embedded in that question— sharp, Jewish irony.

The Nazis might have been able to tolerate Heinrich Heine's flirtation with the anemic German water nymphs. But Heine's sharp, Jewish irony irritated even the genial beer-burghers.

To recognize a people, one must listening to what it thinks, sings, dreams, and says. When the great calamity overwhelmed the German-assimilated Jew, when a brutal sergeant-major cult roared: "Out, Jew!" the German Jew woke from his self-justifying dream, from his trance of German culture, and began to run.

But in himself, and with himself, he carried a bastard: a foreign language; a foreign melody. And so long as he does not abort the foreign element he will not be able to discern the way to Jewishness.

A difficult operation. Perhaps it will succeed. It may be that a Jewish village sage will succeed in exorcising the foreign-culture dybbuk who in the course of his wanderings between borders and peoples continues to recite Lessing's fable of "The Three Rings" and Schiller's "Don Carlos."

The same is true of the Jewish-Polish assimilation viscerally alienated from the soul of the Jewish folk and from its colossal resources. The shades of Krasiński's *Unholy Comedy* and the symbols of Wyspianski's *Wedding* are in a place altogether different from the images of the Baal Shem and Reb Levi of Berdichev, both of blessed memory.

I do not deny the beauty of the foreign mythos. But now, in this historic moment when a people is in the midst of an inward consolidation, one has basically to forget what is foreign in order to find that which is one's own—and thereby to find one's self.

The finest achievements of Jewish literature never lost contact with Jewish folkways and particularly with its folklore.

Is it, in general, possible to have a living literature without basing it on folklore? The answer is a resounding "No!" The best proof of this is the new Hebrew literature, the new Hebrew theater, and the like. Their Hebraism makes the matter clear and simple.

The Diaspora has fragmented the Jewish people linguistically and culturally. The fragments have to be gathered together to create wholeness, organicity.

Behind Hebraism, there stands Zionism, a mighty national renaissance movement. The resurrection of the Hebrew language is a heroic effort to synthesize a national form that would put together that which the Diaspora has cast away. Zionism, the movement that has carried out, in our time, the idea of a Jewish nation, has, and not coincidentally, thrust forward the language that in itself embodies the greatest cultural creation of the Jewish people—the Bible, the language in which Jews have expressed their life in the epoch of their national independence. These two symbolic-romantic arguments had the power to create a new Hebrew literature and culture.

But is that new Hebrew literature an organic expression of Jewish folklife and its folklore?

It may sound like a paradox if I should say that Bialik* was the last of the Jewish poets writing in Hebrew. But it is indeed true. Bialik's intimate contact with Yiddish folksong (*shirei ha'am*), with the Slavic terrain, the Diaspora landscape (*shirei hahoref*), demonstrate that: the snow-covered terrain in Yiddish folksong, the tremor of the Jewish spirit on that very banner of the Slavic countryside. All that was missing for the song to be a classic was that it should be sung in Yiddish.

The greatest of the new Hebrew poets was stimulated by Yiddish folksong. Bialik's intimate contact with Yiddish and with its literature was the new Hebrew literature's last contact with its Jewish folkloristic foundations. After Bialik, Hebrew literature distanced itself farther and farther from the Diaspora and its folklore. Left to itself it was, as it were, suspended in midair. It is to its biblical references that are operational in the Hebrew language itself that the literature owes the pathos intrinsic to it. It is because of that literature's link to the Palestinian landscape that one particularly feels that it lacks an organic-creative folklore.

So it borrows its melody from the Arabs, and Arab melody bears on its wings the substitute for a Hebrew folksong. When the Palestinian Worker's Theater Ohel wants to present a biblical play, *Jacob and Rachel*, it makes use of the clothes and gestures of the desert Bedouins.

Basing itself on the idea that the Patriarchs must have acted and spoken this way, Ohel created a Bedouin, not a Hebrew play, even though its *Jacob and Rachel* was performed in Hebrew.

In the history of cultures, the new Hebrew experiment is not the only endeavor of a people to support and to build and enlarge a literature without a folkloric base. The most classic example is poetry in the Latin language before the time of the European humanists.

There is no denying the poetic value of late Latin literature. But without Roman folklife, which creatively affected its folklore, the new Latin literature was and remained an empty blessing.

Living folklore is the black earth out of which, organically, there grows a living, effective literature. The folklore is a salient indicator by means of which one can clearly recognize and experience the pluses and minuses, the possibilities of one or another national literature.

The crown of English folk creativity is the ballad. The crown of English literature is the drama. The acute feeling for the substance of drama that the English folk had manifested by singing its ballads slowly ripened until it achieved its highest dramatic vision in Shakespeare.

The crown of Jewish folk creativity is its folk humor, the Jewish joke, which has achieved renown even among Gentiles. That acute feeling for the humorous which is so evident in Jewish folk creativity slowly ripened until it achieved its highest classical manifestation in Sholem Aleichem. When we consider the active-heroic role of the English in world history and the passive-heroic role of the Jews in modern world history we may perhaps understand why this is so and not otherwise.

Generally, drama is the problem child for Hebrew as well as Yiddish literature. A people with such a dramatic past and such a tragic present has not, in its literature, achieved drama. The Bible itself provides us with a great number of dramatic personages—and yet not one of them, to this day, has been given dramatic form, either in Hebrew or in Yiddish literature. Until now, the fratricide of Cain, the tragic figure of King Saul, the Hamlet of Jewish history; the motif of the Jewish Iphigenia—the story of Jephtah's daughter—have not found their resolution in the literature of the Jews.

Jephtah's daughter and Iphigenia. Two similarly fated sisters, but without the same luck. The great Greek tragedy writers, the German and French classicists occupied themselves with Jephtah's daughter. But among the Jews, only one writer, Sholem Asch, has dramatized her story in one of his least mature plays.

The complete lack of a feel for drama among the Jewish people made it impossible for the ballad form to develop in its folksong. To this day, what moves them is the Book of Lamentations, that lyric-elegiac dirge in response to that great national tragedy—the destruction of the Temple.

That the link between the ballad and the drama is not merely an assumption of my own that hovers in the air can be demonstrated. All the nations that possessed a feel for drama have the ballad in their folklore and consequently the drama in their literature.

There are two sharply defined lines in Yiddish folklore: the lyric-pathetic and the grotesque-realistic. The lyric-pathetic is tightly linked to the Hebrew tradition, to Jewish religious ecstasy—to the distant past—the wonder tales, the legends. The grotesque-realistic is linked to folk-anecdote and folk-pantomime. In the first line we see Yiddish romanticism in action: Peretz, Leivick, Ignatoff, and others. In the second line, Goldfaden, Sholem Aleichem, Moshe-Leyb Halpern, and so on.

Yiddish romanticism seized and exalted the tone and the style of the religious folk-soul and the tales of wonder generally. Peretz's *Hasidic* and *Folk Tales*, Leivick's *Golem* and *Redemption Comedy*, Ignatoff's *Wonder Tales of Old Prague*. In Yiddish literature, even now, not all the motifs, figures, or problems indicated by religious-romantic folklore have been exhausted.

One thing is worth establishing: in the romantic-pathetic line, the new Yiddish literature encounters Hebrew literature. Moreover, the new Hebrew literature has shown an unusual sensitivity to the romantic-pathetic motifs and tones emphasized by Yiddish folklore, especially as it is found in the Hasidic folktale. Yiddish-religious folklore sustained in itself a soulfulness, a mood of spirituality, that was as old as the Jewish people itself.

In that landscape of the soul, God was still speaking to the light and saying it was good. In that landscape of the soul there walked the holy

Ari and the Thirty-six Righteous Ones. It was in that spiritual landscape that there rose the throbbing figure of the Baal Shem, the youngest mystical legend in all of European folklore.

The Yiddish-religious folklore maintained prayer, like a precious jewel, the lyric *de profundis* monologue of the Jewish soul with the Creator of all the worlds; the intimate lyric resonance of the Psalms up to the amazing complaints of Reb Levi Yitskhok of Berdichev, of blessed memory: lyric, mutinous, and devout.

Yiddish literature could not ignore that living wellspring. No matter how irreligious at times it might have been, it had nevertheless to collide with that folklore treasure which was both a living element in itself and a reminder. When he remembers his mother whispering as she blessed the Sabbath candles, the severe Mendele the bookseller waxes ecstatic. That sober satirist and adherent of the Haskala becomes lyrically exalted. In that prayer, uttered in a woman's archaic Yiddish, there was a sea of love, not only for one's family, but for an entire people; for an entire world.

In the religious folktale not only the Jew but the human being was revealed. And it was his recognition of this fact that helped Peretz achieve his artistry.

Not everything that the pathetic-romantic line in Yiddish folklore indicated found a response in the new Yiddish literature. But whenever Yiddish literature turns again to that wellspring it will have that Columbus-feeling of the discovery of new motifs, symbols, and beauties.

The second parallel line indicated by Yiddish folklore for itself and for Yiddish literature has quite a different character. This line is more worldly, with almost no links to tradition. It is against, and slightly beyond, pathos, realistic, but even more so. A realism that borders on the grotesquely fantastic, like the Jewish reality of the past couple of hundred years. And that particular part of Yiddish folklore swarms with buffoons and fools, with pranks and barbs, with curses and wordplay, with jokes, tricks, and frivolity. It is true that even in this part of Yiddish folklore, strong, pious accents are to be found. The love song of the seamstress, the song of family, the lullaby, children's songs, and the like.

Whoever it was who synthesized the Purim play with folksong became the creator of the Yiddish theater. Raisins and almonds, Goldfaden's Tzingentang—the licentious masked ball plus pious folk spirit. The Yiddish folk theater rose on a broad base of folklore. The farther that theater has moved away from its folkloristic base since Goldfaden's time, the more ignoble it has become.

But the basis is there, and a return is always possible. Sholem Aleichem is deeply rooted in Yiddish folk anecdote. Anecdotes and witty sayings add a great deal of uniqueness and charm to his work.

If Peretz is the highest expression of the romantic-pathetic line, then Sholem Aleichem is the highest artistic expression of the realistic-grotesque line.

What constitutes the grotesque?

Listen to what a simple Jewish man of the people says. "Well, so I was on my way."

And in that manner of speech one notices the curious leap beyond precision.

Sholem Aleichem grasped the manner of speech of the Yiddish-speaking Everyman. His inclination to monologue. The monologue that is essentially theatrical though not dramatic. Thematically, Sholem Aleichem is rooted in the Jewish way of life. In Jewish-Yiddish folklore. His mode of expression is a classic example of the realistic-grotesque line. The rabbi of Chelm was the prototype of his Rabbi Yusifl of Kasrilivke. "The Haunted Tailor" is based on a Chelm tale, and so on. The task of any organic literature is to have a folkloric base. That implies a living people. And to respond to the problems, motifs, and forms which that people has nurtured in its creations.

For us, Goethe, in his ripest work, *Faust,* is an example of the highest artistic perfection and organic rootedness in the creation of his people. The Faust motif, as is well known, is a German folk motif. It was in the Middle Ages that the German folk began to whisper the tale about the wonderful magician, Doctor Johannes Faust, who sold his soul to the devil. In Goethe's work that motif received its highest expressive formulation.

But what is noteworthy is that the great German writer understood not only the folk motif but also the forms that German folklore indicated it could take. The dialogues in *Faust* are written in so-called dog-gerel verse, the verse in which the German "Purim players" improvised their Shrove Tuesday plays. The lyric intermezzos of the great Faust tragedy, the Gretchen songs and others, are written in the tone and style of the German folksong.

The folk and genius were united. Each with the help of the other.

1939

♦ ♦ ♦ *Notes*

p. 3   *Midrash:* A body of post-Talmudic literature of biblical exegesis.

p. 4   grandfather's cup: This refers to the *kiddush,* the blessing over wine.

p. 9   Sabbath-goy: A Gentile employed to do the work that Jews are forbidden to do on the Sabbath.

p. 18   *all right:* The words are in English in the Yiddish text.

p. 18   Gemara: The Talmud. Also spelled Gemora.

p. 18   *Amar Abai:* "Abai said." Abai was a second-century Babylonian sage. Abraham is imagining Isaac reading from the *Gemara.*

p. 19   *lamed-vov:* Cricket (also grasshopper), named after the Thirty-Six Good Men.

p. 19   the cat has washed itself: A sign of guests soon to arrive.

p. 21   mandrakes: The mandrake is a forked root that looks vaguely like a man. On that account, it was believed to ensure fertility to a woman who possessed it. See Gen. 30.16.

SONGS OF THE MEGILLAH

p. 30   Purim (Casting of Lots): The Jewish holiday that comes in early spring and celebrates the triumph of the Jews over wicked Haman as the story is told in the Book of Esther.

245

p. 30   *Megillah:* The Scroll, or Book of Esther.

p. 37   *pan:* A Polish nobleman.

p. 42   Succoth: The Feast of Tabernacles.

p. 42   To "him": A euphemistic way of referring to a Hasidic rebbe, or master.

p. 43   Shavuoth: The Feast of Weeks (Pentecost).

p. 49   "*Vayhi . . . vayhi bimey*": "Now it came to pass in the days of . . . ," the words with which the Book of Esther begins.

p. 55   Adar: A month in the Jewish calendar, late February to late March.

p. 56   *hamantash:* Literally, Haman's pocket; the three-cornered pastry eaten during Purim.

p. 56   *The Essential Jew:* In Yiddish, *dos pintele yid,* literally, the essential dot of Jewishness.

BALLADS

p. 82   Tisha b'Av: The ninth day of Ab, commemorating the destructions of the Jerusalem Temple.

OCCASIONAL POEMS

p. 91   Baal Shem: Israel ben Eliezer, the Baal Shem Tov, literally, Master of the Good Name (ca. 1700–1760), the charismatic founder and first leader of Hasidim. Through oral traditions and legendary tales he became known as an exemplary saint; he was recast at the turn of the twentieth century into a pantheist and neoromantic figure.

p. 94   Saint Besht: *Besht* is an acronym for the Baal Shem Tov.

p. 104   Rabenu Tam: Rabbi Jacob ben Meir (ca. 1100–1170), the grandson of Rashi and the leading Talmudic scholar of his age. *Tam* also means fool, or simpleton.

p. 105   *shikses:* Young Gentile women.

p. 105   Reb Levi Yitskhok: Levi Isaac ben Meir of Berdichev (ca. 1740–1810), a third-generation Hasidic master who brought the movement into central Poland. His Yiddish prayers that pleaded the cause of the Jews before God are preserved in folk memory. For Manger's version, see pp. 169–70 of this book.

p. 105   *tfiln:* Phylacteries.

p. 105   Hasid: An adherent of the religious movement founded by the Baal Shem Tov.

p. 106   *Shimenesre:* The Eighteen Benedictions, recited three times a day.

AUTOBIOGRAPHICAL EPISODES

p. 113   Shlomo Bikel (1896–1969), a Yiddish literary critic and leader of Jewish cultural life in Romania during the twenties and thirties; a lifelong friend and supporter of Manger.

p. 115   Franz-Joseph's birthday: Francis Joseph I of Hapsburg, emperor of the Austro-Hungarian empire, 1848–1916; a revered figure among his Jewish subjects.

p. 122   *treyf:* Food that is not kosher, and therefore forbidden to Jews.

p. 124   *mentsh:* Literally, a person; usually used approvingly as describing a mature, responsible person.

p. 124   *suke:* The lean-to or hut Jews eat in during Succoth, the Feast of Tabernacles.

p. 132   *Leichenbagegenish:* The meeting with the corpse (German).

FICTION

p. 139   Messiah wine: The wine reserved for the righteous at the time of the coming of the Messiah.

p. 141   *zaddikim:* Saints or holy men.

p. 146   Khaim-Nogid: the "rich man."

p. 146   Korah: Led a revolt against Moses in the desert (Num. 16); in rabbinic lore associated with great wealth.

p. 146   Yohanan-the-Cobbler Street: comically named after Johanan ha-Sandelar, a rabbi of the first half of the second century C.E. Basing himself on the folk-etymology of his name, Yohanan the Sandal-Maker, Manger turns him into a working-class hero.

p. 147   the zaddik of Sadgura: the Sadgur dynasty, founded by Israel Friedman of Ruzhin (1797–1850), was the most opulent of Hasidic courts. His son, Abraham Jacob, lived 1819–1883.

p. 158   Messiah-Ox: The fabled ox whose flesh the righteous will be able to eat at the time of the coming of the Messiah.

p. 164   Manger's heavenly conclave includes the Hasidic masters Abraham Joshua Heschel, the rabbi of Apt (Opatów) (1765–1822), and Yaakov Yitskhok Horowitz, (d. 1815), the "Seer" of Lublin.

p. 164   Nahman of Horodenka (d. 1780), a disciple of the Baal Shem Tov.

p. 165   *mezuzahs:* Small tubes containing an inscribed strip of parchment attached to the doorpost of houses in which Jews live.

p. 165   The Maggid of Kozienice: Israel ben Shabbetai (1733–1814), a famous Hasidic preacher.

p. 166   Grandfather of Shpola: Aryeh Leib of Shpola (1725–1812), a miracle worker and faith healer, whose acts on behalf of the poor were the subject of numerous legends.

p. 169   The rabbi of Sasov, Moishe Leib (1745–1807).

p. 169   The Rabbi Velvl of Zbarazh (1819–1883).

p. 173   Preacher of Dubno: Jacob ben Wolf Kranz (1741–1804), a renowned preacher who used parables, fables, and stories to appeal to a popular audience.

p. 182   to *khazer:* The pun turns on the similarity between the two words: *khazir,* meaning pork (or pig), and *khazer,* meaning to repeat (for a lesson).

p. 194   Mayofes Dance: A degrading dance related to Polish mistreatment of Jews. The words are Hebrew for "How beautiful art thou . . ." and are taken from one of the songs sung at home on the Sabbath.

p. 199   *kometz alef:* The Hebrew vowel sound, *kometz,* indicates that the letter under which it is written is given an "aw" sound. In this case, the *alef* is pronounced "aw."

p. 199   *kometz gimel: Kometz,* as just above; in this case, under the letter *gimel* it produces the sound "gaw."

p. 218   *shames:* A synagogue caretaker.

p. 222   *asher-yotser* prayer: The prayer after toilet use.

p. 223   Nussn the Wise: A parody of Nathan the Wise, the eponymous hero of a play by Gotthold Ephraim Lessing, later adapted for the stage by Friedrich von Schiller.

p. 226 Hamsun: Knut Hamsun (1859–1952), Norwegian novelist, playwright, and poet.

p. 226 *Maestoso Patetico:* A poem composed in 1922 by the Yiddish expressionist poet Peretz Markish (1895–1952).

p. 230 Shomer: Pen-name of Nokhem-Meyer Shaykevitsh (1846–1905), the author of sensational potboilers read mostly by women.

p. 232 Sh. Niger: Shmuel Niger (1883–1955), the most prolific and authoritative critic of Yiddish literature. His essay "The Humor of Sholom Aleichem" appears in *Voices from the Yiddish: Essays, Memoirs, Diaries,* ed. Irving Howe and Eliezer Greenberg (Ann Arbor: University of Michigan Press, 1972).

p. 236 "Ozon": An acronym for the Polish paramilitary antisemitic organization Obóz Zedenczenia Narodwego (Camp of National Unity), founded in 1937 by Colonel Adam Kol.

p. 238 Bialik: Hayyim Nahman Bialik (1873–1934), the major Hebrew poet of the twentieth century.